# Racism and the Press

This book presents the results of an interdisciplinary study of the press coverage of ethnic affairs. Examples are drawn mainly from British and Dutch newspapers, but data from other countries are also reviewed. Besides providing the reader with a thorough content analysis of the material, the book is the first to introduce a detailed discourse analytical approach to the study of the ways in which ethnic minorities are portrayed in the press. The approach focuses on the topics, overall news report schemata, local meanings, style and rhetoric of news reports.

Highly original, accomplished and penetrating, the book is the fruit of a decade of research into the question of racism and the press.

The author is an internationally known scholar in the field of discourse analysis, and the first who has addressed the problem of prejudice and racism from a discourse perspective.

The readership for *Racism and the Press* is as interdisciplinary as the book itself: ethnic studies, mass communication and media studies, sociology and linguistics.

**Teun A. van Dijk** is Professor of Discourse Studies at the University of Amsterdam. After earlier work in text grammar and psychology, his present fields of expertise are news analysis and the study of racism in discourse. Professor van Dijk is the author/editor of several books in each of these fields, and founding editor of the international journals *TEXT* and *Discourse and Society*.

**Critical studies in racism and migration**
Edited by Robert Miles
*University of Glasgow*

# Racism and the Press

Teun A. van Dijk

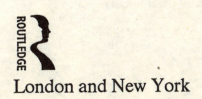

London and New York

First published in 1991
by Routledge
11 New Fetter Lane, London EC4P 4EE

Simultaneously published in the USA and Canada
by Routledge
a division of Routledge, Chapman and Hall, Inc.
29 West 35th Street, New York, NY 10001

© 1991 Teun A. van Dijk

Typeset from the author's disks by
NWL Editorial Services, Langport, Somerset, England
Printed and bound in Great Britain by
Biddles Ltd, Guildford and King's Lynn

*British Library Cataloguing in Publication Data*
Dijk, Teun A. van (Teun Adrianus), *1943–*
    Racism and the Press.
    1. Great Britain. Race reporting newspapers
    I. Title
    070.449305800

*Library of Congress Cataloging in Publication Data*
Dijk, Teun Adrianus van, 1943–
Racism and the press/ Teun A. van Dijk.
p.   cm.
Includes bibliographical references.
1. Racism in the press – Great Britain.   2. Racism – Great
Britain.   3. Mass media and race relations – Great Britain.
I. Title.
PN5124.R29D55   1991                    90–39276
070.4'493058'0941 – dc20                CIP

ISBN 0-415-04733-1
        0-415-04734-X (pbk)

# Contents

# Illustrations

# Preface

Racism remains one of the most pernicious problems of white society. Though often less blatantly and overtly than in the past, it continues to permeate racial and ethnic relations in Europe, North America and other westernized countries. Resistance and protests against this social, economic and cultural oppression of minorities have brought about limited civil rights gains during the past two decades, but the fundamental relations of inequality have hardly changed. Indeed, one of the main strategies of the ideological framework keeping white dominance in place is precisely to deny or to play down the prevalence of racism and to blame its victims for the persistent inequalities that are its outcome. Many white people may no longer believe in white racial supremacy. They may in principle even endorse values of social justice. However, massive legal and scholarly evidence, as well as the available accounts of the personal experiences of minorities, also show that white people and institutions still engage in the many daily practices that implement the system of white dominance, and seldom challenge its underlying beliefs and ideologies.

This continued existence of the ideological and structural dimensions of racism presupposes complex processes of reproduction. In my earlier work of the 1980s I have shown that discourse, language use and communication play a prominent part in this reproduction of the ethnic consensus of white groups. This is particularly true for all forms of elite discourse, including that of the mass media in general, and that of the daily press in particular. Other research in several countries has repeatedly demonstrated that ethnic and racial minority groups always have been, and continue to be, portrayed negatively or stereotypically by the press, for example, as a problem, if not as a threat. Similarly, ethnic minority group leaders and institutions are still considered less credible sources, while minority journalists are seriously discriminated against in hiring, promotion and story assignments. Again, in these respects the press is hardly different from most other institutions and organizations in white society.

These incontrovertible results of earlier scholarly work are the starting point of the present study, which focuses on ethnic affairs reporting in the 1980s. Thus this study does not primarily aim to show again that, as a whole, the Press is part of the problem of racism. Rather, against the background of the increased subtlety and indirectness of public discourse about race relations, also in the media, it will answer the question how exactly the Press is involved in the continuity of the system of racism. That is, we need to know which detailed textual structures and strategies are brought to bear by journalists in the discursive reproduction of the ideological framework that legitimates the ethnic and racial dominance of the white group.

Besides the usual content analysis which provides the necessary figures that show the overall prevalence and distribution of some of the properties of ethnic affairs coverage, this detailed analysis of textual structures requires the more refined, qualitative approach provided by discourse analysis. This new cross-discipline in the humanities and the social sciences aims at a broadly conceived study of the many forms of text and talk that characterize social life. Against the background of the developments in this new discipline, I have earlier argued that discourse analysis should also pay attention to both the study of media discourse and to the critical examination of the discursive mechanisms involved in the reproduction of ethnic prejudices and racism.

The present study combines the theoretical, descriptive and critical goals of this earlier work by focusing on the most crucial communicative means of the reproduction of racism, namely, the Press. Such a discourse analytical approach pays attention to the major levels of news discourse structure, such as topics, overall schematic forms, local meanings, style and rhetoric, as well as their relations with cognitive processes of production and understanding, and their socio-cultural and political contexts. To enhance the readability of this book, these analyses are kept rather informal, whereas each descriptive chapter begins with a theoretical introduction intended for those readers who are not familiar with discourse analysis.

Results of my earlier study of everyday conversations about minorities and ethnic relations strongly suggest how prominent a role the daily newspaper plays for white people in the definition of the ethnic situation and the construction of an interpretative framework for the understanding of ethnic events. After an earlier book about the portrayal of minorities in the Dutch Press, and several papers paying attention to special dimensions of the media coverage of ethnic affairs, this book provides a descriptive and theoretical integration of a decade of research into this role of the Press in 'north-western' societies.

This research and especially the writing of this book has been an arduous enterprise. The overwhelming task of analysing many thousands of newspaper articles and the lack of research funds and assistants proved to be a serious challenge. Being vastly labour-intensive, systematic content analysis is itself a daunting job. The much more detailed discourse analysis of so many data is virtually impossible, and self-defeating unless applied to representative selections of the Press coverage. At many points of this study, therefore, I had to make sometimes painful choices and limitations. Instead of the originally planned analysis of the Press in several countries in Europe and North America, this study focuses on the British Press, with occasional analyses of the Dutch Press, although I briefly report results of earlier research in other countries. Also, in order to make this book accessible to a broad public, I not only had to trim down a much larger study to the size of the present book, but also had to avoid the sometimes highly sophisticated analyses of contemporary discourse studies. The problem of racism in the Press is too important to make this critical enquiry accessible to only a small number of discourse analysts. Therefore, I hope that the present version of this study will be useful to all those interested in racism and the Press.

In particular, I hope that this book will stimulate more research. Despite the wealth of earlier evidence, we need many more, and more detailed studies of the ways the western media deal with ethnic affairs. Many countries still lack systematic content and discourse analyses of their major newspapers. For other countries, we only have data about a few local newspapers, or about past decades of coverage. Also, despite its obvious value, much earlier research is superficially content analytical, and thereby unable to convey the sometimes subtle details of prejudiced or stereotypical reporting. I therefore hope that this study will inspire more students and scholars in the humanities and social sciences actively to join the struggle against racism and to engage in the detailed and explicit analysis of the many dimensions of the discursive reproduction of racism by the Press in their own countries. They will discover that the complexity of the textual, cognitive and socio-cultural processes involved is a serious analytical and theoretical challenge, but also a very rewarding way to bridge the gap that still exists between scholarship and society. If popular artists can inspire many young people by bringing 'rock against racism', academics may try to stimulate their students and readers with 'research against racism'.

I hardly need, in this Preface, to justify my criticism of the Press, and especially of the sometimes appalling practices of right-wing journalists in Britain, who may be second to none in the world in propagating racial hatred. However, to brand individual journalists or newspapers as 'racist' was not the purpose of this work. The problem of the reproduction of racism by the media is much more complex. Its structural and ideological ramifications require a more fundamental approach, accounting for the political, economic and socio-cultural role of the Press as a whole in white-dominated societies. In this framework, also the seemingly 'tolerant' quality Press, as well as readers, advertisers, politicians, academic researchers and many institutions may be directly or indirectly involved in this role of the Press. That is, although journalists are responsible for their own actions, these are embedded in complex relationships for which they cannot take the whole blame.

Nevertheless, I hope that journalists will also profit from this book, if only by seeing more clearly the implications of their everyday routine writing (or non-writing) about race. The ultimate aim of my research on racism and the Press is this: to make journalists, scholars and readers become more critical and more sensitive to the sometimes subtle role of news discourse in the maintenance and legitimation of ethnic inequality in society. Indeed, I sincerely hope that the readers of this book will no longer be able to read about ethnic affairs in their newspapers without routinely asking a few obvious questions, such as: Why is this topic newsworthy? Why does this topic or this information get so much (or so little) attention? Does this topic or this word challenge or maintain stereotypes or prejudices about minorities? Who are speaking and who are (or are not) allowed to give their opinion? Whose interests are defended? From whose perspective is this report written? Is discrimination or racism denied, mitigated or trivialized?

Once we have learned to ask such questions we are no longer 'innocent' newspaper readers. And once we have learned how to answer them critically, that is, from the perspective of true ethnic and racial equality and justice, we have begun to challenge part of the consensual and ideological underpinnings of racism, especially if our next question is: What are we going to do about it?

## CALL TO THE READERS

Research on the reproduction of racism in the Press is complex, difficult and time consuming. This means that it needs to be a collective, interdisciplinary and international enterprise. I have suggested that much more research is necessary in many countries. I also realize that the research reported here is far from perfect and hardly complete. This means that the continued study of this important issue would highly benefit from your critical comments, suggestions, examples, experiences or own research results. Therefore, if you would like to make such a contribution, I would be grateful if you could send it to me at the following address: University of Amsterdam, Department of General Literary Studies, Programme of Discourse Studies, 210 Spuistraat, 1012 VT Amsterdam, the Netherlands.

# Acknowledgements

During the decade of research for this book, I have become indebted to many people, too many to name individually, and I hereby would like to thank them all. However, special thanks are due, in the first place, to my students, who participated in several research seminars on racism and the Press, collected data, coded newspaper reports, and wrote research papers that were helpful for my own work. Without their assistance, the quantitative content analyses in particular of this study would have been impossible. In various stages of this research, Piet de Geus has provided invaluable assistance with the statistical processing of the data.

I am indebted to the Commission for Racial Equality in London for providing me with clippings of the British Press and to the British Council for a travel grant to collect these clippings. Bob Miles has helped to trim down this study to the size required by his series, and I am grateful for his valuable time and patience.

Special thanks go to Gabe Kaimowitz for his stimulating energy in fighting racism as a lawyer and communication scholar, and for having supplied me with clippings from US newspapers, and to Luciano Vitacolonna for regularly sending me clippings about recent ethnic events in Italy.

As with my other work on discourse and racism, I owe most to Philomena Essed. Her continued interest in my work, her love, our numerous discussions about the issues dealt with in this book, and especially her own innovative research on everyday racism have been a decisive stimulating force behind this study.

Amsterdam, October 1990

# 1    The study of racism and the Press

What doubt can there be that the most subtle and implacable foe of our coloured people here is the Press.
(From a letter to the Editor of *The Times*, 21 October 1985)

## ETHNIC EVENTS

### Ethnic event 1: the immigration of refugees

During the first few months of 1985, large groups of Tamil refugees appeared at the borders of several countries in western Europe, soon followed by other Third World refugees. The governments of these countries reacted in a remarkably homogeneous way to this arrival of people whom they often subtly defined as 'economic' refugees: they either sent them back or grudgingly admitted them to await decisions by the bureaucracies and the courts about their requests for political asylum. It soon appeared that these decisions were largely unfavourable for most of the newcomers: many were sent back to where they came from, and sometimes risked harassment, if not imprisonment or death upon their return.

To prevent future predicaments of the same sort, several European governments, in view of the planned abolition of their internal borders in 1992, got together ('conspired' would probably be a better term) to establish a common policy for dealing with non-European (that is, non-white) refugees. The context of this policy is revealing: it was part of a larger framework that dealt with international crime and terrorism. While at first discredited as 'economic' refugees, those who sought asylum were now redefined as the perpetrators of another variant of transborder crime: immigration.

Of course, these events also hit the headlines of the media. In the Netherlands alone, hundreds of news reports, background articles and television items were dedicated to what one conservative newspaper called the 'invasion' of some 3,000 Tamils. As a consequence, what was initially a group of people practically unknown to the majority of the population, soon became a prominent object of public attention and discussion. The official panic of the political elites about what they saw as a deluge of poor Third World peoples arriving at their doorsteps soon led to a corresponding media panic. Before long, this barrage of negative media coverage, especially in the conservative Press, also affected large parts of the public, which expectedly was easily persuaded to resent the 'threatening' presence of another non-white, foreign group that would undoubtedly aggravate already serious unemployment and housing shortage and take a share of 'their own' welfare. These reactions were later used as a legitimation by the conservative Press and the authorities to continue their anti-immigration policies. In the years that followed, the Press in the Netherlands, but also in other west European countries, continued to pay special attention to the issue of refugees. What once was primarily a humanitarian issue, now had become an ethnic and political 'problem'.

## Ethnic event 2: the 'riots' in Great Britain

In the United Kingdom, in the early autumn of 1985, several British cities experienced serious social disturbances in their poor, pre-dominantly West Indian or Asian, neigbourhoods. As was the case a few years earlier, Handsworth, Brixton and Tottenham witnessed widespread violence and fights between mostly West-Indian youths and the police, which left several people dead and many wounded, and which resulted in millions of pounds' worth of damage.

As may be expected, television, the 'quality' Press and the tabloids all paid considerable attention to these events. Again, the definitions of these events by the political elites were prominently displayed, if not endorsed, by most of the media and especially the conservative Press: the 'riots' were the criminal acts of black inner-city youths, and a fundamental attack on the civil order. They should not be seen as caused by ethnic inequality, oppression, or discrimination nor as the expression of socio-economic frustration and rage. The appropriate response to such criminal acts of violence, therefore, should be to strengthen and support the police in their containment of these forms of urban unrest. The prejudice about blacks as a 'problem', if not as 'violent' or even 'criminal' people, thus became further strengthened.

## Ethnic event 3: the Rushdie affair

In the spring of 1989, the Ayatollah Khomeini of Iran issued a *fatwa* (a 'licence to kill') against the British writer Salman Rushdie, who according to Khomeini had betrayed Islam in his book *The Satanic Verses* by his scandalous fictional account of the life of Muhammad. In the UK itself, but also in many other countries, this death threat of the Iranian leader, as well as earlier and later protests against the book by fundamentalist Muslims in Bradford and other cities, became one of the most prominent Press stories of the year. The western governments and virtually the whole Press were shocked and enraged about what they saw as international terrorism and fundamentalist intolerance. The western population at large, this time including most intellectuals, also participated in a contemporary variant of the old schism between Islam and Christianity, in which mutual accusations of intolerance and lack of respect for religious and cultural values were exchanged during a bitter 'ethnic' conflict. What hitherto had remained the slogan of right-wing groups or racist parties suddenly became a widely shared opinion also among liberals: 'They have to adapt themselves to "our" norms and values'. In this way, the Press not only contributed to the legitimation of prevalent prejudices against the Muslim minorities in the western countries, and against Islam and Arabs in general, but also emphasized the socio-cultural superiority of white, western or European values and cultures. A few months later, in France, an even more complex conflict arose between Muslim traditionalism, French educational policies and anti-sexist values, on the occasion of the 'scarves' that some Muslim girls were wearing at school. One of the indirect results of this conflict was that the *Front National* won local elections and thus again obtained a seat in Parliament.

## Ethnic events and the media

These are only three of many other 'racial' or 'ethnic' stories that appear in the media, which extensively report issues of immigration, racially based social disturbances and socio-cultural conflicts between the dominant majority and immigrant or other minority groups. In the USA, this was also the case during the Civil Rights Movement in the 1960s and, in the following decades, during the increasing immigration of Asian refugees, Mexican workers and of people who fled from civil war in Central America.

This special media attention implies that such events are newsworthy. We also saw that these reports may voice official definitions of such events, for instance by the dominant political groups, the bureaucracies, or other elites. These definitions may again be conveyed to, and accepted by large segments of the public. Thus, in our three examples, a panic among the political and cultural elites soon led to a media panic, which in turn inspired large scale popular resentment. This reaction of the white public to the elite definitions of the ethnic situation was largely fed by existing prejudices and stereotypes about ethnic minorities or (other) Third World peoples, beliefs which again largely developed because of earlier reports about similar or other 'ethnic events'.

This book examines in detail the ways the white media, and in particular the Press, cover such 'ethnic' or 'racial' events. We want to know which of these events are reported in the Press, and which events tend to be ignored, and why. In particular, we examine *how* such events are reported and what the consequences are of such reporting for the formation or change of the ethnic beliefs of the readers. In other words, this book deals with the Press's 'portrayal' of ethnic minority groups, ethnic relations, and the special role of political or other elites in this communication process. This analysis should give us insight into the role of the media in the maintenance and legitimation of ethnic power relations and, more specifically, in the reproduction of racism in western (or westernized) societies.

## A MULTIDISCIPLINARY APPROACH

The study of the representation of ethnic minorities in the Press requires a multidisciplinary approach: (1) The enquiry into the role of the Press in the reproduction of racism requires a socio-political analysis. (2) The analysis of news reports needs to be based on recent work on the structures and functions of news discourse. (3) The ways readers understand and memorize such news discourse is a topic that presupposes a cognitive psychological account. (4) The formation and change of ethnic beliefs, attitudes, or ideologies should be studied in the framework of new developments in the study of communication and social cognition. (5) And finally, these various lines of enquiry are to be in turn embedded within the broader framework of the study of racism in the social sciences.

The internal coherence of this multidisciplinary study is provided by a broadly conceived discourse analysis, as outlined below. Such an approach pays attention to the structures of media discourse, to the cognitive, social, and political structures or processes that define their 'context', and especially to the multiple relations between text and context.

However, owing to space limitations this study focuses on the analysis of the structures and contents of news reports themselves, and only occasionally relates these with their cognitive, societal, political, or cultural contexts. Although we shall also provide some quantitative data of the coverage of ethnic affairs, our discourse analysis goes beyond traditional content analyses by its systematic account of various structures of news reports in the Press.

Many studies of racism focus on general, macro-level, societal or political aspects of racism and neglect the various micro-levels of the actual expressions, manifestations and mechanisms of the reproduction of racism, including the discursive, cognitive and interactional dimensions of ethnic group dominance. As outlined in the theoretical framework sketched in Chapter two, our discourse analysis approach does not aim to replace such macro-approaches, but is meant as a necessary complement to them.

## A CRITICAL, ANTI-RACIST PERSPECTIVE

No research is free of norms and values or their implications. This is particularly true in the humanities and the social sciences, where norms and values are themselves objects of analysis. The study of the role of the media in the reproduction of racism is a prominent illustration of such an assertion. At every level of our analysis, we encounter ideologically based beliefs, opinions, and attitudes. This is true both for news reports as well as for our own approach to their analysis and evaluation.

Therefore a thorough scholarly study of the role of the Press in the reproduction of racism can and should also have an important critical dimension. If our data and analyses support the conclusion, already established by much previous research (see below), that at least some Press reports or newspapers, or even the white Press or media in general, contribute to the reproduction of prejudice and racism and the maintenance of ethnic dominance and inequality in society, we shall not hesitate critically to evaluate such a role.

Centuries of experiences of ethnic minority groups, massive legal evidence, as well as a wealth of research have shown that our 'north-western' societies still show many forms of institutional and everyday discrimination and racism (see Chapter two for references). However, this book does not intend to prove again what has already been established without any doubt. Rather, it wants to study and explain in detail *how* racism comes about and how it is perpetuated by the Press, and examine whether there are historical changes, geographical variations, or differences between newspapers in this respect.

Since we also maintain that all forms of racism against Third World peoples in western society are inconsistent with the basic norms and values of our purportedly democratic and pluralistic social order, and a serious threat to the principle of equal rights and justice for all, the anti-racist point of view and aims of this book need no further justification.

## RESEARCH FRAMEWORK

This study is part of a larger project, carried out at the University of Amsterdam since the early 1980s, that deals with the relations between discourse and racism. The main assumption guiding this research is that ethnic prejudices or ideologies are predominantly acquired and confirmed through various types of discourse or communication, such as socializing talk in the family, everyday conversations, laws, textbooks, government publications, scholarly discourse, advertising, movies and news reports. Since many of these types of text and talk are formulated by members of various elite groups, and since the elites control the public means of symbolic reproduction, it is further assumed that the reproduction of ethnic ideologies is, at least initially, largely due to their 'preformulation' by these elites, which therefore may be seen as the major inspirators and guardians of white group dominance. Our earlier research strongly supports the seemingly bold thesis that a country or society is as racist as its dominant elites are. It is one major aim of this study to provide further support for this thesis.

The interdisciplinary strategy of this earlier research is similar to the one taken in this study of the media. For a specific discourse type, it is first established *what* is being said or written about ethnic minority groups or about ethnic relations in general. This analysis yields an account of the contents of discourse, namely, in terms of global topics and more local meanings. However, textual analysis pays special attention to *how* such contents are formulated, that is to style, rhetoric, argumentative or narrative structures or conversational strategies. In conjunction with results of other research about socially shared ethnic prejudices, hypotheses are being formulated about the detailed contents and structures of these prejudices, and how these relate to structures of text and talk. On the basis of these theoretical and empirical analyses, it is finally proposed how white in-group members tend to express and communicate their ethnic attitudes to other members of the group and how such attitudes are spread and shared in society.

Most of this earlier work has been done on high school textbooks and especially on everyday conversation (van Dijk, 1984, 1987a, 1987b). In the study of talk among white group members about ethnic minority groups, it appeared that the media play a vital role in the acquisition and uses of opinions about minority groups. This earlier research also shows that the media convey public knowledge, as well as expressed or implicit opinions, about social groups and events most majority group members have little direct knowledge about. More important, the mass media provide an ideological framework for the interpretation of ethnic events. This framework may also act as a legitimation for prejudices and discrimination against minority groups. Thus, the strategic sentence 'You read it in the paper every day' is a well-known move in the argumentative defence of prejudices expressed in conversation.

Another major result of this earlier work on everyday talk among white people is the apparent ambivalence of expressed ethnic opinions. Prejudiced speakers tend to focus on topics or stories that may be interpreted as expressions of negative opinions about minorities. At the same time, however, they are aware of general social norms or laws that prohibit racial discrimination. In general terms, they may even share such liberal principles. At least implicitly, they know that negative talk about minorities may be heard as racist. Therefore, such talk will often be accompanied by disclaimers, that is, by strategic moves of positive self-presentation, as is the case in such well-known formulas as 'I have nothing against blacks (Turks, etc.), *but* ...'.

It may well be the case that this ambivalence is partly due to the media coverage of ethnic affairs. People on the one hand may read about, and selectively remember, events that they interpret as 'proving' the negative characteristics of minority groups. On the other hand, the more liberal media at least also report about cases of discrimination and prejudice. That is, general social norms are not only acquired during socialization or formal education. They are continually reformulated and specified for new social situations, and this happens especially in public discourse, such as news reports, opinion articles, editorials, television programmes, novels or movies.

Thus, if white readers show this kind of ambivalence, it is likely that the same is true for white journalists. Therefore, we should also analyse news reports with the aim of reconstructing the dominant interpretation frameworks for ethnic events among reporters and editors. Such frameworks, if confirmed through other kinds of research into the opinions of news-workers, may in turn explain why media discourse is ambivalent about ethnic affairs, and why an item about ethnic crime may appear side by side with an item about discrimination. Or why during the urban disorders in Great Britain in 1985, editorials in the popular Press may, just like the speakers in conversations recorded in our previous research, say that 'they have nothing against the black community, *but ...*'. Note, though, that the continued existence of discrimination and racism in western societies shows that the ambivalence may be largely attitudinal and ideological: as soon as real or imaginary competition, interests or conflicts are at stake, the actions of the dominant group may no longer be ambivalent at all.

Within the larger framework of my earlier research on discourse and racism, then, the present study deals with the contents and structures of news discourse, while at the same time analysing their relations with the ethnic attitudes or ideologies of news-makers and the public. Whereas the next chapters focus on the discourse structures of ethnic reporting, the final chapter specifically focuses on the ways readers have 'processed' the information and beliefs about a number of ethnic topics reported in the Press. To establish further coherence with the overall research framework, we also pay attention to the general discursive context of the reproduction of racism. That is, we shall occasionally see how other types of discourse, for example, those of the political elites as well as that of the general public, are related to media discourse.

## MATERIALS AND RESEARCH PROCEDURES

The materials used for our empirical investigation consist of all types of news discourse that appeared in the British Press during the second part of 1985. Selected were all news reports, background and feature articles, columns and editorials about ethnic affairs published between 1 August 1985, and 31 January 1986. A representative sample of both quality and popular national newspapers were thus studied in detail, namely, the *The Times*, the *Guardian*, the *Daily Telegraph*, the *Daily Mail*, and the *Sun*, which together published more than 2,700 articles about ethnic affairs during this period. Clippings were obtained from the media files of the Commission for Racial Equality (CRE) in London. Double checking for accuracy showed that this collection was remarkably complete. 'Missing' items are estimated to amount to approximately 1 per cent of the coverage.

To make the analysis up to date, we also briefly examined the coverage of ethnic affairs in the same newspapers, plus the *Independent*, for the first six months of 1989. This coverage appeared to be much less extensive than that of 1985, and amounted to some 1,200 news items. In order to provide a comparative perspective, we also report some results of a study of the major newspapers of the Dutch national Press, of which we also analysed the Press coverage for the second half of 1985 (about 1,500 items). Finally, to show the international implications of this study, and to emphasize the fact that the Press portrayal of ethnic affairs has similarities in many European countries and in North America, we also make occasional remarks and give brief reviews of studies about the coverage by and analyses of newspapers in some other countries.

In the course of this book we use approximate political or ideological labels to identify the overall policies and practices of these newspapers. These are no more than handy ways to summarize complex ideological configurations. What for one reader or journalist is a conservative newspaper may be a more or less liberal paper for another reader, or in another country, or vice versa. In this case, we have simply followed our own evaluation of the newspaper's position. Thus, for the British Press, we systematically use 'liberal' for the *Guardian*, 'conservative' to denote all other newspapers studied and, more specifically, 'right-wing' for the *Telegraph*, the *Mail* and the *Sun*. We comment upon the positions of the Dutch Press later. General statements throughout this book are carefully made relative to these categories. If we say 'the Press', then we mean 'in principle all major newspapers, independent of their political or ideological position', and the same is true for references to the liberal, conservative or right-wing Press, as explained above.

All news reports were coded for a number of standard properties, such as name of the newspaper, date, discourse genre (such as news report, background article, or editorial), minority and majority actors (and whether these were quoted or not), size, presence and size of photographs, and overall subject matter (such as immigration, race relations, education or crime). Finally, a necessarily more subjective summary of the major topics of the item was recorded, expressed in a number of propositions formulated in simple clauses, for example, 'The Home Secretary said that the riots were criminally inspired.' Scoring the news items was done with the help of trained students from various disciplines in the humanities and the social sciences who took part in research seminars on racism and the Press. The numerical data recorded on the coding forms were first processed with a data base programme and then statistically analysed by the well-known SPSS (Statistical Package for the Social Sciences) program. These data yield the quantitative results of this study.

Next, in order to study the assumed effects of ethnic reporting on the public, we carried out in-depth interviews among some 150 newspaper readers in Amsterdam and some other Dutch cities. These interviews were transcribed in detail and the analyses carried out on these literal transcriptions. The interviews focused on recent and more distant ethnic events the readers could have read about in their respective newspapers. The major events remembered and reproduced in these interviews, however, pertained to the immigration of Tamils and other refugees. A summary of the results of the analysis of these interviews is given in Chapter nine.

Although we refer to them only in passing, we have made use of a variety of materials that might provide further insight into the production conditions of news discourse about ethnic affairs, such as letters from various editors to the author, empirical studies, and journalistic accounts of ethnic opinions of news-makers and generally about reporting on race relations. These materials also include findings about practices of hiring (or excluding) minority journalists in the Press, both in Europe and the USA, partly based on our own informal survey carried out among the most prominent newspapers in western Europe.

The different types of discourse materials collected for this study amount to many thousands of newspaper articles, transcript pages, letters, and copies of other texts. Even these extensive analyses are necessarily partial. Thorough analysis of a single text, in a sophisticated discourse analytical framework, would require many days of work and would result in many dozens of pages of research results. It is obvious that this type of precision cannot be attained for thousands of texts. Therefore, the respective textual levels dealt with in the next chapters will be illustrated with examples taken from a limited number of prominent stories in the ethnic affairs coverage of 1985, such as the urban disturbances, the Honeyford affair and conflicts in other schools, the case of the Black Sections in the Labour Party, racial attacks against Asian families, affirmative action, etc. Throughout the respective chapters, this may require some repetition, which is however necessary to illustrate how 'the same story' can be analysed at different levels.

Because of the large number of news reports, this qualitative discourse analysis is combined with a more classical, quantitative 'content analysis' of news reports (Krippendorf, 1980). Both content analyses and discourse analyses, however, are integrated within a more complex, interdisciplinary framework of socio-political and ideological theory formation and analysis. Also, to ensure that this book is accessible to a broad public, technical aspects of discourse analysis have been avoided. Indeed, we should define the overall approach and method of this study as a form of informal discourse analysis.

## RACISM AND THE MASS MEDIA: EARLIER WORK

It has been emphasized above that this book need not prove again that the media in white-dominated societies participate in the reproduction of racism. Experiences and analyses by minority groups as well as other, scholarly, evidence have repeatedly shown that the dominant media in various degrees have always perpetuated stereotypes and prejudice about minority groups. In this section we only summarize some of the more prominent results of this earlier work, whereas the next chapters occasionally refer to some of their detailed findings, also by way of comparison with our own analyses. Note though that despite the hundreds of informal and anecdotal studies of the portrayal of minorities in the Press, there are few detailed and systematic content analyses of the broader 'ethnic' coverage of the national Press in specific countries, and no international, comparative studies (for bibliographical details, see Snorgrass and Woody, 1985; van Dijk, 1989c). Most relevant research has been done in the USA, the UK, and West Germany.

## North America

### The Kerner Report and other early studies

Whereas regular Press reporting of racial affairs in the United States was virtually non-existent before the 1954 *Brown* decision of the Supreme Court, the issue of equal rights was finally put on the official white agenda after that decision received attention in the media. However, Press reporting of ethnic affairs came under political and academic scrutiny only in times of 'racial crisis'. This was particularly the case during the Civil Rights Movement. Just as this happened twenty years later with the coverage of the 'riots' in the UK, which will be analysed in this book, the US media extensively paid attention to the 'race riots' in various US cities in the 1960s. The Kerner Commission, set up to investigate the causes of these 'civil disorders', was also asked to study the performance of the Press, especially after repeated accusations that media coverage of the black community in general, and of the urban disorders in particular, was itself part of the problem. After many interviews and large scale content analyses, the commission found that although the media

> had made a real effort to give a balanced, factual account of the 1967 disorders ... the portrayal of the violence that occurred last summer failed to reflect accurately its scale and character. The overall effect was, we believe, an exaggeration of both mood and event and ... ultimately most important, we believe that the media have thus far failed to report adequately on the causes and consequences of civil disorders and the underlying problems of race relations.
> (Report of the National Advisory Commission on Civil Disorders, 1988, p. 363)

It will be interesting to see whether the British media in the 1980s have done a better job when reporting the disturbances in the the UK and whether the media still write 'from the standpoint of a white man's world' as the Kerner Commission put it in its report. Relevant to note also are the comments of the black communities, which were even more critical of the Press than of television. One interviewer of the commission recorded the following opinion, which was found to be 'echoed in most interview reports the Commission had read':

> The average black person couldn't give less of a damn about what the media say. The intelligent black person is resentful at what he [*sic*] considers to be a totally false portrayal of what goes on in the ghetto. Most black people see the newspapers as mouthpieces of the power structure.
>
> (p. 374)

One of the reasons for black resentment of the Press, besides the perception of journalists as being part of the white power structure, was that newsmakers generally rely on the police for their information about what is happening during the disorders, and tend to report what the officials are doing and saying rather than the opinions and actions of black citizens. These are precise evaluations, which we may test in our analysis of the Press accounts of current ethnic conflicts. Finally, among its other findings, the commission concludes that there are virtually no black journalists and recommends that news-makers introduce a voluntary code for balanced reporting. We shall see below that the findings and conclusions of this report inspire much later work on the media portrayal of ethnic or racial affairs, and that they continue to be valid in other western countries.

The other early studies in the USA about the coverage of the 'racial crisis' are journalistic accounts of the role of the media (Fisher and Lowenstein, 1967; Lyle, 1968). They are mildly self-critical in that they realize, just like the Kerner Commission, that the Press has paid insufficient attention to the backgrounds of the civil unrest, that is, to the serious problems with which blacks are confronted, such as segregation, discrimination, and lacking adequate education, housing, and health care. Also, the predominant white perspective and the criminalization of blacks in virtually all reporting are discussed in these early critical assessments (see also Johnson, Sears and McConahay, 1971; Knopf, 1975).

Compared with these moderately critical assessments by white news-makers (mostly about the media in general, seldom about their own newspaper!), the black participants of the conferences from which these early studies emerged were more straightforward. Charles Ivers, a worker for the NAACP (National Association for the Advancement of Colored People), like the black reader of *The Times* (quoted at the beginning of this chapter twenty years later) dryly concludes 'The Press has been and is one of the worst enemies, along with the police, that the Negro has in Mississippi' (Lyle, 1968: 68). Another black commentator pointed out that before the disorders in Watts, the media were never to be seen in the ghetto, whereas they now pay extensive attention to the disturbances, and continues as follows:

> Another complaint is that the Press won't print the truth about America, that it is a racist country. Yet that fact is responsible for the problems we have today. They won't print it because they are part of the racism that exists in America. They don't hire black people, or they hire one or two so they can say 'Well, we've got one and others are to come'.
> (Lyle, 1968: 75)

We quote these early statements about the role of the Press in times of 'racial crisis' because they are directly relevant later in this book, when we examine in detail how the British Press performed its task when covering the 'riots' in Handsworth, Brixton and Tottenham in the autumn of 1985 – that is, exactly twenty years after the black revolts in Watts, Newark, Chicago and other US cities. They allow us to answer the question whether the Press coverage of ethnic affairs in general, and of 'racial conflict' in particular, has changed during these twenty years.

## Current assessments

Twenty years later Carolyn Martindale, in one of the first systematic and historical studies of race reporting in the US Press (Martindale, 1986), partly confirmed the findings of the Kerner Commission and found that the sharply increased coverage of black Americans during the 1960s continued in the 1970s. More than before, the Press now also devoted stories to the 'normal life of the black community ... showing blacks in the context of the total American society' (p. 106), while also paying more attention to the causes of black protest. Most newspapers (except the *Boston Globe*) also showed improvement in the attention paid to the problems that American blacks face when trying to participate 'fully in the social and economic opportunities of the country'. As is the case for the *New York Times*, however, underlying causes of social protests sometimes remain under-reported in favour of 'facts, quotes and numbers'.

Despite the improvements when compared to coverage in the 1960s and before, Martindale's review of the scholarly literature of the 1970s also concludes that newspapers still remain focused on stereotypical and negative issues such as crime and conflict. Now that the discontent of blacks is no longer expressed in a violent way, the newspapers largely seem to have lost their interest in the racial situation. Also according to black leaders and journalists, the media convey the impression that after the Civil Rights Movement and the advances in the situation of black people, the racial problems in fact have been solved, whereas many problems have hardly changed since the 1960s. And despite increased hiring of black journalists, equal participation of black and other minorities in the media is still far from realized.

In their introductory book on media and minorities Wilson and Gutiérrez (1985) also pay attention to the Press and show that coverage and employment have gone through several phases, that is, through what they call the 'exclusionary', 'threatening-issue', 'confrontation', 'stereotypical selection' and 'integrated coverage' phases. The authors observe that much of the coverage of blacks, Latinos and other minorities during the last twenty years has remained in the stereotypical selection phase, in which minorities are still often portrayed as too lazy to work and involved in drugs, and more generally as 'problem people', that is, as people who have or who cause problems. Occasional success stories reassure majority readers that minorities are still 'in their place', whereas the few who escape this place are not a threat to the majority. The major Press perspective in the coverage of ethnic affairs remains that of 'us' versus 'them'. Integrated coverage would mean that minorities are represented equally in all types of news, not only in crime or conflict news, but also in economics or foreign policy news.

In one of the few content analyses of the recent portrayal of blacks in the USA, Johnson (1987) examined the performance of the local media in Boston, including the prestigious *Boston Globe*, and also found a scarcity of news stories that challenge racial stereotypes. Rather, white news-makers 'are more likely to report stories that align with their preconceptions of blacks', such as blacks being drug pushers, thieves, dirty, troublemakers, violent or failing students, on the one hand, or as (only) involved in sports or entertainment, on the other hand. When whites and blacks are portrayed together, white news actors are represented as more powerful and in control, and even on race issues the media often prefer to interview whites as experts. Another important conclusion of this study is that the concept of 'racism' remains taboo in the Press. Instead, euphemisms such as 'disadvantaged' or 'under-privileged' are used to denote the victims of racism. Indeed, racism for many whites is seen as a thing of the past.

Daniel and Allen (1988), in an agenda-setting study, showed that what holds for the daily Press also applies to the leading news magazines. Comparing the coverage of blacks in *Time* and *Newsweek* with the agenda for blacks of the National Urban League, they found that topics that are crucial for blacks, such as maintaining past civil rights gains, including affirmative action, or alleviating poverty, were not at all the focus of the news magazines. These followed the Reagan doctrine of 'self-help' and were more interested in eliminating alleged 'reverse discrimination'.

That problems of coverage remain closely associated with discriminating hiring practices was also established by a subcommittee of the US House of Representatives, after hearing evidence from many minority organizations (Minority Participation in the Media, 1984). George T. Leland, chairman of the committee, summarizes the bleak situation of minority portrayal and hiring in the media in the following unambiguous terms: 'It is clear to any objective observer of the television industry that the record of the industry with regard to portrayal of minorities and enunciation of minority concerns is, and historically has been, abysmal' (p. 1).

That this conclusion based on massive evidence not only applies to television but also to the written Press repeatedly emerges from current enquiries, facts, and figures. Thus, several reports summarized in the *New York Times* in 1988, as well as in a special issue about blacks and the media of the NAACP magazine *The Crisis* (June–July 1989), find that only 2 per cent of 12,226 newspaper editors are black, that promotion is very slow and that 60 per cent of the daily newspapers in the USA do not employ a single black journalist (see also Greenberg and Mazingo, 1976).

In a more extensive scholarly paper, Mazingo (1988) re-examined Warren Breed's classic study on social control in the newsroom (Breed, 1955) for its present application to the role of black reporters on policies and practices of news coverage. She found that there are still serious impediments, partly based on implicit policies, to the contribution of stories about blacks and the choice of a black perspective on news, despite the fact that many black reporters surveyed responded that their presence in the news-room had affected black news coverage.

Concluding this brief selection of studies of the Press coverage of ethnic affairs in the USA, we find that there have been modest, if sometimes only cosmetic, changes during the last three decades, but that both coverage and hiring are still far from ideal, to put it kindly (van Dijk and Smitherman-Donaldson, 1988). Newspapers, news magazines or television alike have their own white agenda, which remains focused on minorities as problem people, who tend to be covered especially when they satisfy a number of stereotypical conceptions or expectations. Issues that are particularly relevant for the black community, such as continuing forms of segregation, discrimination and racism, the lack of affirmative action, and the fundamental condition of poverty, tend to be ignored or explained away in an ideological framework; this was politically sustained during the Reagan administration, advocates 'self-help' and assumes that the advances since the Civil Rights Movement have put an end to racism and the dominated position of minority groups. Similarly, although hiring of minorities by newspapers has improved since the 1960s, there are still many newspapers without minority journalists, whereas the other newspapers effectively limit access of qualified minority journalists to higher editorial or managerial positions.

## Canada

While there are few general studies of the coverage of minorities in the Canadian Press, there is more detailed work on local coverage. Thus, in one of the most extensive content analyses of the coverage of minorities in the Press ever undertaken, Indra (1979) examines the history of the Vancouver Press. Analysing three major periods, starting from the beginning of this century, she shows how the Press reacted to immigrant groups that settled in British Columbia. Western European, and especially English, immigrants were consistently portrayed throughout this period as the ideal immigrants, whereas French Canadians, South and East Europeans, East Indians (for example, Sikhs), Chinese, Japanese and more recently Latin American immigrants were variably ignored, vilified, and mostly described in stereotypical, if not blatantly racist, terms. She also shows, however, that there are considerable contradictions, ambiguities, and especially historical changes in this Press portrayal of ethnicity and immigration. If Chinese, among others, were represented (and treated) as a threat to white jobs in the beginning of this century, present portrayals are much more subtle, but may remain influenced by prominent criteria of ethnicity. As elsewhere in the popular Press, she found that currently the association between specific ethnic groups, such as French Canadians or black Americans, and crime, conflict or violence, was an important feature of Press reporting about ethnic affairs.

On the whole, therefore, the (local) Canadian Press also maintains an ethnocentric, and what Indra calls a 'white, middle-class, middle of the road North American' perspective. Additionally, ethnic coverage has been predominantly male-oriented: attention for minority women, throughout this century, has been insignificant (women are explicitly mentioned in only 5 per cent of all items). Finally Indra interestingly observes that the present newspaper studied, that is, the Vancouver *Sun* 'never commented on its own presentation of ethnicity and only allowed public input about its coverage on the carefully controlled letters to the editor page' (p. 508). We shall show later that this is one of the most characteristic features of Press performance generally, and for the coverage of ethnic affairs, in particular.

## Western Europe

### *The United Kingdom*

The situation in the European Press in many respects resembles that in North America as far as its coverage is concerned, whereas hiring practices of minority journalists are even worse. The studies of the portrayal of minorities, immigrants, or ethnic affairs, carried out since the early 1970s, generally arrive at similar conclusions, of which we again select a few prominent ones that may serve as a background for the research reported in the remainder of this book.

Undoubtedly the most original and influential early study of the role of the Press in the reproduction of racism has been that by Hartmann and Husband about ethnic news coverage in Britain during the 1960s (Hartmann and Husband, 1974; Hartmann, Husband, and Clark, 1974). More detailed results of their work will be reviewed in later chapters of this study, and here we only focus on their general conclusions. The authors emphasize that rather than call their book 'Race and the Mass Media' it is appropriately called *Racism and the Mass Media*, because it is not 'race' but 'racism' that is the problem of race relations in the UK and its media. Combining unique survey data about ethnic attitudes with content analyses of the Press, the authors conclude:

> One effect of this emerging news framework has been that the perspective within which coloured people are presented as ordinary members of society has become increasingly overshadowed by a news perspective in which they are presented as a problem.... Most importantly – and this is the essential feature of the Press treatment of race – coloured people have on the whole not been portrayed as an integral part of British society. Instead the Press has continued to project an image of Britain as a *white* society in which the coloured

population is seen as some kind of aberration, a problem, or just an oddity, rather than as 'belonging' to the society.

(Hartmann and Husband, 1974: 145)

From their survey data the authors also conclude that the media on the one hand have positively conveyed the information that minority groups suffer from discrimination, but that on the other hand they have also helped to shape the impression among the readers that 'coloured people' represent a problem and a threat, for instance because of immigrant numbers or the use of social resources.

Critcher, Parker, and Sondhi (1977), in their study of news coverage in the provincial Press of the UK (the West Midlands) during the 1960s, essentially arrive at the same conclusions as those of Hartmann and Husband for the national British Press, that is, 'that the media perpetuate negative perceptions of blacks and define the situation as one of intergroup conflict'. Thus routinized (crime and human interest) news about minorities is more than just everyday news about 'white people with black faces', and heavily imbued with the significance of colour, which essentially lead the journalist to an 'active collusion with racist definitions'. Similarly, 'political problem news' is found to be 'white power' news, where white politicians, including Enoch Powell, are able to define the ethnic situation and have vastly more access to the Press than black people, where white liberals are attacked when discussing race relations, and in which hostility is reported in relation to the white working class. Finally, 'social problem' news shows that whereas some of the news definitions in some areas (such as protests) may be the same as for specific white groups (such as students), the emphasis on cultural differences in housing, education, language, religion, dress, or other areas of culture, leaves no doubt about the specificity of white reporting about ethnic minority groups in Britain.

A few years later, Troyna (1981) replicated Hartmann and Husband's research approach in a study of the Manchester and Leicester Press and, again, the results are surprisingly similar to those found for the national Press of the 1960s. Race relations are essentially defined in a negative way, involving negative stories about Asian refugees coming to Britain, the accommodation of homeless families in expensive hotels, racial attacks, or the activities of the National Front and its opponents. Contrary to 1960s reporting, the news focus in the mid-1970s changed from immigration problems to the problems perceived to result from the presence of these immigrants in the country. Qualitatively, the coverage essentially remained the same: from an 'external threat', minorities now became treated as 'the outsider within'. On the other hand, while the National Front's policies may not be supported by the majority of the Press, it is nevertheless represented as a legitimate participant in British politics.

The findings of these British studies go beyond the important results of systematic content analysis. Contrary to most studies in the USA, for instance, they are embedded in theoretical frameworks which combine results from social psychology, sociology, political science, and cultural studies. Some of this work has emerged from the important Cultural Studies paradigm in the UK, as inspired by the early work of Stuart Hall and his collaborators at the Centre for Contemporary Cultural Studies (CCCS) in Birmingham (Hall *et al.*, 1980). It is also in this tradition that a thorough and influential study of the political and media panic of 'mugging' was made (Hall *et al.*, 1978). These studies relate details of 'race' coverage with a more explicit study of socially shared racial attitudes, the political economy, or accounts of general news values and other ideologies underlying news production as well as news reading. The detailed attention paid, first by Hartmann and Husband (1974), to the relations between news coverage of ethnic affairs and the knowledge, beliefs, and attitudes of the public at large, provide fundamental insights into the role of the media in the reproduction of racism in white dominated societies.

## West Germany

Besides these studies in the UK, and our own earlier work on the Dutch Press (for example, van Dijk, 1983, 1988b, 1988c, 1988d), West Germany is the only country in which scholars have undertaken systematic content analyses of the coverage of ethnic affairs. After Delgado's early book (Delgado, 1972), more recent studies have been carried out at the universities of Bielefeld and Münster. Thus, in their study of the local Press in Bielefeld, Ruhrmann and Kollmer (1987), developed a micro-sociological framework that analysed news about foreigners (*Ausländer*) in terms of a theory of everyday knowledge and the reconstruction of reality. They found that, either through indifference or through prejudice, the local papers construct xenophobic everyday 'theories' of and for the population at large. Foreigners are thus mainly portrayed as criminals, as a threat to national German resources, as a problem, and as essentially passive in their decisions and behaviour. The presence of ethnically different Turkish *Gastarbeiter* is thus essentially construed as a problem that also has an important cultural dimension, so that foreigners can in principle only be accepted when they assimilate themselves to the dominant German culture.

Along similar theoretical lines, Merten and his associates (Merten et
al., 1986) carried out an extensive analysis of the coverage of 'foreigners'
in the most influential news media in West Germany. Again, crime and
violence are major issues associated with immigrant workers (especially
Turks), who also more generally – together with refugees – are
portrayed as appearing in negatively defined events. The tabloid Press
especially confirms popular prejudices about issues of safety and
overpopulation. The study of these authors clearly shows that *Ausländerfeindlichkeit* (animosity against foreigners), especially in the conservative
and tabloid Press, both reproduces and shapes widely shared racist
attitudes both among right-wing political and other elites, as well as
among the population at large.

### Other European countries

Although in most other European countries there have as yet not been
systematic content analyses of the portrayal of ethnic affairs in the Press,
there have been interesting case studies. Thus, Ebel and Fiala (1983)
made a detailed discourse analysis of the coverage of proposals by
right-wing groups in Switzerland to limit what these call *Überfremdung*
(over-alienation). Similarly, Windisch (1978, 1982, 1985, 1987), in
a series of interdisciplinary studies of xenophobic common-sense
reasoning, analysed the letters sent to Swiss newspapers on this and
related issues. Wodak and her associates in Vienna paid special
attention to the various anti-Semitic discourses, also those of the Press,
occasioned by the election of President Waldheim (*Projekt 'Spache und
Vorurteil'*, 1989). In Italy, the discussion on the new presence of
non-white immigrants is quite recent in the Press, and has as yet only
produced some journalistic accounts (for example, Balbi, 1988). There
is a surprising lack of Scandinavian studies on the coverage of minorities
or immigrants in the Press (see, however, about the Swedish Press,
Hedman, 1985). The same is true for the other European countries, as
well as for Australia and New Zealand.

### Conclusions

The main conclusions of more than two decades of research on the
relations between the Press and ethnic minority groups or immigrants
are hardly ambiguous or contradictory. Most blatantly in the past and
usually more subtly today, the Press has indeed been a main 'foe' of black
and other minorities. As a representative of the white power structure,
it has consistently limited the access, both as to hiring, promotion, or

points of view, of ethnic minority groups. Until today, its dominant definition of ethnic affairs has consistently been a negative and stereotypical one: minorities or immigrants are seen as a problem or a threat, and are portrayed preferably in association with crime, violence, conflict, unacceptable cultural differences, or other forms of deviance. While paying extensive attention to these racialized or ethnicized forms of problems or conflict, it failed to pay attention to the deeper social, political, or economic causes and backgrounds of these conflicts. From the point of view of a 'white man's world', minorities and other Third World peoples are generally categorized as 'them', and opposed to 'us' and, especially in western Europe, as not belonging, if not as an aberration, in white society. Similarly, events in the ethnic communities are defined by the white authorities, such as the police and the politicians, and minority voices are effectively excluded.

These conclusions of earlier research are the point of departure of an investigation that pays attention to the, hitherto largely neglected, details of ethnic affairs coverage: *how* exactly does the Press represent ethnic affairs, and how, thus, does it contribute to the reproduction of racism in society.

## TO BE OR NOT TO BE A RACIST

A few final remarks are in order about the implications of this study. First, our analysis of the Press does not mean that journalists are the only elite group involved in the reproduction of racism. On the contrary, academic scholarship, for instance, has also often contributed to the propagation of racist beliefs and the denial of racism (Essed, 1987; Unesco, 1983).

Secondly, we realize that most white people, including white journalists, resent being called 'racist'. It is not surprising, therefore, that faced with the evidence of research on the Press coverage of ethnic affairs, many journalists tend to resort to a number of defence strategies. If not wholly ignoring such research in the first place, these strategies may involve the usual denials ('We are not racist, but ...'), affirmations of good intentions and apparent counter-examples ('We have also written positive things about minorities ...'), or more direct attacks against the researchers. Such reactions deserve study in their own right, but – apart from our own experiences with editors of Dutch newspapers – we have few data about these journalistic reactions to scholarly critiques of their practices, or other inside information about the ethnic attitudes of journalists in the Press room (see, however, Morrison, 1975; Hollingsworth, 1986).

However, this book is not interested in branding individual journalists or even single newspapers as 'racist'. As we shall see in more detail in the next chapter, racism is a structural and ideological property of white group dominance and therefore characterizes the Press as a whole. If moral judgements are to be passed at all, the crucial criterion is whether there are newspaper directors, chief editors and reporters who challenge the dominant ethnic consensus, try to write within an explicitly anti-racist perspective and who practise equal rights in hiring decisions and work assignments. It is also within this framework that we shall examine the repeated attacks against anti-racist forces in society, especially in the conservative Press. This will also allow us to make necessary distinctions between different newspapers and countries. Despite the structural position of the Press as a whole in the reproduction of white group power, there are obvious differences (as well as fundamental similarities) between the liberal quality Press, on the one hand, and right-wing popular tabloids, on the other hand, and these differences will be pointed out also in our analyses.

# 2 Theoretical framework

## INTRODUCTION

The first component of the multidisciplinary framework that organizes our research is a more general study of racism, and deals with assumptions about the ways in which prejudice and racism are reproduced in north-western societies. These assumptions are themselves based on a theoretical analysis of the notion of reproduction and on general observations about the nature of ethnic inequality and power relations between minority groups and the dominant, white majority. This analysis provides the societal and institutional macro-context of the reproduction of racism through the mass media.

Secondly, the role of the media in the reproduction of racism can only be properly understood and explained in terms of an account that combines political, cultural, and societal dimensions of media organizations at the macro-level with interactional, discursive, and cognitive aspects of news-making and news reports at the micro-level. In this analysis, news-making routines, ideological frameworks of journalists, and relations between the media and other societal institutions, need to be examined in relation to the contents and structures of news reports. This part of the framework links societal macro-structures with the micro-structures of social cognition and social practices of the reproduction of racism in news-making.

Thirdly, the special role of the Press needs to be assessed in terms of its uses by the readers and the ways readers process news structures. Therefore, we also briefly examine the social cognitions of readers about ethnic minority groups, and the ways they reproduce media information in conversations as a function of such social cognitions. This final step in the theory extends the study of the reproduction of racism towards the cognitive, social, and ideological functions of the media in society as a whole. In this chapter we sketch the overall outline as well as a number of important concepts of these three major components of our theoretical framework.

## RACISM

Numerous studies as well as the continuing experiences of minority group members with overt or more subtle forms of ethnic or racial prejudice and discrimination have shown that western societies are racist. Although carried out in different, and even opposed, theoretical or methodological perspectives, such studies generally arrive at similar overall conclusions. Thus, in the 1980s alone, we may mention the following studies, among many others, about racism in different western countries: in the USA: Dovidio and Gaertner, 1986; Essed, 1991; Katz and Taylor, 1988; Omi and Winant, 1986; Schuman, Steeh, and Bobo, 1985; in the UK: Barker, 1981; CCCS, 1982; Gilroy, 1987; Husband, 1982; Jenkins and Solomos, 1987; Miles, 1982; Mullard, 1985; in West Germany: Hoffmann and Even, 1984; in the Netherlands: Essed, 1991; van Dijk, 1987a; in France: Taguieff, 1988; and in Europe generally: European Parliament, 1986. For survey and introduction to the various approaches to racism, see Miles, 1989.

However, despite the empirical evidence and theoretical analyses of various aspects of racism, or similar forms of group dominance, presented in these and other studies, much confusion and differences of opinion remain about the specifics and precise delimitation of the concept of racism. Therefore, instead of reviewing the large number of different approaches, we shall only give a summary of our own conception of racism. This theoretical framework will then serve as the point of departure for the more specific question about how racism is reproduced in contemporary western (European or Europeanized) societies. In order to avoid complexities that are not relevant for this study, we ignore ethnicism or similar forms of 'racial' or ethnic group dominance in non-western societies or in other historical periods of western societies.

Contemporary racism is a complex societal system in which peoples of European origin dominate peoples of other origins, especially in Europe, North America, South Africa, Australia, and New Zealand. This relation of dominance may take many forms of economic, social, cultural and/or political hegemony, legitimated in terms of, usually negatively valued, different characteristics ascribed to the dominated people(s). Before we discuss this system of dominance, however, a few remarks are in order about the very notion of racism.

## The history and concept of racism

Historically, one major characteristic selected as the basis for the categorization and negative evaluation of non-western peoples has been perceived differences of bodily appearance, primarily skin colour. These real or imaginary differences later developed into folk taxonomies about different 'races', which as from the eighteenth and nineteenth centuries were supported by pseudo-scientific arguments about inherently associated moral or socio-cultural characteristics of these 'races', usually leading to the conclusion that the 'white' race was superior to the other races. This European ideology of racial superiority was often used to motivate, explain, or legitimate the exploitation, oppression, or extermination of non-European peoples of other 'races', from the earlier periods of imperialist western expansion, slavery and colonialism until the Holocaust of the Jews by the Nazis in World War II (Gossett, 1963; Jordan, 1968; Kuper, 1975; Miles, 1989: 11–40; Todorov, 1989; Unesco, 1983).

This well-known historical background of contemporary western racism is often used as an introduction to various and contradictory claims about the nature of racism. For instance, since it has been scientifically shown that there are no 'races', and that therefore such 'races' cannot have inherent moral or socio-cultural characteristics, the notion of 'racism' is sometimes found to be misguided. It would, for example, precisely presuppose the notion of 'race' (see Banton, 1977). Also, 'racism' is often denounced, and thereby denied, as a mere rhetorical or political term, and not as a theoretical concept (for a critical analysis of this position, see Essed, 1987). These positions ignore the evidence that the racial taxonomies of popular and pseudo-scientific representations of different peoples were not only real social constructions with very real social consequences, but also that they are still alive today. We would hardly declare Christianity, or religious intolerance, dead by establishing that God does not exist. That is, modern racism need not presuppose the biological notion of race or its associated racial hierarchies, but presupposes their continued socio-cultural construction as it is adapted to the current historical context (Omi and Winant, 1986).

For the same reason, racism is not presently defunct because most white Europeans are no longer assumed to believe in their 'racial superiority'. Especially since World War II and the Holocaust, dominant norms and values have discredited such an ideology, and hence the legitimation of group dominance in such terms. This does not imply, however, that the social constructions of race are no longer associated with moral or socio-cultural evaluations that may be expressed in other terms, as we shall see in more detail later. Indeed, textbooks, the media and other forms of public discourse are today still replete with propositions that state or imply the belief in the moral, political, cultural, or technological superiority of white, western 'civilization' when compared to those of (mostly non-white) Third World peoples, including those groups that migrated to the north-western countries.

## Racism and ethnicism

Although these arguments alone justify the adequacy and hence the continued political and theoretical relevance of the notion of racism, the complex pattern of group dominance in western countries requires a more differentiated conceptualization, which also has its historical roots in western culture. That is, immigrants of non-western origin, or peoples of Third World countries generally, are not only or primarily categorized and (negatively) evaluated in terms of bodily appearance (whether or not conceptualized as different 'races'), but also on the basis of cultural, that is, 'ethnic' characteristics. Throughout western history, such social representations have been used to distinguish in- and out-groups according to a variable mixture of perceived differences of language, religion, dress or customs, until today often associated with different origin or bodily appearance. This may mean that, for example, Turks or Moroccans who migrated to western European countries may become represented and evaluated along a cultural dimension similar to the representation of Africans, South Asians or West Indians using a mixed 'racial-ethnic' dimension.

We see that this 'ethnic' positioning of self and others may underlie the same hierarchization as that based on 'race', which may in turn give rise to and legitimate a system of ethnic dominance or exclusion, that is, ethnicism. While seen as morally less reprehensible, the emphasis on culture and cultural differences has become the modern variant of racial differentiations of earlier western ideologies. Hence, racism is being transformed into ethnicism (Mullard, 1986).

Instead of using a dual or even multiple set of basic theoretical terms, we use the term 'racism' in a more general sense, as it also has become adopted in political contexts of resistance, denoting both racism in the strict sense as well as various forms of ethnicism. Therefore, when we speak of 'racism' in this book we refer to the type of racism or ethnicism prevalent in western countries, both against 'black' groups, including peoples of African origin and those of (South) Asian origin, as well as against specific, such as Mediterranean or Arabic, peoples or immigrants from the 'borders' of Europe, or against Hispanics in the US. For an historically special case of ethnicism, that directed against Jewish people, we will however retain the usual term 'anti-Semitism'.

Finally, in order to distinguish racism, as a general term, from various forms of intra-European ethnicism, such as in the case of the British dominance over the Irish, or of what is presently sometimes called the *razzismo* of North Italians against South Italians, the latter forms of ethnicism may also be called 'regionalisms'. These are not merely socio-culturally based (for instance on language or religion), but also politically and economically grounded. Although the ideological basis of these different forms of ethnicism may differ as to the set of criteria by which 'difference' is socially constructed, the structural consequences for the position of the respective dominated groups may be very similar. Note, however, that for historical reasons (slavery, colonialism), and in particular contexts, racism against Third World peoples, notably against peoples of African origin, may very well have substantially different implications from the various forms of ethnicism among different western peoples. This is particularly the case in the United States, where blacks continue to be subjected to forms of racism that cannot simply be compared to the ethnicism of Anglos against, for instance, Irish and Italians (Omi and Winant, 1986).

## Racism as structure and ideology

In this conceptual framework, then, we assume that racism (including ethnicism) is a system of group dominance. The analysis of contemporary racism, thus, requires the study of the structures and processes of this type of dominance, primarily in Europe and North America. This system is both 'structural' and 'ideological'. That is, it embodies both political, economic, and socio-cultural structures of inequality, and processes and practices of exclusion and marginalization, as well as the socio-cognitive representations required by these structures and processes.

These two major dimensions of racism are mutually dependent on each other. Structural inequality, for example, manifesting itself in discriminatory arrangements and practices at all levels of society, is here analysed as a dimension of racism only if it is supported by corresponding cognitions (prejudices, ideologies) of the dominant group about dominated groups and about race or ethnic relations. And conversely, racist cognitions are systematically (socially, politically, culturally) developed and relevant only when enacted in the practices that define structural inequality. This dialectic of the structural and ideological dimensions of racism is extremely complex. We shall however try to unravel some of its properties in our analysis of the functions of the media in the reproduction of racism and return below to a further analysis of the role of ideology in this process of reproduction.

## Structural inequality

As such, many general aspects of the structural dimension of racism in western countries are fairly well known, and need not be detailed here (see the references given above). Thus, ethnic minority groups are systematically subjected to societal arrangements and practices that, at least for the group as a whole, are the implementation of a less powerful social, political, economic, and cultural position than that of white Europeans. Despite laws and norms that prohibit discrimination, minorities generally have less access to material or symbolic resources, such as immigration and settlement rights, adequate jobs, housing, education, health care, safety, welfare, legal defence, respect, status, and other conditions that define full equality.

## Contemporary racism

Despite very general historical constants, structural forms of inequality change as a function of changing social representations and different societal structures. It has been repeatedly observed, for instance, that the more overt and blatant forms of legal and social structures and everyday practices that define ethnic or racial discrimination are slowly being replaced by more implicit, indirect, subtle, or otherwise less open, though not necessarily less effective or insidious, forms of dominance and inequality, variously called 'new', 'modern', or 'symbolic' racism (Barker, 1981; Dovidio and Gaertner, 1986). We have seen that one aspect of this change is the apparent displacement of racism by ethnicism, through an ideological substitution of the relevance of 'race' by that of the rich set of socio-cultural factors.

One of the implications of this transformation of racism into ethnicism is the development of an ideology that recognizes socio-cultural differences between different ethnic groups, but denies differences of power, and hence the dominance of western culture. That is, such an ideology suggests a 'pluralism' of cultures and therefore of ethnic relations, in which all ethnic groups (including the white one) have equal power. As a consequence of this 'multi-cultural' approach to ethnic relations, anti-racist perspectives, which focus on ethnic dominance and power, tend to be discredited as too 'radical', or even as a form of 'inverted racism'.

These changes in the nature of racism have contributed in some countries, such as in the USA, to considerable improvements in the overall position of minorities, but on the other hand such changes may be temporary, superficial, or only effective for some segments of minority groups or for some sectors of society. Overall, the economic or socio-cultural position of minority groups, as well as the sustaining ideological representations, may have changed only minimally or super-ficially. Opposition may no longer be directed against the principle of equal rights, but against the serious implementation of that principle, for instance in various forms of affirmative action. Similarly, ideologies may perhaps no longer be premised on the belief that whites are a biologically superior 'race', but assume that other ethnic or racial groups happen to be 'backward' along other dimensions. It is within this framework of contemporary racism that we need to examine the special role of the Press.

## The specificity of racism

Note that these forms of inequality closely interlock with, but are conceptually independent of, other forms of social inequality, such as those resulting from class or gender differentiation. That is, the social stratification of ethnic minority groups may partly be explained in terms of class, as is the case for the different social formations of the dominant majority group, but 'race' or ethnicity is a special dimension of socio-economic positioning. Structures of class may be transformed in such a way that ethnic minority groups may be assigned to systematically lower levels, such that the position of large segments of these groups may be forming an 'underclass' (Omi and Winant, 1986; Solomos, 1989). Similarly, minority women may be subjected to special forms of 'gendered racism', which combine general forms of sexism (shared with white women) and general forms of racism (shared with minority men), with a position and experiences that are specific for non-western women (Essed, 1991). The same is true for any other dimension used to define the hierarchies of in-group versus out-group dominance, for instance those based on religion, language, or other cultural dimensions, which may also take on special characteristics when combined with racial or (especially non-western) ethnic group membership.

## Dimensions of dominance

A few remarks are in order concerning the notion of 'dominance'. The structural forms of ethnic group hierarchization are systemic and global. They hold for overall group relations, and need not define each individual group member, sub-groups, or specific social situations. For instance, a white employee may well have a black boss, and a large city in the USA may well have a black mayor, and blacks may sometimes get equal or even preferential treatment in some situations, jobs, or career tracks (for instance in sports or music). However, they are precisely the exception that proves the rule and may also be interpreted as strategic forms of 'ethnic group management'. At present, these exceptions do not fundamentally affect or determine the system, although they may be symptoms of systemic change. The black boss may, at work, have control over the white worker, but his or her structural position need not be recognized by the white worker, and in other contexts the same black boss may be subjected to various forms of discrimination. Thus racism is as dominant in western countries as is capitalism, even when some western countries (still) have communist mayors, ministers, or professors.

Similarly, the prevailing nature of racism as a system does not mean that all white people are necessarily, let alone inherently, 'racist'. White group dominance, and hence racism, are part of a specific historical process which involves western imperialism, capitalism, and colonialism, among other fundamental factors. Racism is not only itself a form of group power, but fundamentally also a function of other forms of power. Indeed, racism may be instrumental in the support or legitimation of these other forms of power. In the present historical context, whites collectively participate in a system that is in their common, and often also individual, best interest, both nationally and internationally. It is therefore not surprising that the dominant ethnic consensus among white Europeans is coherent with this structural arrangement. However, this consensus and its structural base may change, sometimes in ways that are beneficial both for the dominant and the dominated groups, for instance when socio-economic improvements in the situation of minority groups may avoid open conflict and when affirmative action may lead to the education, employment, or promotion of much needed minority workers.

Also, segments of the white group may well oppose and challenge racism, and thus become allies of minority groups, for instance in anti-racist teaching or political action. Again, such real or apparent exceptions to structural dominance do not debilitate the system, but may sometimes even strengthen it. Exceptions make the system of dominance more flexible or less rigid. They allow some 'space' to internal group opposition, and they enable the incidental expression of moral values (for instance, those of equality). In other words, both structurally and ideologically, they are not fundamental contradictions but manifestations of the strategic flexibility of the system of ethnic dominance. It is also in this perspective that we need to examine the role of the Press in the reproduction of ethnic dominance relations in society.

## The reality of racism

This conceptual analysis of racism needs some concrete support from current experiences with, and research into, the reality of racism in everyday life in Europe and North America. Thus, the Committee on the Status of Black Americans of the National Research Council, recently published its extensive report, *A common destiny: Blacks and American Society* (Jaynes and Williams, 1989). Despite its moderate views about half a century of black–white relationships in the US, the committee concluded from a mass of empirical evidence that although significant changes have taken place in the lives of black people in the US, the gap between white and black progress is still far from closed. The chapter on 'racial attitudes and behaviours' similarly concludes that although racial prejudices and practices have changed in the direction of increasing acceptance of egalitarian values, their implementation in concrete action may not always be realized: 'the overall preponderance of the evidence indicates that the existence of significant discrimination against blacks is still a feature of American society' (p. 156).

Contemporary racism is not always subtle and indirect, however. In many western countries ethnic group members continue to be victims of serious harassment by the police or of racial attacks, including arson and murder, by extremist white groups and individuals. On the day this section was revised (28 August 1989), the newspapers reported that in Paris seven people burned to death as a consequence of a racial arson attack. The same day, the Press also carried the story of a young black in New York having been shot to death by a gang of white youths. Such attacks are far from exceptional in the USA, France, West Germany and the UK. Indeed, they have become so common that much of the white Press pays only limited attention to them, sometimes even blaming the victims. The coverage of such attacks in the UK, is one of the issues we address in this study.

While these are common events, they are extreme, and defined as forms of ethnic oppression that are presently placed outside of the consensus. They do not define the forms of everyday racism, where discrimination may take very subtle forms (Blauner, 1989; Essed, 1991). These are sometimes difficult to prove in court, partly also owing to restricted admission of evidence, by discrediting (minority) witnesses or because of (white) racist judges (Gordon, 1983). Also, laws against discrimination are often seriously unenforced, if not subtly boycotted, for example, by police officers (Institute of Race Relations, 1985). If adopted at all, principles of affirmative action may similarly be flouted by responsible authorities (Braham, Rhodes and Pearn, 1981; Jenkins and Solomos, 1987). Thus, despite some legal and moral constraints, the notion of western, democratic, or pluralist freedom also allows considerable freedom to discriminate. The overall result is that ethnic minority groups as a whole, or their members individually, remain in an unequal, subordinated, economic, social, or cultural position (Bhat, Carr-Hill, and Ohri, 1988). Thus, they continue to be under-represented in most white institutions (except in prison), underemployed, underpaid, under-rated, and underpriviliged. That is, they are generally underneath and an underclass. Similarly, they are problematized, marginalized, or inferiorized in most domains of society.

Of course, the realities of racism vary historically and regionally. Thus, the ethnic situation in Western Europe is different from that in the USA, South Africa, Canada, and Australia, and there are also differences among European countries. The causes of these differences are multiple, such as colonial history, results of slavery, the political economy of migrant labour, cultural history, the political system, and the origin or the size and culture of the immigrant (or native) population. Essential for the study of racism, however, is that we understand the profound similarities defining the various forms of ethnic or racial dominance in these countries.

## REPRODUCTION

Groups can remain dominant only if they have the resources to reproduce their dominance. This is not only true economically, but also socially, culturally, and especially ideologically. Hence, it is essential for the reproduction of racism that also the 'means of ideological production', such as education and the media, are controlled by the white dominant group, as we have seen in Chapter one. Along the lines of class formations and divisions this dominance is complex and contradictory. This is also because of the politically and economically subordinate position of the academic elites, who have partial control over symbolic power resources, for instance in the professions, education, the media, or the arts (Bourdieu and Passeron, 1977; Bourdieu, 1984). However, along racial and ethnic lines this is not the case: in all western countries, virtually all leading positions, including those in the domain of cultural reproduction, are occupied by whites. Thus, if only because it is taken for granted, white group dominance is much better organized and more persuasively legitimated than any other kind of dominance in these societies. This means that white elites control the contents and structures of the system of ideological ethnic representation, which is essentially a form of positive group self-(re)presentation. In other words, through education and the media the white group controls the definition of the ethnic situation. Given the social, economic, and cultural position of the major newspapers in western countries, it may therefore be expected that the white Press shares in the overall system that sustains white group dominance. Assuming the crucial legitimating role of ideology in a society where the overt discriminatory practices of ethnic group dominance are legally forbidden, we may even hypothesize that this role of the Press is vital.

The notion of reproduction, repeatedly used above, needs further theoretical analysis, since it plays such a crucial role in this study (see for example, Giddens, 1979). By 'reproduction' we mean the dialectical interaction of general principles and actual practices that underly the historical continuity of a social system. Reproduction may be analysed at the societal macro-level, at the micro-level and along the macro–micro dimension. At the macro-level, a system is historically reproduced when its general principles (processes, rules, laws, structures) remain more or less the same over time, as is the case for such different systems as the English language, racism, or the Press, despite possible changes or variations in the actual historical or contextual manifestations or realizations of the system.

Continuity and change of social systems, however, depend on the relations between principles at the macro-level and practices at the micro-level (Knorr-Cetina and Cicourel, 1981; Alexander, Giesen, Münch, and Smelser, 1987). Trivially, the English language continues to exist as long as there are language users who speak or read it. Similarly, the Press is reproduced as a socio-economic or cultural institution as long as there are journalists and readers engaged in practices of news-making and reading, and as long as there are newspapers.

The same is true for the reproduction of the societal system of racism, the continued existence of which also depends on repetitive practices of discrimination in everyday life (Essed, 1991). Under the influence of particular social, political, or historical context factors, the actual practices of these systems may vary, and if such variation becomes systematic, the system may also change. However, as long as the same basic principles are not changed, the overall system remains the same.

These macro–micro relations between system principles and practices are both top-down and bottom-up. A top-down relation is for instance that of 'governing' or 'ruling': practices are monitored or controlled by the general principles of the system, for example, when speakers of English observe the rules of grammar, when journalists follow the everyday routines of news-gathering and news-making, or when white individuals adopt the discriminatory practices of their group. The strength or strictness of ruling may be different for each system: the rules of English grammar may be stricter, that is, allow less freedom of application, than the principles of news-making.

The ruling of practices by a system requires that members at least implicitly know the system. Hence, parallel to socio-economic systems, there are cultural and cognitive systems of knowledge and beliefs, which are however also social, since they may be shared by all, most, or many members of a group. Without these cognitions, there is no link between the social system and its functioning, between groups and their members, or between principles and practices (Cicourel, 1973). We return to this important socio-cognitive aspect of reproduction below.

Note that this top-down ruling of social systems is not a form of (causal) determination: owing to the partial freedom of individual action, individual members may deviate from system principles, for instance by breaking the rules, by not respecting the prevailing norms, or by following the principles of another system. This deviation may take any form between unconscious variation and conscious resistance. If such deviations or variations are systematic and generalized, the system itself may change or ultimately cease to exist. This means that besides top-down ruling, reproduction also has a bottom-up complement, that is, implementation or application: members follow system principles and thereby confirm the system, or they may vary or deviate from its principles and thereby challenge and eventually change the system – or even produce another system.

The reproduction of racism may also be analysed at these different levels and along these various dimensions. We may study the historical continuity and change of economic, societal, cultural or political system principles of racism, at a macro-level, but also analyse these processes along the vertical dimension of ruling and application: how are racist beliefs and practices enabled or controlled by the system, and how do everyday practices of social members confirm, challenge, or even change the system?

More specifically, when accounting for the role of the Press in the reproduction of racism, we may first examine how the Press as an institution is organized and related to other political, societal or cultural institutions involved in the reproduction of racism, and how, thus, the Press contributes to the continuity of the system of racism at the macro-level. Secondly, actual news practices may be examined for their dialectic of confirmation and change of this overall role of the Press in the reproduction of racism. It is this latter dimension of the notion of reproduction that is being studied in this book.

## SOCIAL COGNITION

Besides the macro–micro distinction underlying the analysis of reproduction, there is another important dimension that needs to be conceptualized in more detail. At the micro-level of societal structure, we talked of social practices of actors or group members. We also saw that such practices presuppose knowledge and beliefs shared by all, most, or many other group members, that is, various types of 'social cognition' (Fiske and Taylor, 1984; Wyer and Srull, 1984) or 'social representation' (Farr and Moscovici, 1984). That is, the reproduction of systems, such as the system of racism, also has an important cognitive dimension, again at several levels of generality or abstractness. It is this cognitive dimension of racism that is often called its 'ideological' dimension, a term we provisionally used above, but which we shall shortly define in a more specific way.

In traditional sociological terminology, cognitions were usually referred to with the term 'consciousness', a notion which is vague and therefore theoretically not very useful. Thus, we distinguish between personal knowledge and beliefs about unique situations, events, and experiences, represented as so-called 'models' in episodic memory, on the one hand, and systems of group knowledge, attitudes, norms, and ideologies, represented in 'semantic' or rather 'social' memory, on the other hand (van Dijk, 1987a). These different cognitive systems have different representations, that is, specific contents and structures, and also different cognitive and social uses or functions, requiring the application of different cognitive strategies.

From a societal point of view, general group knowledge, attitudes, or ideologies may be characterized at the macro-level. In the same way as social processes at the macro-level may be reproduced by practices at the micro-level, these macro-level beliefs of a group may be confirmed or changed at the micro-level of individual beliefs, which in turn control personal practices and social interaction. For the system of racism also,

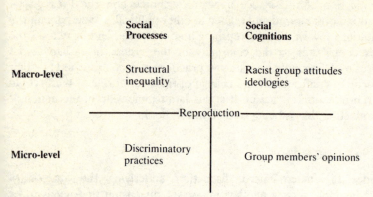

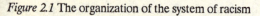

| | Social Processes | Social Cognitions |
|---|---|---|
| **Macro-level** | Structural inequality | Racist group attitudes ideologies |
| | ──────────Reproduction────────── | |
| **Micro-level** | Discriminatory practices | Group members' opinions |

*Figure 2.1* The organization of the system of racism

both this bi-level organization (macro-processes versus micro-practices) and duality (social structures versus social cognitions) are necessary to explain the continuity and the possible changes of racism. Thus, as a whole, the Press may sustain the system of racism, but individual newspapers or journalists may well challenge this system. Indeed, individual resistance against the social dominance of a system is a necessary, though not sufficient, condition of change (see Figure 2.1).

## Ideology

Within this framework of analysis, ideology plays a crucial role. It is here defined as the basic and general, that is, shared, socio-cognitive system of a group, culture, or society (for other approaches, see also CCCS, 1978; Rosenberg, 1988). It is the fundamental interpretation framework that monitors the development of knowledge and attitudes, provides coherence to such cognitions, and brings them in line with specific group goals and interests. Thus ideologies organize sets of attitudes, for instance about minority groups, about women, or about the environment. Ideologies themselves are also organized along specific dimensions, which explains similarities among ideologies, for example, about minorities and about women. The organizational function of ideologies also involves the development, selection, combination, and application of societal norms and values. In the development of a racist ideology, for instance, people may assign more weight to the value of in-group solidarity and allegiance, than to equality of different groups.

Hence, an ideology is a cognitive 'machine' or – in more contemporary parlance – the fundamental 'programme' that generates the group attitudes which sustain optimal group reproduction, both in relations of dominance as well as that of resistance.

We see that ideologies provide the cognitive foundation of group reproduction, including the reproduction of its 'position' in social structure or culture, and the goals and interests associated with this position (Barrett, Corrigan, Kuhn and Wolff, 1979). This process of ideological reproduction usually means that group members tend to favour the acquisition, confirmation and application of precisely those systems of beliefs and opinions that may be used to monitor the practices that benefit the in-group and its members. However, just as people may be forced or persuaded, socially or economically, to act against their best interests, their cognitions or ideologies may also be influenced in a way that does not result in an optimal realization of their goals. This does not mean that we conceive of ideologies as essentially 'false' forms of consciousness, as is the case in many traditional theories of ideology (see, for a historical survey, Larrain, 1979). In the technical sense used here, ideologies are merely basic cognitive systems for the goal-directed and interest-related interpretation and representation of social reality. These systems may or may not be ideally tuned to the reproduction of group interests, they may or may not embody 'false' statements of facts, and they may be developed by both dominant and dominated groups. Thus, an ideology is not characterized by its truth value, but by its effectiveness and functions for the cognitive organization and reproduction of groups.

This possible discrepancy between group ideology and group interests implies that power relations in society can also be reproduced and legitimated at the ideological level. To control other people, it is most effective to try to control their group attitudes and especially their even more fundamental, attitude producing, ideologies, because in that case the others will behave out of their own 'free' will in accordance with the interests of the powerful. The exercise of power in modern, democratic societies is no longer primarily coercive, but persuasive, that is, ideological. Structural dominance may in this way be transformed into hegemony, that is, into a system of dominance sustained by a system of acceptance and legitimation shared also by dominated groups, thus diminishing their potential for resistance (CCCS, 1978).

Despite many contradictions and conflicting goals and interests of the various elite groups, it is therefore crucial that their power also extends to the control of the means of symbolic production, such as the media, which play such a decisive role in the development of the ideologies of the population at large (Chomsky, 1989; Golding, Murdock and Schlesinger, 1986; Herman and Chomsky, 1988). We suggested that this manipulation process may result in a form of ideologically based consensus that supports the dominance relations in society. This process is neither simple, nor straightforward. Power not only invites compliance but also provokes resistance, and its supporting ideologies may condition the formation of counter-ideologies, which may not only be developed by the dominated group, but also be partly supported by some fractions of the dominant group (Abercrombie, Hill and Turner, 1980; Morley, 1983).

It should be strongly emphasized that our cognitive approach to ideology does not imply that we take ideologies as collections of individual or personal beliefs and opinions. On the contrary, although defined in terms of cognitive representations, ideologies are at the same time *social* systems, shared by social groups. They are acquired, used, and changed in social situations. Similarly, both their cognitive organization and their social functions are not limited to the domain of 'ideas', but have a material basis or expression in institutions and the social practices of agents as group members. To keep our conceptual analysis effective, however, these institutions or practices are not themselves part of such ideologies, even if they are controlled by them. That is, we have a more specific conception of ideology than in most other recent studies, where ideologies are defined rather loosely as combinations of specific forms of 'consciousness' and social practices, and even as the 'state apparatuses' that sustain or organize such ideologies (Althusser, 1971).

The same is true, more specifically, for the analysis of ethnic attitudes and ideologies. Thus, prejudice in our view is not a personal opinion about other groups, but a shared group-based attitude towards another (mostly dominated) group, and hence often associated with relations of group dominance and power (van Dijk, 1987a). It might even be hypothesized that in such a system of dominance it is only the dominant group that has (and needs) prejudices as a means of cognitive control and reproduction, whereas the dominated groups have (and need) judgements in order to resist and survive in the system of dominance. We shall come back to a more detailed discussion of the precise structures and functions of such ethnic prejudices later. This approach to the cognitive dimensions of racism implies that racism for us is not just a racist ideology (for this position, see for example, Miles, 1989), because we have defined racism in such a way as to include also structural, institutional arrangements as well as racist practices.

## Ideology and ethnic dominance

In the domain of ethnic relations, all white people in principle benefit from the discriminatory practices and cognitions that define the racist system, for instance in employment, housing, and education. Hence, unlike minority group members, most white people seldom have material goals and interests that motivate the development of an anti-racist ideology. Up to a point the same is true at the ideological level: most white people are not daily confronted by a system of public discourse, for instance through the media, that provides the necessary elements for the construction of such a counter-ideology. The few elements that are available are of a very general, normative, or ethical nature, such as laws against discrimination and norms of social equality and justice.

In present western societies, these normative principles provide the consensual boundaries of the system of ethnic dominance. They may result, for instance, in the official rejection of explicitly racist parties. The overall ideological result, thus, is a 'modern' or 'moderate' form of ethnic dominance, as noted above. This moderate racism presents and legitimates itself on the one hand through official principles of tolerance and equality within a pluralist political system, but on the other hand it is not consistently anti-racist. Consistent anti-racism would imply the abolition of white group dominance in all domains of societal and private life, including both everyday discriminatory practices as well as their controlling prejudiced beliefs, attitudes, and ideologies. That such a process of change is fundamental and complex is not because of the nature of the change in present power relations and structural arrangements. It also requires a fundamental transformation of ideological systems which we found to have been developed during many centuries of political, economic, and cultural western dominance over non-western peoples.

It is against this background of ideological processes and the manufacture of the ethnic consensus within the white group that the Press plays its vital role. More than any other form of public communication and discourse, the media have the ability to contribute the shared elements that define the ethnic situation and that develop or change the ideological framework used by white people to understand and control ethnic events and relations. They provide specially selected 'facts' and preformulate preferred meanings and opinions. If the Press endorses the ideology that legitimates white group dominance, it may be expected that it will ignore, discredit, marginalize, or problematize anti-racist positions and groups.

This also means that anti-racist individuals and groups need to 'counter-read' the newspapers, that is, by reinterpreting the 'facts' and preferred meanings along the lines of their beliefs and opinions as defined by their counter-ideology. This is possible only if they obtain information, argumentation, and legitimation from other sources, such as white radical media, minority media, specialized publications, or other forms of alternative social information processing.

## STRUCTURES AND STRATEGIES OF NEWS

In order to relate these overall societal dimensions of racism, ethnic power relations, the media and the role of ideology, to the local levels of news and news-making, we need to know more about news-gathering routines in media organizations and about the detailed structures of media discourse. That is, we need to examine in detail how the reproduction of racism by the media at the macro-level is actually reproduced at the micro-level of news-making and news reports. It is this micro-level focus that inspires our analysis in this book (see also van Dijk, 1985b, 1988a, 1988b).

Sociological work on everyday news-gathering converges with earlier studies of news values, and shows that the organization of 'news-beats' as well as the definition of newsworthy events are determined by powerful professional and social ideologies and organizational routines (Gans, 1979; Tuchman, 1978). Thus, powerful elite groups and institutions, especially in the corporate and political domains, are able partly to control their access to, as well as their portrayal in the media. They have effectively organized access through press offices, press releases, press conferences, and in addition they have partial control over news-gathering and portrayal by strategic leaks, personal contacts, financial incentives, or various forms of retaliation against non-complying reporters or newspapers (Bagdikian, 1983; Hollingsworth, 1986; Paletz and Entman, 1981).

This does not mean that elite groups are always portrayed positively. However, it is relevant that they are prominent news actors (participants, including passive or neutral ones) in the first place, that their voice is heard, and that their opinions are presented as credible and legitimate, even when the Press may disagree about details of their policies and actions (Golding, Murdock and Schlesinger, 1986). In this respect, the role of the oppositional Press – unlike the 'radical media' (see Downing, 1984) – is little different from that of other, opposed, power groups, such as the parties of the official opposition, the unions or some sections of the symbolic elites, as in education, academic research, or the arts. Indeed, some newspapers may act as the voice of such oppositional groups, as long as they remain within the boundaries of a flexible, but carefully guarded consensus of legitimate dissent (Herman and Chomsky, 1988). It may even purport to speak 'for the people' when large sections of the readers are assumed to oppose specific acts or policies of some elite groups.

These constraints define rather specific features of news-making and news structures. They condition the assignments given to reporters, the choice of primary beats, the nature of interviewing, the strategies of 'checking out' facts, the credibility and hence the changes, or lack of them, in Press releases, and generally the discursive 'work' of journalists. Within this framework of news-making, elite groups and their actions are by definition newsworthy (Galtung and Ruge, 1965; Golding and Elliott, 1979). Their opinions will be asked and quoted credibly, and their description will generally be respectful. Thus, at all levels of news-gathering, defined as a complex system of source text processing, and at all levels of news report structures, the social, economic and cultural power relations may indirectly become reproduced (Davis and Walton, 1983; Hall, Hobson, Lowe, and Willis, 1980).

Structures of headlines, leads, thematic organization, the presence of explanatory background information, style, and especially the overall selection of newsworthy topics are thus indirectly controlled by the societal context of power relations (Glasgow University Media Group, 1976, 1980; van Dijk, 1988b, 1989a). It is therefore crucial for this study to examine in detail these relationships between societal power relations on the one hand, and the precise structures of news reports, as they are mediated through the practices and social cognitions of the reporters and the editors of the Press, on the other hand.

Important in such a study is the assumption that the elite versions of the 'facts', their definitions of reality, will tend to prevail over those of other, non-dominant groups. In our examples, given in the previous chapter, about the Tamil refugees, the West Indian 'rioters', and the Muslims who protested against Rushdie's book, we have seen what such a dominant definition of ethnic events entails. In other words, it is at this point that we must relate white group power and ideologies with their reproduction in and through the media.

Despite its dependence on other power elites, it should finally be emphasized that the Press does not passively participate in the reproduction of power. We have seen that it may voice conflicting interests, represent legitimate opposition groups, or even sometimes speak 'for the people'. On the other hand, its own contribution to the reproduction of power also has important specific and autonomous features. That is, the Press also produces its own dimension of the power structure. Through its specific discursive and cognitive strategies of selection, emphasis, focusing, exaggeration, relevance assignment, description, style, or rhetoric it has a powerful role in the final definition of the situation. Even when leading politicians sometimes formulate the events with due restraint as a 'problem', the tabloids may in their own terms redefine them as a drama.

This may happen not only for ideological reasons, but also because of special media functions. Thus, besides the communication of information and the formation of opinion the media are expected to entertain, if only to boost sales. In other words, the reproduction of power, and hence the reproduction of racism, by the media is to be carefully defined also as a semi-autonomous productive practice, with its own complex ideological framework, its own cultural codes, and its own political economy.

## PUBLIC REPRODUCTION

The process of reproduction ultimately finds its rationale with the public at large. In democratic societies, little power can be legitimated and hence be truly effective without some form of popular support or consent. Here we confront the vital role of the media. Beyond the traditional and controversial study of 'effects', therefore, we need to know how the media definition of the ethnic situation affects the beliefs of the public.

Strategic processes of decoding, semantic and pragmatic inter- pretation both at the global and local levels of discourse, the construction of textual and situational representations in memory, and the activation and application of knowledge or other beliefs, require complex cognitive theories in order to explain what exactly 'happens' when readers read a news report and process its information (Graber, 1984; Gunter, 1987; van Dijk, 1988a). Besides, by general cognitive principles, and by socially shared knowledge, these processes are in turn constrained by personal, situational, and more general social and cultural constraints of understanding, newspaper reading, and mass communication. It may be expected, therefore, that interpretations stored by readers may show considerable variation as a function of, for example, class position, education, and culture (Morley, 1983). Indeed, as is the case for the media themselves, the readers are not passive, but active processors of information. They do not simply register conveyed meanings, but construct them. And this is only the first step in the process of public reproduction, to which we return in Chapter nine.

The next steps involve even more complex, and as yet hardly understood, processes of opinion and attitude formation, which are controlled by underlying norms, values, and ideologies, and which in turn are the basis for social action. Media research in the future will have to pay detailed attention to the cognitive representations and strategies involved in the formation and changes of these various forms of social representations. Results of this research will also explain how exactly prejudices or other ethnic attitudes and ideologies are conditioned by the complex interaction of represented media discourse and already existing beliefs of the readers.

## ELITE RACISM

Within the theoretical framework presented above we need to emphasize one particular thesis, that is, that the reproduction of racism by the Press is a specific kind of what we call 'elite racism' (van Dijk, 1987d). This thesis is derived from results of much earlier work on racism and the role of the Press in society. It not only implies that the various elites have a special set of racist ideologies and practices, but also that their position allows them to 'preformulate' those of the population at large, and thus to produce and reproduce the white ethnic consensus.

One of the complex arguments used in the derivation of this thesis is, for example, that although racism is in the interest of the whole white group, it will most of all benefit the (power of the) elites. Since the dominant white media and their ideologies are inextricably related to these political, social, and corporate elite groups, and mediate, legitimate, or even directly support white elite power, it is also in their interest to play their crucial, 'symbolic' role in the reproduction of the ethnic consensus and, in fact, to participate itself in its (pre)formulation. Specific and autonomous media power in this case is defined by the fact that in present-day societies the mass media have nearly exclusive control over the symbolic resources needed to manufacture popular consent, especially in the domain of ethnic relations. This means that anti-racist ideologies can be successfully marginalized and thus excluded from popular opinion formation. We shall later see in more detail by what strategies and structures of news production and news reports the Press is involved in these processes of reproduction. This analysis will also show that this process is complex and far from straightforward, exhibiting internal contradictions as well as many variations, for instance, between different types of newspapers and countries.

The assumptions formulated above not only suggest that the dominant Press does participate in the reproduction of various modes of elite racism, but also how it is likely to do so. Thus we may expect that any group or proposal that advocates weakening of white group control, and especially of political and corporate control (for example, political organization of minorities, serious forms of affirmative action or energetic measures against discrimination), will be attacked with the media's own, symbolic strategies. These may range from overt verbal abuse to more subtle forms of marginalization, such as limiting access, biased reporting and quotation, or discrediting. It may therefore be predicted that for the right-wing Press especially, the main opponents will generally be the following:

politically, the radical left;
ethnically, the most militant minority groups (for example, young
    black males);
socially, pro-minority welfare organizations; and
culturally, those who are symbolic competitors for the definition of
    the ethnic situation, for example, anti-racist educators, scholars,
    writers, as well as some politicians.

It may also be expected that those groups that combine these societal dimensions will be the major targets of the Press, although norms and values that restrict blatantly racist writing may lead to more virulent attacks against, perhaps, prominent white anti-racists of the left than against black groups.

## THE DISCOURSE ANALYTICAL APPROACH

For the systematic analysis of the contents and structures of ethnic reporting in the Press our overall approach is discourse analytical. This means that we study news reports as a particular type or genre of discourse, and not simply as an unanalysed 'message' as would be the case in traditional mass communication research (van Dijk, 1985b, 1988a, 1988b). Before we begin with the concrete analysis of news reports, let us briefly summarize what discourse analysis amounts to (for details, see van Dijk, 1985a).

Discourse analysis is a multidisciplinary approach to the study of language use and communication in their socio-cultural contexts. Against the background of the classical tradition of rhetoric, modern discourse analysis emerged in the late 1960s and early 1970s from different but related developments in anthropology, ethnography, linguistics, poetics, psychology, micro-sociology, mass communication, history, political science, and other disciplines in the humanities and social sciences interested in the analysis of 'text' or 'talk'. The many directions in contemporary discourse analysis have in common a detailed study of the various levels or dimensions of natural discourse, such as everyday conversations, institutional dialogues, stories, argumentation, media discourses (such as news reports, advertisements or television programmes), and many other genres of text or communicative events.

Whereas this focus on the systematic study of textual or conversational structures is the more specific task of discourse analysis, the interdisciplinary relevance and the explanatory frameworks for it derive from the analysis of the relationships between 'text and context'. That is, discourse analysis specifically aims to show how the cognitive, social, historical, cultural, or political contexts of language use and communication impinge on the contents, meanings, structures, or strategies of text or dialogue, and vice versa, how discourse itself is an integral part of and contributes to the structures of these contexts. For the analysis of news in the Press this means, among other things, that we show how social or political structures are also manifest in the meanings or organization of news reports, and how such news reports may in turn contribute to the formation or change of social cognitions of the readers or the reproduction or legitimation of power of elites, as we have indicated above.

## Structural analysis

In a 'structural' description of texts themselves, we usually make a distinction between different levels and dimensions of analysis, where dimensions, so to speak, 'vertically' cut across different 'horizontal' levels. The 'surface' structure levels in such a description are those of syntax and style, word formation, sound structures (such as intonation) and graphical presentation (such as lay-out of news reports). These surface structures, or forms, are described as 'expressions' of the underlying levels of the meanings, reference, or functions of words, sentences, paragraphs, or whole texts, which are analysed by the semantic component of a linguistic grammar or a theory of discourse. Conversely, we say that surface forms are being 'interpreted' in terms of meanings or reference.

Together, surface forms and their underlying meanings, when used in a particular communicative situation, realize specific social acts, that is, so-called 'speech acts', such as assertions, questions, promises, threats, or accusations. The analysis of such social acts typically performed by verbal utterances, takes place in a pragmatic enquiry. Thus, news reports usually have the pragmatic function of an 'assertion': they state what is supposed to be unknown to the reader. Editorials on the other hand may also have the function of an accusation or a recommendation.

One of the major differences between discourse analysis and linguistics is that linguistics is usually limited to the study of grammar, that is, the analysis of the surface structures and meanings of (isolated, abstract) sentences. Discourse analysis goes beyond the sentence boundary and studies structures of discourses as a whole, while using data derived from naturally occurring text and talk. For the study of meaning and speech acts, this means, among other things, that we usually make a distinction between local or micro-structures (those of words and sentences, partly analysed also in linguistic grammar, but also coherence relations between sentences), on the one hand, and global or macro-structures, on the other hand. We shall see that the topics or themes of a news report, often expressed in the headline and lead, are examples of these global meanings of a news report. Similarly, in a pragmatic approach of discourse, we find that since news discourses usually consist of many sentences, they are not realizing sequences of unrelated (local) assertions, but that these speech acts are also coherently related, and that together they may function as one overall, macro-speech act of assertion.

In a way that is similar to the syntactic forms of sentences which express the structures of underlying meanings, we further assume that the overall meaning of a text is organized by a global schematic form, a so-called 'superstructure'. We shall see, for instance, that news reports have such an overall schematic structure, consisting of conventional categories, of which headline and lead, together forming the 'summary category' of the news report, are familiar to the newspaper reader.

Across these different micro- and macro-levels of form and meaning, discourse analysis distinguishes various dimensions of analysis. For instance, in order to express the same underlying meaning, surface structures of different levels may vary as a function of personal and social positions of the speaker, the discourse genre, the social situation, or the wider cultural context. The overall result of the specific choices that characterize each of these possible contexts and that are made among various alternatives, is called the 'style' of a discourse. For instance, specific lay-out, words, or sentence structures are rather typical of news in the Press and would occur less or not at all in everyday conversations or in scholarly reports. Similarly, because of different lay-out and printing type, different sentence structures and different word choice, the style of a popular tabloid will usually differ from that of a quality newspaper, usually as a function of a different socio-cultural context, namely, the intended reading public.

Another dimension that cuts across different levels of discourse is that of rhetorical structures, which may be those of sounds (such as alliteration and rhyme), sentence structures (for example, parallelism) or meaning (such as metaphor, understatements, or irony). Whereas style tells us something about the attitudes or social context of the speaker or about the type of communicative event, rhetorical structures are geared towards the reader, and are used to enhance the effectiveness of the text by calling special attention to specific expressions or meanings.

Finally, spoken discourse genres not only consist of surface forms, meaning, speech acts, style and rhetoric, but also have an interactional nature, as is the case in everyday conversations or institutional dialogues, such as meetings and interviews of different kinds. Thus, spoken discourse consists of structural units called 'turns', which are defined by speaker changes and which follow each other according to specific turn-taking rules. This interactional aspect of talk also requires an important strategic analysis of discourse: speakers try, optimally, to realize their communicative or social goals, and go through different functional moves to realize those goals. Besides wanting to convey their intended meanings, they may want the hearer to do something, or to present themselves as positively as possible (the well-known strategy of face-keeping), or to persuade their listeners. This dimension is relevant in an analysis of news only when we study news interviews or news programmes in broadcasting. In our study of the ways news about ethnic affairs is understood and processed by the readers, we have conducted interviews that may also be examined in terms of this so-called conversational analysis.

## Contextual analysis

Once such a structural analysis has been made, we may proceed to establishing relationships with the context (of course, we may also start out by analysing the context and then the text). For instance, we may want to know how specific textual structures, such as headlines in the Press, different categories of story-telling and argumentation, or a specific style or rhetorical device impinge on the reader or listener, as we already suggested above. That is, we are then interested in the actual processes of decoding, interpretation, storage, and representation in memory, and in the role of previous knowledge and beliefs of the readers in this process of understanding (van Dijk and Kintsch, 1983). Such cognitive representations and strategies involved in actual discourse processing may themselves be influenced by the social and political contexts of the language users, such as their gender, class, or ethnic group membership, or the nature of the communicative situation (classroom, courtroom, or news-room).

A multidisciplinary analysis of the discourses of the Press systematically deals with these different levels, dimensions, and contexts of news about ethnic affairs. Besides these structural and contextual analyses, however, we also provide some quantitative data about the frequencies and distribution of such structures, as is also done in classical content analysis. The following chapters offer an analysis of the overall meanings or topics of news, first those expressed in the headlines. Then we proceed to more local aspects of news reports, such as meanings of sentences, style, and rhetoric. Each of these analyses is proceeded by a brief theoretical introduction for readers who are not familiar with discourse analysis.

## CONCLUSIONS

The elements of the theoretical framework that inspires the research reported in the next chapters suggest that the reproduction of racism by the media is not a simple and straightforward process. A multidisciplinary approach appears to be necessary to formulate the major issues involved in its analysis. Thus the role of the media in the reproduction of racism cannot be isolated from the general properties of racism and white dominance in society, including the structural and ideological organization of that form of group power. This means that the role of the Press as a corporate, social, and cultural institution needs to be analysed in relation to other institutions, such as those of the polity or the economy.

This book, however, will focus on how these relationships at the macro-level are 'translated' at the micro-level into everyday routines of news-gathering, news-writing, editing, printing, distribution, and reading at the level of actual social practices. At this level, very subtle details of interaction with actors or elite institutions, of source text processing, and of the composition of news reports, need to be attended to. In particular, we shall examine the textual or symbolic implications of our general working hypothesis, that is, that the Press participates in the various modes of what we have called 'elite racism'. In this way, we are also able to link properties of the coverage of ethnic affairs with the more global elite role and position of the Press in the reproduction of racism in society. Such an analysis also requires a study of the cognitive processes involved in the comprehension of news reports by the readers and in the formation and change of ethnic attitudes and ideologies, and how these depend on the structures and contents of news reports about ethnic affairs. These various dimensions of the coverage of ethnic affairs require the complex theories and subtle methods of current discourse analysis, which specifically focuses on the relationships between detailed textual structures of news, on the one hand, and the cognitive, social, political, and cultural structures of their contexts, on the other hand.

# 3 Headlines

## STRUCTURES AND FUNCTIONS OF HEADLINES

Let us begin our analysis of news reports about ethnic affairs where such reports begin themselves: the headline. Headlines in the Press have important textual and cognitive functions. They therefore deserve special attention. As every newspaper reader knows, they are the most conspicuous part of a news report: they are brief, printed 'on top', in large bold type, and often across several columns. Their main function is to summarize the most important information of the report. That is, they express its main 'topic', a notion we discuss in the next chapter. Grammatically, headlines are often incomplete sentences: articles or auxiliary verbs may be deleted. This may sometimes lead to vagueness or ambiguity, which may also have a special ideological function, for instance when the responsibility for an action must be concealed. We shall come back to this specific aspect of grammatical style in the following chapters.

Headlines also have an important cognitive function: they are usually read first and the information expressed in the headline is strategically used by the reader during the process of understanding in order to construct the overall meaning, or the main topics, of the rest of the text before the text itself is even read. Indeed, often readers do not read more than the headline of a news report. Headline information is also used to activate the relevant knowledge in memory the reader needs to understand the news report. Thus, as soon as the word *riot* is used in the headline, the reader will activate relevant general knowledge about riots, that is, a so-called 'riot script'. This script monitors the interpretation of the details of the rest of the text.

Headline information is used by the reader as an overall organizing principle for the representation of the news event in memory, namely as a so-called 'model of the situation'. For instance, after having read one or several news reports about the Handsworth 'riot' in the UK, the readers who have understood these reports have built a personal memory representation, that is, a model, of that particular disturbance. Headline information signals the reader how to 'define' the situation or the event. This 'top-level' information of the text will therefore often also serve as the top level of the mental model the readers build of that event.

Headlines often have ideological implications. Since they express the most important information about a news event, they may bias the understanding process: they summarize what, according to the journalist, is the most important aspect, and such a summary necessarily implies an opinion or a specific perspective on the events. Thus, journalists may 'upgrade' a less important topic by expressing it in the headline, thereby 'downgrading' the importance of the main topic. In other words, headlines are a subjective definition of the situation, which influences the interpretation made by the readers. Defining an event as a 'riot' may lead to a different interpretation of the news report, and hence to a different model of the situation, from when the event is defined as a 'disturbance' or a 'protest'. Since the headline has such a powerful influence on the interpretation of a news report, readers would have to make an extra effort to derive an alternative main topic from the text. Generally speaking, the information in the headline is also the information that is best recalled by the readers. This means that headlines have a particularly important function in influencing the use readers will make of this information on later occasions (Schwartz and Flammer, 1981; van Dijk and Kintsch, 1983).

Finally, headlines also have an important role in the everyday routines of news production. Just like the readers, journalists use summarizing headlines to understand and memorize the information they get from the discourses of their many sources, which may well define the situation for *them* as they in turn do it for the reader. Often, headlines are not written by the reporters themselves, but by special editors, who not only think of the best summary for a news report, but also take into account what they think will be a 'catchy' title for the readers; readers may decide to read a news report, or not, only on the basis of the information contained in the title (Garst and Bernstein, 1982).

Thus, headlines of news reports about ethnic affairs summarize events that the white newspaper, reporter, or editor finds most relevant – for the white readers, that is. In other words, these headlines at the same time define and evaluate the ethnic situation, as the white Press sees it. In cognitive terms such a definition of the situation amounts to the expression of the top of the mental model of the ethnic situation, that is, how news-makers have mentally represented an ethnic event. Given the prominence of headlines in the semantic and cognitive representations of the news report, and hence their role in further processing and memorization, this definition of the ethnic situation is crucial.

Given their semantic, cognitive and ideological relevance in processes of communication, especially for news topics about 'race', which presuppose complex social attitudes and ideologies, this chapter pays special attention to the contents and structures of these headlines. We focus on headlines in the British Press. Elsewhere we have already reported on the headlines in Dutch ethnic news (van Dijk, 1988c). However, we shall also make comparisons with other data and research results, when available. We begin our analysis with some quantitative results, and then proceed to the qualitative study of the headlines. In the next chapter, we pay attention to other aspects of the topical structure of news reports about minorities.

## HEADLINES IN THE BRITISH PRESS

### Frequencies

We examined a corpus of 2,755 headlines, all about race, taken from *The Times* (576), the *Guardian* (670), the *Daily Telegraph* (705), the *Daily Mail* (524), and the *Sun* (280). We see that except for the *Sun*, the national newspapers each have more than 500 news reports, published during a period of 6 months (from 1 August 1985 to 31 January 1986). Since there are 162 weekdays during that period, we see that most of the Press published an average of at least 3 items per day, which is more than the usual amount of Press coverage about minorities. Indeed, during the first six months of 1989 the same newspapers had only 974 news items, that is, only about a third. One obvious explanation for this discrepancy is of course the massive coverage of the 'race riots' in September and October 1985, during which 938 reports on race were published, an average of 7 items per day per newspaper! This is a first indication of the importance assigned in the Press to urban violence, especially the kind of violence associated with minority groups. August 1985 and January 1986, each with about 2 items per day, are more 'normal' months for the coverage of minorities, although still more than in 1989.

## Words

The first property of the headlines we examine is the use of words, that is, their lexical style. Words manifest the underlying semantic concepts used in the definition of the situation. Lexicalization of semantic content, however, is never neutral: the choice of one word rather than another to express more or less the same meaning, or to denote the same referent, may signal the opinions, emotions, or social position of a speaker (see Chapter eight for details about the notion of style). To describe the civil disturbances in Britain in 1985, the headlines may use such words as *riots*, *disturbances* or *disorders* among many other words. We have seen above that such a choice of words in newspaper headlines plays an important role. Not only do they express the definition of the situation, but they also signal the social or political opinions of the newspaper about the events. That is, headlines not only globally define or summarize an event, they also evaluate it. Hence, the lexical style of headlines has ideological implications.

We begin the analysis of the words and other properties of the headlines with a study of their common characteristics. Then we examine more specifically the headlines on some major issues in the different newspapers in order to see whether and how the newspapers provide different definitions and evaluations of the ethnic situation.

### A note on quotes and references

Here, as well as in the next chapters, actual words used in the Press are written in italics, when we focus on the words themselves. When words or phrases of the Press are merely quoted without further analysis, we use double quotation marks. Semantic concepts (the meanings of words) are enclosed by single quotes. Examples of full quotations or headlines written on separate lines, are printed in ordinary, roman, type, without quotation marks. Headlines are always printed in small capitals.

### The urban disturbances

Since most of the news items deal with the urban unrest in September and October 1985 and its aftermath during the next months, it is not surprising that the most frequent headline words are *police* (occurring in 388 headlines) and its synonyms ('policeman', 'policewoman', 'PC', 'WPC', 'constable', etc.) and *riot* (320 headlines) (see Table 3.1). The social unrest, for the majority of the Press, is defined with the more obviously dramatic and negative term *riot*, rather than with the more

*Table 3.1* Most frequent words in the headlines of five British newspapers, August 1981–January 1986

| | | | | | | |
|---|---|---|---|---|---|---|
| 388 | police | 40 | mob | 27 | Tory |
| 320 | riot | 39 | day | 27 | Tottenham |
| 244 | black | 39 | murder | 26 | family |
| 200 | race | 39 | woman | 26 | plea |
| 88 | city | 38 | fear | 26 | section |
| 85 | row | 38 | teacher | 26 | time |
| 84 | attack | 36 | communicate | 26 | world |
| 81 | Asian | 36 | hate | 25 | group |
| 77 | Hurd | 35 | ban | 25 | immigrant |
| 67 | racist | 35 | victim/ize | 25 | protest |
| 66 | MP | 34 | immigration | 25 | raid |
| 66 | school | 34 | white | 25 | win |
| 65 | head | 33 | death | 24 | kill/er |
| 65 | Honeyford | 33 | London | 24 | Kinnock |
| 63 | Handsworth | 32 | claim | 24 | power |
| 61 | report | 32 | plan | 23 | children |
| 60 | council | 32 | union | 23 | hit |
| 55 | Britain | 31 | racism | 23 | threat |
| 54 | inquiry | 30 | leader | 22 | youth |
| 53 | job | 30 | minister | 21 | parents |
| 48 | fight | 30 | shoot | 21 | speak/speech |
| 48 | law | 30 | work/er | 21 | strike |
| 47 | Brixton | 29 | Grant | 21 | terror/terrify |
| 47 | charge | 29 | racial | 21 | Thatcher |
| 46 | face | 29 | rule | 22 | talk |
| 45 | chief | 29 | warn(ing) | 21 | comment |
| 45 | man | 29 | blame | 20 | deal/er |
| 44 | Labour | 28 | order | 20 | fail/ure |
| 41 | call | 27 | end | 20 | peace |
| 41 | court | 27 | Jarrett | 20 | Powell |
| 41 | home | 27 | left | 20 | told |
| 41 | violence | 27 | street(s) | 20 | urge(nt) |

neutral terms *unrest* or *disturbance*, which each occured only twice, or *disorder* (12 occurrences). The presence and actions of the police, as a main actor in the news, adds to the negative definition of this first situation in which minorities are involved: together with the concept of 'riot', the urban disturbances are thus primarily situated in the domain of law and order (for details about the disturbances of 1985, see Benyon and Solomos, 1987; Gifford, 1986).

It is not surprising that the third major concept is *black*, occurring both as an adjective and as a noun. Given the cultural and political knowledge of the readers, this concept, together with *police* and *riot*, defines the basic proposition of many headlines, as in 'blacks riot with the police'. Indeed, the prominent presence of the concept of 'black' in the headlines suggests that the disturbances are primarily defined in terms of ethnic background or colour. They are not defined as 'urban' or 'social' forms of protest or unrest, or as actions of 'youths', but specifically attributed to black people, usually young males, despite the fact that about 30 per cent of the participants were white. Even from this superficial analysis of the frequency of words or concepts in the headlines, it already becomes clear that the disturbances are not merely vaguely associated with blacks, in which case blacks could also have the role of victims. Rather, the cause of the 'riots' is essentially attributed to black youths as active agents, an assumption we shall further examine when we study the syntactic and semantic structures of the headlines.

Similarly, reports about minorities are also firmly connected to the concept of 'race' or 'racial', words that together occur 219 times in the headlines. Words such as 'ethnic groups' or 'minorities' hardly occur, and their relative infrequency suggests that ethnic relations for the British Press are primarily seen in terms of racial categories, that is, in terms of colour or appearance, as was also the case in the 1960s (Hartmann, Husband and Clark, 1974). Although the word *Asian* is quite frequent (80), more specific group terms, such as *West Indian* (8) occur much less. Also *immigrant* has become much less frequent than before. Comparison with our Dutch data shows that the headlines of the Press in the Netherlands generally prefer specific names to denote minority groups, for instance, 'Turks', 'Moroccans', 'Surinamese', or 'Tamils', and sometimes generic terms such as 'foreigners' and 'refugees' (van Dijk, 1988c). Headline identification of minority groups by race or colour in the Dutch Press is rare.

The style register of violence is amply represented in the headlines. *Death*, *murder*, *terror*, *attack*, *violence*, *shot*, *shooting* and similar words can be found in hundreds of headlines (see Table 3.1). Whereas they may be expected in the coverage of the disturbances, it should be noted that they also frequently appear in reports about other events. Together with the notions of 'riot' and 'police', they essentially define the negative ethnic situation as much of the British Press sees it. Here are a few typical examples from different newspapers (all examples are from 1985):

HUNDREDS OF POLICE CLASH WITH MOB IN BIRMINGHAM RIOT
    (*Times*, 10 September)
CARNIVAL NO-GO AREA ANGERS DRUG POLICE (*Mail*, 26 August)

THE TICKING TIME BOMB. 'QUIET DAY' THAT TURNED TO NIGHT OF
   FIRE TERROR (*Sun*, 11 September)
WEST INDIAN GANG INVADED PUB IN REVENGE RIOT (*Telegraph*, 23
   August)
POLICE BLAME RIOT ON DRUG DEALERS (*Guardian*, 16 September)

The tabloids are the most outspoken with their negative headlines,
and do not shun constant references to mobs, terror, attacks, murder,
and related notions of the violence register. These notions are not only
reserved for minority actors: racist attacks and white violence are
occasionally also associated with such negative terms. It should be
emphasized though, that even in such cases the general association
between violence and race remains, whether blacks are seen as victims
or as perpetrators of crime and violence. Since headlines are often
syntactically ambiguous or unclear, agency may even be difficult to
establish. Indeed, it is the collocation of concepts that is important in
the headlines.

Even events that are non-violent in themselves may be described
metaphorically with 'aggressive' notions, such as 'attack', 'clash', or
'tackle'. In this respect, British headlines generally appear rather
aggressive. Even routine political and social relationships and minor
conflicts are often expressed with words from the aggression and
violence registers, or with military metaphors. We do not know whether
this is also the case for the coverage of other issues, but the presence of
aggressive terms in the headlining of race relations neverthelesss
establishes an overall association between race relations and serious
trouble and problems, if not violence.

## Other ethnic subjects

As may be expected, the other frequent words denote the other major
agents and locations of ethnic news events of 1985. Perhaps most
interesting is the massive interest in the case of Honeyford (the
headmaster of a Bradford school suspended because of his racist
writings). This case is especially prominent in the right-wing Press,
which defines it as an attack on the freedom of speech, if not as a form
of reverse 'racism'. Note though that from a different point of view, this
topic is also extensively discussed in the *Guardian*.

Whereas the urban disorders and other violence associated with
blacks are massively present in the headlines, white violence is much less
prominently displayed. *Discrimination* gets headline status in ten
reports only, whereas *prejudice* occurs only twice in more than 2,700

reports! (The reverse is true in the Dutch Press reports of the same period, when discrimination is quite frequently headlined.) The words *racist* and *racism* occur 67 and 31 times respectively in our table. However, these words are usually placed between 'scare' quotes, suggesting journalistic distance or scepticism, if not ridicule about such an accusation. This is a first indication of the biased opinion of much of the Press about racism: black violence gets much more, and more negative, attention than white racist violence, such as racial attacks against Asians. Often the notion of 'racism' is mentioned in a sub-title, or refers to racism abroad. The same is true for the more frequent word *racist*, which also often occurs in quotes or associated with allegations that are obviously found ridiculous. That these quotes and contexts are not just general journalistic convention, may be seen from the *Guardian*, which uses them much less than the conservative and especially the tabloid Press. The standard concept used for violence against minority groups is 'racial/racist attack', which occurs in a few dozen headlines, especially in the reports about arson attacks against Asian families.

## The 1989 coverage

The 1,184 headlines of the 1989 ethnic affairs coverage are dominated by a few major ethnic stories, such as the Rushdie affair, the deportation of Viraj Mendis, the Silcott affair, the case of separate Muslim schools, and the immigration of Kurdish refugees. This time, *black* is the most frequent headline word (occurring in 95 headlines), followed by *race* (75), which demonstrates the continued prominence of 'race' in the definition of ethnic events in 1989. The salience of the Rushdie affair in the headlines also shows in the frequency of *Rushdie* (65) and *Muslims* (64) in the definitions of the situation. Similarly, also the name of Viraj Mendis, the Sri Lankan refugee and Tamil supporter deported to Sri Lanka, often (42) appears in the headlines. Other frequent words in these headlines are *school*, *Labour*, *immigrant*, *student*, *white*, *Vauxhall*, *Hurd*, *ethnic*, *threat*, and of course *police*. The frequency of 'school' is due to the prominent issue of separate Muslim schools, and Labour and Vauxhall are mentioned often because of the Vauxhall by-election, in which Labour substituted a white candidate for a local black candidate for this parliamentary seat. The frequency of *Silcott* and *students* is due to the initiative of students nominating Silcott, a black man convicted for murder of a policeman (Blakelock) during the Tottenham disturbances in 1985 (see pp. 62–4), as their honourary president, to express their protests against his trial, which according to prominent human rights organizations was scandalously biased.

Although the death threat by Khomeini and the various forms of protests by fundamentalist Muslims against *The Satanic Verses* give rise to occasional panicky and aggressive reporting and headlining, we found that the 1989 headlines on ethnic affairs are on the whole less aggressive than those in 1985. Among the words from the 'aggression' style register that occur at least 10 times in the headlines, we only find *threat*, *row*, *attack* and *death*. This time words such as *mob* hardly occur in the headlines (although they do in the text of the reports themselves). In other words, if judged by the lexical style of the definition of the situation expressed in the headlines, ethnic reporting in 1989 has become less negative and aggressive. Further research is necessary to determine whether this is a manifestation of a more general tendency towards more subtlety in race reporting in the UK.

## Headline structures

We also need to pay attention to the relations between words in the headlines because these relations also describe the roles of, and the relationships between the news actors. After all, the police or young blacks may be mentioned as 'agents' of an action, but also appear in the semantic category of 'patients', that is, as actors who undergo an action, for instance as victims of aggression or as the object of accusations. At the same time, we may examine whether such roles are associated with positive, neutral, or negative actions. For instance, the police may be specifically represented as the responsible agent of neutral or positive actions, and blacks may be typically represented as the responsible agents of negative actions.

For this analysis, we coded all headlines and counted how often special roles, actions, or relationships occurred for the major news actors. Some special actors (for example, Honeyford) and events (for example, the 'riots') were coded separately. Tables 3.2 and 3.3 give the frequencies of these categories for five British newspapers. We first briefly examine some figures, and then analyse the headlines in a more qualitative way.

First inspection of Table 3.2 shows that a large number of headlines are conceptually unspecific, that is, they cannot be identified as a summary of an ethnic event: examples are "SAFE SEAT" and "UNEASY ALLIANCE". In all newspapers, especially in the right-wing Press, minority actors seem to be more frequent than majority group actors, but if we add the special majority group categories of the government, the police or a prominent individual, majority groups are more frequent in headlines. That is, they are more prominent in the definition of the

*Table 3.2* Frequencies of actors in the headlines, August 1985–January 1986

| Categories | Times | Sun | Tele-graph | Mail | Guardian |
|---|---|---|---|---|---|
| Total number of articles | 576 | 280 | 705 | 524 | 670 |
| Unclear | 150 | 61 | 192 | 142 | 177 |
| Minority actors | 93 | 52 | 131 | 70 | 93 |
| Majority actors | 51 | 10 | 49 | 31 | 63 |
| Neutral predicates | 131 | 22 | 58 | 49 | 108 |
| Negative predicates | 126 | 81 | 115 | 108 | 92 |
| Positive predicates | 29 | 8 | 38 | 14 | 22 |
| Government, Parliament, parties | 47 | 9 | 47 | 23 | 43 |
| Police, judiciary | 88 | 36 | 118 | 80 | 105 |
| Action groups | 0 | 0 | 0 | 0 | 1 |
| Stereotypes | 0 | 0 | 3 | 7 | 1 |
| Anti-racist actions | 7 | 0 | 1 | 1 | 0 |
| Majority indiv: Honeyford, Powell | 20 | 19 | 34 | 32 | 40 |
| Race relations | 67 | 70 | 119 | 108 | 178 |
| Racist attacks | 5 | 2 | 9 | 8 | 13 |
| Riots | 98 | 52 | 115 | 71 | 84 |
| Inter-ethnic conflict | 0 | 2 | 1 | 3 | 2 |
| Other agents | 0 | 0 | 1 | 0 | 0 |
| Unclear white/black agents | 3 | 32 | 41 | 30 | 21 |
| Immigration | 25 | 4 | 27 | 12 | 36 |

situation. As may be expected, government actors are more prominent in the quality Press than in the tabloids, which generally have less political or policy news on ethnic affairs. We have already seen earlier that the police and the judiciary category is one of the most prominent single actors in news about ethnic affairs.

With the exception of the *Guardian*, all newspapers have headlines in which negative predicates (for example, those denoting actions) are more frequent than neutral ones. This is particularly obvious in the right-wing Press. Positive predicates are exceptional in news reporting about ethnic affairs in all newspapers (the *Telegraph* has relatively most of them). An example of such a headline is "POLICE SAVE ASIANS", which puts the police in a positive light. The same event, a racial attack, could have been summarized by the headline "WHITE RACISTS ATTACK ASIANS", which more clearly identifies the agents of the crime, and which would better render the negative evaluation of these racist attacks. Many of the neutral predicates refer to speech acts, such as declarations or accusations. Of the special event or action predicates we examined, 'riots' and race relations are most frequent, and much more prominent than, for instance, anti-racist actions or racial attacks against minority groups.

Table 3.3 shows the frequencies of some of the relations between these different headline actors in ethnic minority news. If an actor is mentioned before the predicate then it is an active agent, otherwise it is

*Table 3.3* Frequencies of relations in the headlines, August 1985–January 1986

| Categorical relations | Times | Sun | Tele- graph | Mail | Guardian |
|---|---|---|---|---|---|
| Minority: Neutral predicate | 22 | 11 | 20 | 15 | 26 |
| Minority: Negative predicate | 19 | 25 | 32 | 16 | 14 |
| Minority: Positive predicate | 4 | 1 | 4 | 4 | 5 |
| Majority: Neutral predicate | 23 | 0 | 9 | 6 | 20 |
| Majority: Negative predicate | 9 | 1 | 14 | 6 | 7 |
| Majority: Positive predicate | 3 | 0 | 10 | 2 | 7 |
| State/parties: Neutral predicate | 26 | 4 | 11 | 10 | 21 |
| State/parties: Negative predicate | 2 | 0 | 4 | 2 | 2 |
| State/parties: Positive predicate | 4 | 1 | 3 | 1 | 3 |
| Police/judiciary: Neutral predicate | 31 | 2 | 13 | 12 | 34 |
| Police/judiciary: Negative predicate | 21 | 4 | 6 | 8 | 25 |
| Police/judiciary: Positive predicate | 4 | 1 | 13 | 4 | 2 |
| Neutral predicate: Minority | 10 | 3 | 7 | 10 | 11 |
| Negative predicate: Minority | 11 | 7 | 14 | 8 | 16 |
| Positive predicate: Minority | 10 | 3 | 13 | 3 | 7 |
| Neutral predicate: Majority | 3 | 1 | 3 | 4 | 7 |
| Negative predicate: Majority | 5 | 7 | 6 | 5 | 2 |
| Positive predicate: Majority | 1 | 0 | 2 | 0 | 2 |
| Neutral predicate: State/parties | 3 | 0 | 2 | 0 | 2 |
| Negative predicate: State/parties | 1 | 1 | 3 | 0 | 0 |
| Positive predicate: State/parties | 0 | 0 | 1 | 0 | 0 |
| Neutral predicate: Police/judiciary | 12 | 1 | 5 | 7 | 6 |
| Negative predicate: Police/judiciary | 6 | 11 | 23 | 21 | 13 |
| Positive predicate: Police/judiciary | 2 | 2 | 2 | 3 | 3 |

the passive 'patient' or the beneficiary of an action. In the right-wing Press, minority agents are mostly associated with negative predicates. Majority agents tend to be more often associated with neutral and positive predicates. This is particularly the case for the state institutions and the political parties. The police are mostly a neutral or positive agent, although each newspaper also regularly mentions the police as a negative agent (we shall later see how that is done). If we now examine the actors in their 'passive' (patient or beneficiary) roles, we see that minorities (who are mostly negative agents) are more often described as passive actors of neutral or positive actions (that is, something good is done for them). That is, they are less often defined as victims, while exactly the reverse is true for majority group actors. The police are usually defined as the recipient of negative actions, that is, as victims of the negative actions of others. The same was found for the Dutch Press, in which minorities are seldom headlined as agents of positive action.

Whereas headlines are first and prominent textual categories of news reports, we see that even within the headlines, the ordering of words and concepts may be significant. Therefore we made a separate analysis of the first words or phrases of all headlines, to see which actors or actions tend to be 'topicalized', that is, placed first in a sentence. Often, first position of actors is associated with the role of active agents. About 40 per cent of all headlines have an actor in first position. As a single group, it is the police who occur most often in first position, but taken together minority groups, mostly blacks, are most frequent, as we have also seen above for headlines as a whole. When the police are first actor, however, they are agent of a negative action in only 7 of 171 cases! When put in first position, minorities are agents of negative actions twice as often, especially in the *Telegraph* and the *Sun* (and never in the *Guardian*). Also, in the Dutch Press, if minorities occur in first position, they are usually agents of negative actions. In other words, their negative actions are emphasized twice, first by headlining them and secondly by further topicalizing them in the headline. It is also interesting that in the British Press, unlike political parties and party leaders, the government and the ministries appear very little in first position in the headlines, and if they do, only in neutral or positive roles. Honeyford has the privilege to be the most frequently topicalized individual in this prominent position of the headlines.

These figures confirm what we might have assumed already from the general nature of ethnic reporting and the frequency of headline actors as studied above, namely, that there is tendency for a mirror image to occur in the roles and relations of news actors in the situation-defining headlines of ethnic affairs news: when they are agents, minorities tend to be more often responsible for negative actions, and when they are passive actors then they are less often represented as victims, while the opposite is true for majority actors. This special syntactic encoding of underlying actor roles of minorities and authorities has been often found in earlier research (Fowler, Hodge, Kress, and Trew, 1979; Sykes, 1985; van Dijk, 1988c). In many headlines the ethnic or racial category of the actors is unclear, as is the case for such words as 'mob' or 'rioter'. Previous reporting and the contents of the news report itself, however, hardly leave any doubts about the intended ethnic or racial category of such actors.

## Qualitative properties of headlines

After this analysis of the frequencies of actor roles and predicates in the headlines, we may proceed to the analysis of more detailed, qualitative properties. We shall do so by focusing on the headline definitions of the major stories in the autumn of 1985. Note that the analysis we give is informal, and not a systematic and explicit analysis, such as a grammatical one. Our aim is to reveal the ideological implications of the headlines, that is, from which socio-political position the news events are defined.

### The 'riots'

Since the urban disturbances play such a prominent role in the coverage of ethnic affairs in general, and during the period we examined in particular, let us begin by examining in more detail some of the headlines that define these dramatic events. For illustration, we focus on some of the hundreds of headlines on the disturbances in Tottenham (Broadwater Farm):

BLACK YOUTHS IN DEMO AS MOTHER DIES (*Telegraph*, 7 October)

MOBS IN FIREBOMB RAMPAGE. Police hit by shotgun blasts (*Telegraph*, 7 October)

OFFICER STABBED TO DEATH IN RIOT (*Guardian*, 7 October)

POLICE STONED BY MOB AFTER DEATH RAID. Mum dies during search. (*Sun*, 7 October)

RIOTING MOB SHOOT POLICE. Officer dies after being slashed in neck (*Mail*, 7 October)

AMBUSH ... IRA STYLE. Policemen lured into trap of hate. (*Mail*, 8 October)

WE SAW HIM BUTCHERED. Police fury over the night mayhem turned to bloody murder in Tottenham. Mates tell of a hero copper's last minutes. (*Sun*, 8 October)

The definition of the 'riot' situation is clear in these examples, as we already have seen in the examples given above and in the study of the lexical items of the headllines. The main focus is on violence and crime, not on definitions that imply social causes of the disturbances, which could have been headlined as, for example, "BLACK YOUTHS REVOLT", "FRUSTRATION ERUPTS IN INNER CITIES" or simply "BLACK RAGE HITS THE CITIES". Only the *Telegraph* headline is more neutral here, and also includes the immediate cause of the Tottenham disturbance: the death of a black woman, Mrs Jarrett, as a result of a heart attack during a police raid on her house. The *Sun* mentions her death in a lower level sub-headline, whereas the main headline itself uses the vague and hence ambiguous term "death raid", which does not immediately identify the police as the responsible agents of that raid. Nominalizations like these, instead of full clauses with active verbs, are often used to conceal responsible agency. The criminal actors are primarily identified as a 'mob', and not as a 'crowd', and therefore evaluated in terms of irrationality and lack of control, as is also the case for terms such as 'rampage' and others we have studied above. The use of concepts such as 'vengeance' or 'rage' in order to describe the reaction to the serious consequences of a police raid would be too 'rational' as an explanation of the events. Indeed, they might not only explain, but partly even excuse the disturbances.

As we have already concluded from the frequency of the word "black" in the headlines, the ethnic or racial identity of the "mob" is often prominently displayed: black youths are the main protagonists of this form of irrational crime. On the other hand, the police are represented as victim, mainly because of the murder of a policeman. The death of this policeman, PC Blakelock, is prominent in most of the coverage, and hence in the headlines and situation definitions of the Tottenham disturbance, especially in the right-wing Press. His murder is not only defined as such (and never as a 'casualty' in a fight), but often phrased in even more negative terms, such as "butchered" or "hacked to death", which of course implies an even more negative evaluation of the murderers. The death of Mrs Jarrett, as we shall see in more detail later when we examine the main topics of these reports, seldom reaches headline status: this event is apparently less important, and therefore seldom headlined. Her death is merely an 'accident', and she is a woman, and black. Note finally that the events in Tottenham are also defined in a broader framework of political crime, in other words, as a form of terrorism, when in the *Mail* a comparison is made with IRA ambushes.

Although newspapers may claim to simply state the 'facts' in their headlines, it is obvious that there are many ways to describe the facts, and to highlight and headline them accordingly. Take for instance the three headlines, all published on the same day by the *Telegraph*, about the aftermath of the disturbances, when participants in the 'riots' have been taken to court:

> SECOND BLACK ON MURDER CHARGE (*Telegraph*, 14 December)
> BLACK BRIXTON LOOTERS JAILED (*Telegraph*, 14 December)
> JARRETT SON CLEARED OF ASSAULTING PC (*Telegraph*, 14 December)

Note that when blacks are accused or jailed they are described as "blacks", whereas when they are cleared of an accusation, they suddenly lose colour, and are identified by their name, as is the case of the son of Mrs Jarrett, whose arrest lead to the police raid which sparked off the disturbances. Conflicting with the guidelines of the NUJ (*see* Appendix, p. 255), the newspaper thus defines looters and murderers prominently but irrelevantly as "black" in the headline, thereby emphasizing, even months after the disorders, the association between blacks and crime. This is one of the notorious 'classics' of racist reporting, and we shall meet this focus on black violence and crime repeatedly in the following chapters.

We see that lexical choice, syntax, relevance ordering, ethnic or racial identification and comparisons, among other characteristics, may be used to persuasively define and convey the prevalent definition of the situation: a vicious attack on the police by black (West Indian) youths. Owing to this definition, other aspects, such as the death of a black woman or deep social causes of the disturbances are not accepted as major elements of the definition of the situation, as has also been shown in other studies of the urban unrest in the UK (Benyon and Solomos, 1987; Hansen, 1982; Murdock, 1984; Murray, 1986; Solomos, 1989; Sumner, 1982).

## *Honeyford*

By their sheer frequency, the 145-odd headlines about the Honeyford case already suggest the prominence of this event in ethnic affairs news of 1985. Months passed in which each detail of the fight between the parents of mostly Asian children, as well as the Bradford council, on the one hand, and Honeyford and his supporters, on the other hand, was highlighted. Honeyford had written several articles in conservative publications, in which he attacked the principles of multi-cultural education, and called attention to the 'fate' of white pupils in predominantly 'black' schools, like his own. Because his remarks about the Asian community were hardly flattering, his opponents consequently accused him of racism. This accusation was violently opposed by the entire conservative Press, which saw Honeyford as the victim of radical anti-racists, and which therefore soon variously proclaimed him their hero and martyr. During the autumn of 1985 the affair reached its peak when a court reinstated Honeyford, who was suspended by the authorities in Bradford. The city, however, appealed against the decision, and finally won. Honeyford then left with a "golden handshake".

Whereas the urban disturbances also involve violent actions of black youths, the 'facts' of the Honeyford case are predominantly ideological, and this also clearly emerges in the headlines. More or less neutral headlines refer to the Honeyford case as such and define the decision of the court to reinstate Honeyford:

> HONEYFORD CASE (*Times*, 16 August)
> COURT VERDICT TODAY ON SUSPENDED HEAD AT CENTRE OF ETHNIC DEBATE (*Times*, 5 September)

However, also in *The Times*, which usually is more cautious with headlines that betray its conservative ideology, the headlines soon become more obviously biased in favour of the "race row head", as Honeyford is consistently called by the Press:

> HONEYFORD: WHOEVER WINS IN COURT THE BATTLE GOES ON.
> Andrew Brown on the latest round in the Bradford 'racist' head affair. (*Times*, 3 September)

The perspective here is literally Honeyford's: his statement defines the main headline, and that the "battle goes on" obviously suggests *his*, positively valued, battle against the anti-racists and the Bradford authorities. That the accusation of his opponents is not adopted by *The Times* is obvious from the quotes around 'racist'. Other *Times* headlines speak of a new "threat" to Honeyford, which also clearly defines the perspective of this newspaper (one of Honeyford's articles appeared in *The Times Literary Supplement*).

When Honeyford returns to his school, we have more or less factual accounts of the protests:

> PARENTS PICKET SCHOOL AS HONEYFORD RETURNS. Problem for officialdom as pupils stay away (*Guardian*, 17 September)
> RACE ROW HEAD BACK AT HIS DESK DESPITE DEMO (*Telegraph*, 17 September)

Many headlines, however, are less innocent, and rather overtly betray the position of the newspaper in this "battle". Here are some of the views of the tabloids:

> MOB PROTEST FAILS AS RACE STORM HEAD GOES BACK TO SCHOOL
>     (*Mail*, 17 September)
> THE COURAGE A MOB CAN'T FORGIVE. Why Ray Honeyford's fight is
>     our fight, too (*Mail*, 18 September)
> RENT-A-ROWDY ATTACK FORCES RACE ROW HEAD OUT OF COLLEGE
>     (*Mail*, 17 October)

These headlines first show that the tabloids tend to define as a "mob" any group of people who engage in public actions which the tabloids do not like. In this case, this applies to a group of mostly Asian parents of the Bradford school, who picket the school, and demonstrate against Honeyford's return. For the tabloids, this legitimate protest is redefined as a violent battle, in which the opponents are implicitly qualified as irrational. The many war and crime metaphors (see "Rent-a-rowdy attack") in these headlines also represent the ideological fight as a real fight, and categorize the opponents of Honeyford accordingly as aggressive, violent, and filled with "hate". Once this protest is defined as violence, it is also easier to make Honeyford a hero and martyr: he is the one with courage, who defies a "mob", and not the one who is suspended because he had published racist articles and offended both his Asian pupils and their parents. In such an ideological dispute, in which the white public at large, and especially the readers of the tabloids, are not expected by the tabloid editors to be able to take sides, simply because they are ignorant of what Honeyford wrote, and cannot judge why his position is called racist, it is therefore essential to redefine the situation in other terms, namely that of a violent and aggressive mob against a brave, single man "who only wanted to tell the truth". It is this reformulation of the events that the tabloids assume will appeal to the readers.

*Other issues*

The quality Press is generally less explicit and crude in its headlines about other events during this period. However, as soon as a dispute, row, or clash pitches the authorities against demonstrators of any kind, especially those who are inspired by anti-racist motives, the demonstrators are again consistently defined as "mobs". This is the case when students show that racist or anti-immigration talk will not be tolerated during lectures of visiting ministers or MPs, a case that repeatedly hits the headlines during this autumn:

MOBBED MINISTER BERATES STUDENTS (*Telegraph*, 11 October)

Similarly, when Labour MPs are accused by Tory ministers of having 'represented' immigrants who failed to be admitted by the immigration authorities, the conservative Press defines such immigrants as "dubious", this time *without* using quotation marks:

MPs READY TO GREET DUBIOUS IMMIGRANTS. Blake Baker concludes his report on unwelcome arrivals (*Telegraph*, 3 December)

On the whole, however, it is the tabloids that heavily dramatize and negativize ethnic events. It might be argued that they do so in general, with any kind of problem of conflict, and that therefore their ethnic reporting is simply 'in style' with the rest of their coverage. However, such an explanation would seriously understate the ideological slanting involved: it is not dramatization, exaggeration or negativization in general which is involved. Rather these forms of hyperbole are almost always only ever applied to ethnic minority groups, especially black youths, or directed against anti-racists and the "Loony Left". That is, the drama staged by the tabloids is highly selective, and blatantly favours the white group, the Tories and the authorities.

The only exceptions are some of the headlines about racial attacks. These are correctly identified as "terror" for Asian families. Recall though that the agents of this terror, namely white racist thugs are *not* identified in such headlines. In other words, only half of the situation is correctly identified in such definitions. Even the 'race attacks' themselves may be put between quotes, as if these attacks are only a matter of interpretation:

BEATEN-UP ASIAN IN FIRE TERROR. Latest in series of 'race attacks' (*Mail*, 20 August)

For most other ethnic events, however, the headlined definition of the situation is obvious as soon as young blacks, anti-racists, or the left are involved. Thus, in line with the reporting on the Honeyford case, many headlines deal with various forms of accusations of racism. Instead of simply reporting the accusations, usually between quotes and therefore declaring them dubious, the right-wing Press reverses the charges, and accuses the anti-racists. Here are two examples of the type of headlining and topicalization we shall meet in much more detail later:

THOUGHT CRIME NIGHTMARE (*Mail*, 3 August)
RACIST? NO, I'M BEING VICTIMISED FOR SPEAKING OUT (*Mail*, 14 October)

The use of "nightmare" implies that the accusation of 'thought crime' is not only ridiculous, but again a form of anti-racist terror. Moreover, the words 'thought crime' recall the ideological oppression of Stalinism and fascism, as well as Orwellian associations. This well-known reversal of the facts, that is accusing anti-racists of 'intolerance' instead of those who resent the presence, rights, or aspirations of minorities, is one of the most consistent defence strategies of the right-wing Press. Apparently, through the attacks against racist teachers, employers, or politicians, with whom they agree, they feel attacked themselves. Hence, they do not summarize and headline the fact of the accusation, but headline their own reaction to it.

Finally, among the many other ethnic issues that are thus negatively dramatized in the right-wing Press, are the socio-cultural differences between immigrants, mostly Asian ones, and the dominant culture. One of these differences is what is seen as the custom of arranged marriages, as well as the issue of separate Muslim schools or schools for girls, which were prominently targeted in the headlines in 1989. In 1985, one of these "scandals" discovered, or rather fabricated, by the *Mail* is the:

SCANDAL OF THE BRIDES FOR SALE (*Mail*, 5 August)

For days "terrorized" Asian girls are sympathetically portrayed as threatened by the prospect of being sold to South Asian men who in this way hope to be able to immigrate. The implications and effects of such headlines hardly need to be spelled out. Firstly, even if true, they are primarily intended to emphasize well-known stereotypes or prejudices, because the fate of Asian immigrants, or of women, is usually quite irrelevant for the tabloids. Secondly, the dramatic and scandalous notion of 'women for sale' also suggests sex crimes while at the same time associating immigration with shady practices.

## The 1989 headlines

We saw that in 1989 the headlines are largely dealing with only a few 'affairs', those of Rushdie, Mendis, Silcott, the claim for Muslim schools and refugees. Whereas in 1985 the major villains were young rioting blacks, now the 'threat' to British society (and the Christian West in general), comes from fundamentalist Muslims, first represented as burning Rushdie's *Satanic Verses* in Bradford, then associated with Khomeini's *fatwa* against the author. There is no doubt in the hundreds of news reports, both in the UK, as well as in the Dutch data we have about the case (Minnema, 1989), what the position is of the Press and the authorities:

OBEY OUR LAW OR GO TO JAIL, MUSLIMS WARNED (*Sun*, 
BRITISH ISLAM MUST RESPECT THE RULES (*Telegraph*, 25

However, although most of the reports (and the many letters to the editor) themselves are rather outspoken about Muslims and Islam, the headlines are much less aggressive than in the Honeyford affair and the disturbances of 1985. This change of style does not mean that ethnic affairs and immigration headlines have suddenly become innocent in 1989, as we may see in the following example defining new immigrants from the moment of entry to the UK:

BRITAIN INVADED BY AN ARMY OF ILLEGALS (*Sun*, 2 February)

## CONCLUSIONS

This chapter has shown that headlines are not arbitrary parts or labels of news reports. On the contrary, they formulate the most crucial words of such reports. Their position, semantic role, and cognitive consequences are such that they literally cannot be overlooked. They express the major topic of the report, as the newspaper sees it, and thereby at the same time summarize and evaluate a news event. In other words, they essentially define the situation. It is this definition that also plays a prominent role in the ways the readers understand and memorize news.

Headlines about ethnic affairs, therefore, are essential in the definition of ethnic events. We have seen that, especially in the right-wing Press, this definition is seldom positive, occasionally neutral, and often negative. This is most obviously the case for the 'riots', represented by many hundreds of sometimes blatantly negative headlines, in which the urban disturbances are variously associated, not only with violence, but with the most heinous crimes of irrational "rampaging mobs", mostly consisting of black youths. The lexical style of these headlines is accordingly dramatic and aggressive.

The same is however true for ideological disputes, such as the Honeyford affair, and other cases in which people are accused of racism. Again, the right-wing Press not only dramatizes these conflicts, but also takes an unambiguous position about those accused of racism, for example, by accusing the "mobs" of terrorizing valiant defenders of white rights. Thus the perspective of ethnic groups, or of those who sympathize with them, not only seldom hits the headlines, but is also systematically discredited. If minorities, immigrants, anti-racists or the left are generally defined as a problem in the conservative Press, these headlines may even further emphasize this evaluation by defining them as criminals, deviants, irrational mobs or lunatics. The same is true for the ethnic situation itself, which is not merely seen as a problem, but as a drama of violence, terror, or ideological oppression, of which white people are the victims. We also found, however, that the headlines in 1989 are less prominently negative than those of 1985. We shall see in the next chapters how these definitions of the headlines are further detailed in the rest of the news reports of the Press.

# 4 Subjects and topics

## THE RELEVANCE OF TOPICAL ANALYSIS

In this chapter we pay specific attention to the subjects and topics in news reports about ethnic minorities in the British Press, and give a summary of results from a study of subjects and topics in the Dutch Press. This topical analysis at the same time serves as a more or less informal overview of the contents of the Press portrayal of ethnic relations in the second part of 1985, which is needed to provide some background to the more detailed analyses of the following chapters. That is, we first try to answer the simple question 'What does the Press write, or not write, about racial or ethnic affairs – and why?', and then will proceed to answer the question 'How does the Press write about this issue – and why?'

Topics are an important aspect of news reports and crucial in an analysis of ethnic affairs reporting. Besides their prominent discursive functions, topics reflect many dimensions of the psychology and sociology of news. They represent what news-makers construe to be the most important information about a news event. The selection and textual prominence of topics result from routines of news-making and embody criteria of journalistic decisions about the newsworthiness of events. Therefore, topics also manifest complex networks of professional, social and cultural ideologies (van Dijk, 1988a, 1988b). When such topics are about ethnic minority groups, they also express and reproduce the concerns and the agenda of the prevailing ethnic consensus of the white majority.

Before we proceed to an analysis of the topicalization of ethnic affairs in the Press, we give a brief informal introduction to the theory of topics because it explains why they are so important in news reports and why they may have such a decisive impact on the readers.

## Semantic macro-structures

To understand the notion and the role of topics of discourse, we may use the familiar image of the pyramid when describing the structure of information in news reports. The bottom of the pyramid consists of the complex and detailed information expressed by the respective words and sentences of the text, whereas the topics represent the higher levels of the pyramid. In a news report the top of the pyramid is usually expressed by the headline and the lead. In this way, only a few topics 'at the top' may summarize large amounts of information 'at the bottom'.

In more theoretical terms, topics are defined as semantic macro-structures (van Dijk, 1972, 1977, 1980). These global, overall meaning structures of a text consist of a hierarchically arranged set of macro-propositions, which are derived from the meanings (propositions) of the sentences of the text by way of macro-rules. These rules reduce the complex information of the text to its essential gist. For instance, if we have a story with a sequence of propositions such as 'I went to the station', 'I bought a ticket', 'I walked to the platform', 'I waited for the train ...', we may reduce this sequence by 'summarizing' it with a single macro-proposition, for instance, 'I took the train to ...'. Newspapers do this all the time, and typically express such summarizing propositions in their headlines and leads. Each of these summarizing macro-propositions is what we call a topic. The overall meaning of a text consists of a hierarchy of such topics, because each series of topics may in turn be summarized again at a higher level: the topic of my train journey may be a sub-topic of a story about my vacation in France, for instance. To avoid unnecessary jargon, we henceforth simply use the term 'topic' (and sometimes 'theme') when we refer to macro-propositions derived from a text, and 'topical (or 'thematic') structure' when we refer to its semantic macro-structure.

Unlike topics in everyday storytelling, topics in news reports are usually not expressed in a continuous way. It is not the chronology of the events, but rather their importance, relevance, or newsworthiness that organize news reports. Therefore, what we find is that of each episode of the story the most important, topical, information will be given first, and then later in the text the details 'covered' by that topic. That is, topics in news discourse are delivered 'in instalments'. In other words, and using the image of the pyramid again, the way the information of a news report is actually realized in a text is from top to bottom: we first encounter, or read all high level topics, and then, further down in the text, more specific topics and sub-topics until we arrive at the detailed level of the bottom of the pyramid.

Since topics summarize complex information, they have very important functions in communication. Thus, because they represent the most important or relevant information, they are routinely used to make a summary or abstract of a text. They are also crucial in cognitive information processing, and allow readers to better organize, store and recall textual information in memory. Experimental research has repeatedly shown that topics are usually the best recalled information of a text (van Dijk and Kintsch, 1983).

The construction of topics by journalists and readers requires large amounts of world knowledge. In order to derive the topic 'I took the train to ...' in the example given above, we must know a lot about travelling by train, that is, we must have a 'train-travel' script (for details about such knowledge scripts, see Schank and Abelson, 1977). Many of the topics we thus derive during newspaper reading make use of such scripts, for instance, about civil war, immigration, or riots.

For our analysis of news reports about ethnic affairs in particular, it should be stressed that the formation of topics is subjective: what for one journalist or reader is the most relevant or important information of a text, may not be so for others. Similarly, different readers may also give at least slightly different summaries of the same news story. This means that the headlines and leads of news reports are not objective summaries of the report, but necessarily biased by specific beliefs, attitudes, and ideologies. As we have seen in the last chapter, topics expressed in headlines may be seen as subjective 'definitions of the situation'.

Also, some topics may have a higher hierarchical position in the topical structure than others, and this position can also be manipulated. For instance, it may happen that a lower level topic is 'upgraded' and even expressed in the headline, as we shall shortly illustrate in a concrete example. Since newspaper readers use headlines and leads to guide their process of comprehension of the news report, such biased topical structures may also influence the ways the readers interpret the text – and how they interpret the world. For instance, information about the social backgrounds of the urban disturbances in the British inner cities in 1985 may thus be downgraded in the conservative Press, whereas the criminal aspects of the 'riots' may be upgraded. If readers have no alternative sources of knowledge, it will be difficult for them to construct a different topical structure. This means that the topics as presented by the Press are also the ones that are most likely to be later recalled and used by the readers.

## Models

Topics not only suggest what information is most important in the text, but also what is most important 'in the world'. In our case, this means that topics influence the representation readers construct in their mind of specific ethnic events and situations. Such mental representations of events are called 'models' (Johnson-Laird, 1983; van Dijk and Kintsch, 1983; van Dijk, 1985c, 1987c). Since models are the fundamental cognitive knowledge structures readers build and use when reading reports in the Press, we need to explain briefly what they are, because the notion of model will also be used repeatedly throughout this study.

Models are mental structures of information which, besides the new information offered in a news report, feature information about such a situation as inferred from general knowledge scripts. Thus, when reading about the 'riot' in Handsworth, readers make a model of this particular disturbance on the basis of the information in the news reports, but 'know' much more about it than the newspaper now tells them, because they have more general knowledge about such disturbances or the place where they occur. Hence models are much 'richer' in information than texts, because readers are able to infer large parts of the relevant knowledge themselves. The organization of the text may give strategic hints about how the model of the reader should be organized. Thus, text topics suggest to the reader what is important or less important information in a subjective model of the situation. High level topics in the text may also become high level information in the model. It is this model of the events or situation described by the text, and not so much the mental representation of the text itself, that influences the later recall and uses the readers make of the information from the newspaper.

Besides knowledge about an event or situation, models also feature evaluative beliefs, that is, personal opinions. In the same way as specific knowledge may be derived from general, socially shared knowledge scripts, such opinions may be derived from social attitudes shared by a group, including ethnic prejudices. Hence, models are the central 'interface' between the knowledge and attitudes of the readers, or journalists, on the one hand, and the texts they read, or write, on the other hand. Such opinions may also become part of the main topics of a text and be prominently expressed in headlines or leads. On the other hand, what may be a quite explicit opinion, for instance about minorities, in such a model, may also appear indirectly, for example, in the use of some subtle words or in a specific discursive strategy in a news report. One of the tasks of critical news analysis is to reconstruct the 'underlying' models, and especially the opinions of journalists from such subtle discursive properties (van Dijk, 1989b). Once we know these models, they may in turn give insight into the underlying knowledge and attitudes shared by reporters and editors. The analysis of topics in this chapter, then, aims at an understanding of what according to journalists is the most important information of 'ethnic events' and what general knowledge, attitudes, and ideologies underly this assignment of importance or relevance.

## An example: the Cuban connection in the *Daily Mail*

Before we report some quantitative results of our topical analysis of the British Press, let us start with an illustration of the theory of topics by giving an example from the British Press – a news report from the *Mail* about the aftermath of the Tottenham disturbance: CUBANS IN A LINK WITH RIOT ESTATE. One major actor in this news report is Haringey Council leader Bernard (Bernie) Grant, a black politician whom we shall meet more often in our analyses, because he is one of the most prominent demons of the conservative Press. Tottenham (and the Broadwater Farm Estate) are part of Haringey.

The interesting feature of this report is the ideological manipulation of the topical structure. As we have seen in the previous chapter, headlines usually express the main topic of the report. We have also argued, however, that lower level topics may sometimes be 'upgraded' and reach headline status, whereas topics that would usually make the headline may be 'downgraded'. The report in the *Mail* is a characteristic example of such a transformation of the topical structure. That is, the perfectly innocent visit of some Cuban women to the estate is only part of what council leader Bernie Grant talked about during an interview, and certainly not the encompassing topic of which the rest of the text gives details.

The reason why this sub-topic is assigned such a prominent position, both in the headline and in the lead, may be inferred from the use of the usual abbreviation "riot estate" in the headline, and the expression "before the Tottenham riots" in the lead, which strongly suggests that the visit had something to do with the cause of the disturbances, as if young blacks of the estate had conspired with "Cuban Communists" and had planned the urban disorders. This suggestion of a "Cuban connection" should also be interpreted in light of other accusations in the right-wing Press about the alleged role of radical left-wing "agitators" in the disturbances.

To show how this transformation works, consider the following (first level) topics that 'summarize' the respective paragraphs of the report. These topics are obtained by a deletion of irrelevant details, by generalization, and by abstraction (for details about these procedures, see van Dijk, 1980; for application to news reports, see van Dijk, 1988a):

# CUBANS IN A LINK WITH RIOT ESTATE

**By Anthony Doran**
**Home Affairs correspondent**

CUBAN Communists and young blacks met on the Broadwater Farm Estate some time before the Tottenham riots exploded.

Their meetings were fixed by Haringey Council leader Bernie Grant.

Mr. Grant boasted of introducing the two groups in an interview in the far left magazine London Labour Briefing.

And he made clear his intentions. He said "We have got to get to the activists, get to the grass roots in order to mobilise them"

In July, 41-year-old Mr. Grant led a group of 30 including his white middle-class girlfriend, Sharon Lawrence, a Labour councillor, to Jamaica for a month.

With him went 14 youngsters from the estate, including Floyd Jarrett, whom police were seeking when Mrs. Cynthia Jarrett died in her home, the tragic event that sparked the rioting.

"When we take a party of youth to Jamaica in the summer I am personally hoping to take a party to Cuba for a few days," Grant added in the interview in the magazine.

"We have already established links with some of the women comrades in Cuba who came over, and we took them into Broadwater Farm and had a meal and so on."

Mr. Grant also said in the interview that he was trying to establish links with Nicaragua.

He added: "We need, in London in particular, a new leadership which is prepared to face going to jail on principle, and it doesn't matter if we have to face the whole force of the state against us if we are prepared to stand up and challenge them.

Mr. Grant appealed last night for Tottenham's young people to "step back from violence." He told a council meting: "You cannot fight violence with violence".

He added: "Two people have died in the chain of events which started on October 5.

That is enough. There must be a rethink of how Tottenham is policed and the council is prepared to play a

*Figure 4.1* Article from the *Daily Mail*, 15 October 1985

Reproduced by permission of the *Daily Mail*

1: Mr Grant declared in an interview:

  1.1: Cuban women, introduced by me, visited the Broadwater Farm Estate.

  1.2: We must mobilise young people.

  1.3: We need new leaders, who are prepared to challenge the authorities.

  1.4: We hope to visit Cuba on our next visit to Jamaica.

2: In July, Mr Grant and a group of black youths visited Jamaica.
3: Last night Mr Grant declared:
    3.1: Young black people should not use violence.
    3.2: We must think about new policing in Tottenham.

We see that there are three major topics, namely, the two pertaining to Grant's declarations, one in an interview, the other "last night", and the topic of his visit to Jamaica. According to the ordering and relevance principles of the report, one sub-topic (the visit of Cuban women) of one of these topics (the declarations in the interview) is promoted to main topic and hence emphasized in headline and lead. The other sub-topic, namely his call to mobilize young activists and a new leadership are apparently found less newsworthy, although politically more relevant. More important, however, we also find that the entire last topic, namely his call to refrain from violence, is put at the end of the article, and not mentioned in the headline or lead. We may conclude that in the situation model of this journalist, a call by a 'controversial' left-wing black politician for a non-violence policy is inconsistent with his beliefs about black violence, and will therefore be downgraded, and hence put at the end of the report. Note that by journalistic rule the recency as well as the political relevance of this last declaration would normally have been sufficient reason to put it in the lead and headline. In other words, news production rules are ignored in favour of an ideologically based transformation that upgrades a lower level sub-topic to main topic, while at the same time suggesting a Cuban connection as a cause of the disturbances.

In Chapter six, dealing with local semantic strategies, we shall see how seemingly irrelevant details may be used in the elaboration of such topics. Also in this report we find multiple additions of irrelevant details (whether true or fabricated) that cast a negative or otherwise dubious light on Grant and the young blacks of the Broadwater Farm. For instance, it is said that the review to which Grant gave the interview is "far left", that Grant has a girl-friend, that she is white and that she accompanied him to Jamaica, that also Floyd Jarrett went to Jamaica, that he was sought by the police, and that the death of his mother sparked the disturbances. In other words, there are several subtle moves to link Grant and black youths to the 'riots' through their interest in communism, illustrated by their planned visit to Cuba, the visit of Cuban women and their intention to establish contacts with (communist) Nicaragua.

Note incidentally that the text says that the "police were seeking [Jarrett] when his mother Mrs. Cynthia Jarrett died in her home" and not: "Mrs Cynthia Jarrett died when the police were seeking him ...", which is a quite different way of representing the facts. The first formulation suggests that the death of Mrs Jarrett and the search of the police were quite unrelated, and that the police came to the house when Mrs Jarrett was (already) dying, which is false. We come back to these subtle local properties of syntax and semantics later.

In other words, not only the order and the prominence of topics is highly relevant in telling ideologically biased news stories, but so also are the ways these topics become implemented at the 'local' level of the meanings of words and sentences, for instance by the addition of irrelevant details that can be interpreted in accordance with prevailing stereotypes and prejudices about black people.

## SUBJECTS IN THE BRITISH PRESS

As a first, largely quantitative, step in the study of topics and their organization in British news reports about ethnic affairs, let us consider their overall 'subject' categories. It is somewhat confusing that in earlier research such 'subjects' are often called 'topics' (for example, in Hartmann, Husband, and Clark, 1974), whereas we have defined topics in a different way. Therefore, we use the term 'subject' here to avoid further confusion. A subject is a single concept, such as 'crime' or 'education', which stands for a large social or political domain or a complex issue about which the Press offers potentially an infinite number of specific news reports. Each news report has its own, unique, topics, which do not consist of a single concept but of a more complex structure of concepts, such as a macro-proposition, as in the topic 'Headmaster Honeyford was suspended from his job'. Hence, topics always refer to specific events, actions and people.

Instead of the usually short list of subjects, such as 'immigration', 'race relations', or 'employment', we used a more extended list of subjects that would better capture the specificity of the news in the British Press during the second half of 1985. That is, the vast number of items about the disturbances, and the many articles about headmaster Honeyford and council chief Bernie Grant, were coded separately. Each news item was thus coded for its three most important subjects. In order for information in an item to be categorized as a subject, at least one of its topics (and hence, in practice, at least one paragraph), as defined above, should be within that subject category. Most items are coded by a single subject category.

Table 4.1 shows the frequencies and percentages of these subjects for the 2,764 items we analysed. Many of these subjects are directly or indirectly related to the subject of the disturbances, such as housing, employment, or other social backgrounds in the inner cities, usually discussed only as possible causes of the disorders. The same is true for policing and actions of the courts. Therefore, we counted separately court cases related to the disturbances, 'ordinary crime' court cases, and court cases related to civil cases or discrimination. Similarly, in order to emphasize their special ethnic implications, racial attacks are not counted under crime, but as a separate subject.

The figures of Table 4.1 leave no doubt about the prominence of the 'riots' and their most frequently topicalized aftermath, policing. Although somewhat less in *The Times*, these two subjects together account for a large part (30 per cent) of the coverage on ethnic affairs during this period. Often, they occur together in one item, of course. Except for the *Sun*, which has more on the disturbances than on later policing matters, all newspapers have nearly 20 per cent of their items about the various aspects of policing that are discussed in the aftermath of the disorders. If we add court cases related to the urban unrest, as well as personal consequences of the disturbances (like burial of the victims, actions to help the widow of the killed policeman), and also the general category of social affairs, which almost wholly covers social backgrounds mentioned as causes of the 'riots', then the riot-related topics account for about 40 per cent of all news items! Note that *The Times* pays most attention to social affairs, largely also as background news about the disturbances. The *Sun* on the other hand has virtually no items about the social backgrounds of the urban unrest, nor on the social dimension of ethnic affairs generally, for that matter. In our analysis of topics below, we show in more detail which aspects of the disturbances are, prominently or less prominently, covered.

If we disregard the subjects related to the disturbances, which are of course specific for this period, it is undoubtedly the cluster of race-relations subjects that scores highest: some 600 items (more than 20 per cent) feature race-relations topics. Racism itself is covered relatively little, except in the *Guardian*. Racial attitudes, prejudice, including racist statements and actions (including those by the National Front), receive much more attention, even in the *Sun*, and account for nearly half (281) of all items in this subject cluster. The necessity of a more qualitative analysis of topics is particularly clear in this case. That is, the frequency of this subject cluster might suggest that the British Press is very much concerned about race relations, and in particular about racist attitudes and statements. This is true, but further analysis shows that the concern is not so much with racism, but rather with anti-racism.

The next cluster of subjects is national and local politics, This subject occurs in 517 items (18.7 per cent) and is usually combined with other

*Table 4.1* Frequencies per subject, August 1985–January 1986

|  | Times | | Guardian | | Telegraph | | Mail | | Sun | |
|---|---|---|---|---|---|---|---|---|---|---|
|  | N | % | N | % | N | % | N | % | N | % |
| Government | 58 | 10.68 | 89 | 11.77 | 51 | 7.91 | 18 | 3.56 | 6 | 1.91 |
| Local, city government | 21 | 3.87 | 37 | 4.89 | 45 | 6.98 | 29 | 5.73 | 13 | 4.14 |
| Politics, parties | 44 | 8.10 | 2 | 0.26 | 46 | 7.13 | 29 | 5.73 | 12 | 3.82 |
| Immigration | 56 | 10.31 | 68 | 8.99 | 53 | 8.22 | 27 | 5.34 | 15 | 4.78 |
| Repatriation | 4 | 0.74 | 9 | 1.19 | 7 | 1.09 | 1 | 0.20 | 5 | 1.59 |
| Housing | 9 | 1.66 | 14 | 1.85 | 12 | 1.86 | 9 | 1.78 | 1 | 0.32 |
| Social affairs | 69 | 12.71 | 57 | 7.54 | 48 | 7.44 | 31 | 6.13 | 9 | 2.87 |
| Facilities, funding | 10 | 1.84 | 27 | 3.57 | 23 | 3.57 | 14 | 2.77 | 12 | 3.82 |
| Employment, unemployment | 34 | 6.26 | 39 | 5.16 | 26 | 4.03 | 14 | 2.77 | 7 | 2.23 |
| Education | 25 | 4.60 | 41 | 5.42 | 52 | 8.06 | 39 | 7.71 | 15 | 4.78 |
| Academic research | 0 | 0.00 | 5 | 0.66 | 1 | 0.16 | 1 | 0.20 | 0 | 0.00 |
| Crime | 28 | 5.16 | 54 | 7.14 | 45 | 6.98 | 53 | 10.47 | 26 | 8.28 |
| Drugs | 4 | 0.74 | 2 | 0.26 | 8 | 1.24 | 5 | 0.99 | 1 | 0.32 |
| Illegality | 0 | 0.00 | 8 | 1.06 | 0 | 0.00 | 0 | 0.00 | 0 | 0.00 |
| Health | 3 | 0.55 | 2 | 0.26 | 2 | 0.31 | 1 | 0.20 | 0 | 0.00 |
| Arts | 26 | 4.79 | 26 | 3.44 | 18 | 2.79 | 4 | 0.79 | 4 | 1.27 |
| Religion | 15 | 2.76 | 15 | 1.98 | 16 | 2.48 | 13 | 2.57 | 3 | 0.96 |
| Media | 12 | 2.21 | 19 | 2.51 | 13 | 2.02 | 4 | 0.79 | 7 | 2.23 |
| Inquiries | 18 | 3.31 | 0 | 0.00 | 26 | 4.03 | 18 | 3.56 | 4 | 1.27 |
| Race relations, general | 20 | 3.68 | 37 | 4.89 | 27 | 4.19 | 17 | 3.36 | 13 | 4.14 |
| Racism | 10 | 1.84 | 29 | 3.84 | 19 | 2.95 | 9 | 1.78 | 5 | 1.59 |
| Discrimination | 46 | 8.47 | 46 | 6.08 | 33 | 5.12 | 19 | 3.75 | 11 | 3.50 |
| Prejudice, National Front | 38 | 7.00 | 84 | 11.11 | 61 | 9.46 | 37 | 7.31 | 61 | 19.43 |
| Racial attacks | 15 | 2.76 | 40 | 5.29 | 20 | 3.10 | 14 | 2.77 | 8 | 2.55 |
| Minority attacks | 1 | 0.18 | 9 | 1.19 | 3 | 0.47 | 12 | 2.37 | 10 | 3.18 |
| Demonstrations | 24 | 4.42 | 35 | 4.63 | 33 | 5.12 | 26 | 5.14 | 17 | 5.41 |
| Riots | 50 | 9.21 | 129 | 17.06 | 80 | 12.40 | 88 | 17.39 | 74 | 23.57 |
| Socio-cultural differences | 8 | 1.47 | 5 | 0.66 | 5 | 0.78 | 12 | 2.37 | 2 | 0.64 |
| Racism abroad | 16 | 2.95 | 17 | 2.25 | 9 | 1.40 | 16 | 3.16 | 2 | 0.64 |
| Policing | 106 | 19.52 | 148 | 19.58 | 125 | 19.38 | 96 | 18.97 | 38 | 12.10 |
| Court actions | 26 | 4.79 | 24 | 3.17 | 15 | 2.33 | 11 | 2.17 | 9 | 2.87 |
| Black Sections | 16 | 2.95 | 22 | 2.91 | 13 | 2.02 | 9 | 1.78 | 6 | 1.91 |
| Honeyford | 28 | 5.16 | 44 | 5.82 | 50 | 7.75 | 45 | 8.89 | 32 | 10.19 |
| Affirmative action | 14 | 2.58 | 6 | 0.79 | 14 | 2.17 | 13 | 2.57 | 7 | 2.23 |
| Court cases on riots | 24 | 4.42 | 38 | 5.03 | 45 | 6.98 | 15 | 2.96 | 12 | 3.82 |
| Unions | 10 | 1.84 | 8 | 1.06 | 3 | 0.47 | 7 | 1.38 | 1 | 0.32 |
| Personal consequences of riots | 8 | 1.47 | 3 | 0.40 | 12 | 1.86 | 17 | 3.36 | 19 | 6.05 |
| Grant, Bernie | 9 | 1.66 | 14 | 1.85 | 17 | 2.64 | 20 | 3.95 | 20 | 6.37 |
| Sports | 6 | 1.10 | 9 | 1.19 | 5 | 0.78 | 12 | 2.37 | 10 | 3.18 |
| Human affairs | 6 | 1.10 | 2 | 0.26 | 5 | 0.78 | 10 | 1.98 | 3 | 0.96 |
| Other | 6 | 1.10 | 5 | 0.66 | 8 | 1.24 | 10 | 1.98 | 2 | 0.64 |

subjects, such as the 'riots', policing, immigration, education or the social backgrounds of the inner cities. Government politics is a subject that typically interests the quality Press, in this case *The Times* and the *Guardian*. The *Sun* has very few items about government policy. The tabloids are more likely to focus on local politics, and we shall see later that, in ethnic affairs, this usually means very negative reporting about the alleged mismanagement or anti-racist measures of "loony" left-wing city councils. Party politics accounts nearly for as many items as national politics and is particularly frequent as a subject in the *Guardian*.

"Race-row" headmaster Honeyford has the honour of being the most covered individual during this period. His case alone is discussed in nearly 200 items (7.2 per cent). Note that the percentages of this coverage are highest in the right-wing Press. In the *Sun* the Honeyford items make up more than 10 per cent of the complete ethnic affairs coverage. Also partly related to the Honeyford case are the other items on education, which also score surprisingly highly during this period (172 items, 6.2 per cent). Many of these items have to do with "rows" in schools where a teacher is accused of making racist statements, a point which the right-wing Press usually pays extensive attention to, mostly in order to deny or attack such accusations, as it does in the Honeyford case.

Immigration, with 219 items (7.9 per cent), is an important subject, as it always has been in ethnic coverage in the British and western European Press, also in the items we analysed for the first half year of 1989, which frequently focus on illegal immigration and especially on refugees. Much of the coverage on immigration in 1985 has to do with only a few topics, such as a parliamentary row about Labour MPs accused by Tory ministers of abusing their right to 'represent' immigrants, mostly Asians, and various kinds of immigration scandals, such as faking passports or various forms of illegal entry.

Finally, as expected, crime is also an important subject (206 items, 7.5 per cent, plus some 20 items on drugs). If we count 'riots' and riot-related policing subjects as part of crime, as it is defined by most of the right-wing Press, the subject of crime would reach about 50 per cent of the total coverage! It is not surprising that the percentages for crime coverage are highest in the tabloids (especially the *Mail*), but in absolute terms it is the *Guardian* that has most crime-related items! If we may judge only from these figures, we see that, contrary to what one might expect, liberal newspapers do not necessarily report less on crime – as related to ethnic affairs – than the tabloid Press.

Since each news report may feature several subjects, for which size could not be measured independently, we do not know whether these figures correspond with similar discrepancies in the total size of the coverage of each topic. Table 4.2 shows the average size of the articles in which the respective subjects occur and therefore provide an indirect suggestion of total size. If we know that the average size of the news reports on ethnic affairs in all five newspapers is about 120 sq. cm, that the 161 larger background features are about twice to three times as large (and letters to the editor and columns much shorter), and that the size of the average item is 127 sq. cm, we have an idea which subjects tend to be dealt with in longer items, such as the disturbances, policing, government politics, the social topics and crime. Race relations subjects and education have average length. Court reports, art reviews and racial attack news are smaller. There are however large variations in these figures. On the whole, however, we see that the most frequent subjects, namely those about the urban unrest, policing, politics, crime, and race relations also appear in the longest articles, which suggest that the total space of, and hence the amount of information about, these subjects is also largest.

From these remarks about the frequency, size, and distribution of the major subjects, we conclude that 'riots', race relations, politics, immigration, crime and education (including Honeyford) are the main subject clusters of ethnic reporting in a large proportion of the British Press during the second half of 1985, both in number and in overall size. For race relations, crime, and immigration these results are consistent with earlier research about the content of the British Press coverage of ethnic affairs (see the references given in Chapter one). At the second level of frequency (between 100 and 200 items) we find subjects such as demonstrations.

It is often relevant also to assess which subjects are not at all, or only barely, covered in ethnic affairs news. Our data show that major concerns of the minority communities, such as housing, work, and health are little covered (see also Smith, 1989). If so, this is again mostly the case as background topics in inner-city and riot-related coverage. 'Facilities' is the subject which covers all topics related to the discussion about financial assistance, and other forms of help for the inner cities – again, mostly related to the discussion of the 'riots'. If we disregard the Honeyford case and similar cases in which teachers are in conflict about their racist remarks, education would not score very high. Academic research on race relations is virtually ignored, and only discussed in a handful of items. The few dozen items on the media coverage of ethnic affairs appear mostly in the quality Press. The same is true for arts and religion and the subject of the so-called Black Sections in the Labour Party.

There is somewhat more attention (87 items) for racial attacks, but most of these items appear in the *Guardian*. Apparently, for the

*Table 4.2* Average size per subject (in sq. cm), August 1985–January 1986

| | Times | Guardian | Telegraph | Mail | Sun |
|---|---|---|---|---|---|
| Ethnic affairs | 0 | 0 | 0 | 0 | 298 |
| Government | 153 | 167 | 150 | 127 | 88 |
| Local, city government | 86 | 121 | 126 | 108 | 91 |
| Politics, parties | 122 | 144 | 154 | 155 | 73 |
| Immigration | 149 | 112 | 126 | 119 | 114 |
| Repatriation, | 65 | 234 | 67 | 81 | 193 |
| Housing | 128 | 170 | 160 | 117 | 122 |
| Social affairs | 142 | 208 | 173 | 171 | 133 |
| Facilities | 165 | 158 | 149 | 117 | 117 |
| Employment, unemployment | 158 | 179 | 138 | 100 | 131 |
| Education | 117 | 140 | 119 | 160 | 112 |
| Academic research | 0 | 115 | 194 | 182 | 0 |
| Crime | 106 | 133 | 111 | 187 | 111 |
| Drugs | 283 | 92 | 161 | 101 | 56 |
| Illegality | 0 | 150 | 0 | 0 | 0 |
| Health | 109 | 50 | 94 | 188 | 0 |
| Arts | 103 | 145 | 99 | 37 | 101 |
| Religion | 195 | 108 | 153 | 75 | 227 |
| Media | 93 | 155 | 108 | 104 | 40 |
| Public relations | 124 | 0 | 144 | 162 | 94 |
| Race relations | 169 | 134 | 164 | 115 | 141 |
| Racism | 106 | 140 | 120 | 124 | 106 |
| Discrimination | 145 | 140 | 111 | 113 | 76 |
| Prejudice, National Front | 118 | 132 | 93 | 93 | 100 |
| Racial attacks | 89 | 123 | 110 | 131 | 73 |
| Minority attacks | 240 | 118 | 96 | 187 | 74 |
| Demonstrations | 104 | 120 | 113 | 175 | 77 |
| Riots | 172 | 205 | 171 | 178 | 174 |
| Cultural differences | 149 | 118 | 80 | 151 | 219 |
| Sports | 138 | 146 | 46 | 150 | 141 |
| Human affairs | 190 | 213 | 52 | 79 | 48 |
| Racism abroad | 118 | 169 | 76 | 314 | 32 |
| Policing | 157 | 167 | 150 | 205 | 106 |
| Court actions | 121 | 163 | 109 | 118 | 73 |
| Black Sections | 83 | 109 | 148 | 130 | 73 |
| Honeyford | 124 | 110 | 110 | 129 | 96 |
| Affirmative action | 169 | 121 | 100 | 120 | 111 |
| Court cases on riots | 87 | 113 | 88 | 96 | 89 |
| Unions | 115 | 97 | 103 | 99 | 112 |
| Personal consequences of riots | 74 | 155 | 115 | 55 | 122 |
| Grant, Bernie | 144 | 167 | 181 | 144 | 92 |
| Other | 123 | 30 | 76 | 68 | 109 |

conservative Press, this kind of white violence, which ranges from assaults to murder, is much less newsworthy than the 'riots' or other forms of urban unrest or violence defined as crime. A fifteen to one score on the frequency count (and higher on the total space count) in favour of riot-related items is certainly saying something about how marginally racial attacks are covered (and policed!) in Britain.

These simple frequency counts for major subjects and subject clusters show a few elementary things about race reporting. First, if violence is committed by minorities it usually comes first in the news, as is obvious from the coverage on the urban unrest. Second, this subject will not primarily be related to social backgrounds, but to policing (policies, riot gear, etc.), or criminal causes (for example, drugs, immoral greed). In both cases, the disturbances are essentially related to criminal violence, that is, defined as a subject of law and order. If we add the separate subject of 'other' crimes, we find that the riots/crime/policing topics occur in 50 per cent of the news reports. The next major cluster is race relations, appearing in 20 per cent of the reports. Again, this is not a topic that shows concern for prejudice and discrimination. On the contrary, the right-wing Press especially covers race relations events mostly in an aggressive way, that is, by attacking anti-racist people or measures. The same is true for the hundreds of items on Honeyford and education, which appear in 15 per cent of the news reports. Next, immigration remains a major concern, again covered from a 'defensive' point of view: how do we keep them out? Finally, different political topics will mostly combine with the other ones – and deal with national or local reactions to the disturbances, immigration, education, social affairs, etc.

On the other hand, if we take topics that cover ethnic affairs from the point of view of the concerns of minority groups, that is, the problems they face, or the obstructions and discrimination they experience in immigration, housing, employment, social affairs, facilities, education, culture, relations with the authorities (police, courts, administration), and many other fields of their social life, even this cursory inspection of the figures shows that the Press in Britain is a white Press, and hardly interested in the coverage of ethnic affairs subjects that illuminate the true position of minorities, and the true nature of race relations (as in discrimination and racism). In other words, according to these figures, the British Press does not seem to contribute much to the critical examination of ethnic inequality. Clearly, these conclusions are provisional, and need to be backed up with a more qualitative analysis of the topics in the British Press.

## Actor frequencies

Subjects and topics in the Press are closely related to the news actors involved in them. Instead of providing lengthy frequency tables for the large number of different minority and majority groups (further broken down for newspapers and topics), we briefly summarize our major findings. Of the dozens of minority groups recorded, unspecified minority groups in general, West Indians and Asians are by far the most prominent news actors. West Indians appear in nearly half of all stories that have minority actors, Asians in about a quarter of the items, and unspecified minorities are mentioned in about two-fifths of the news reports. We see that a large part of the minority coverage is about 'blacks', as we have seen before. The occurrence of majority group actors is much more diverse. The analysis of the headlines in the previous chapters already suggests that the extraordinary coverage of the disturbances shows that the police are by far the most frequent majority actors in 1985, appearing in about a quarter of all stories with majority actors. They are followed, at a distance, by the government and the ministries, the city councils, white British individuals and teachers (especially Honeyford), each with somewhat more than 10 per cent of the occurrence of majority actors. It is striking that in ethnic affairs coverage, the Labour Party, appearing in 13 per cent of the news items, is twice as frequent an actor as the Tories.

For each minority group the frequencies of their major social categories were also analysed, such as whether they appear as individuals, men, women, children, institutions, action groups, or political parties. It appears that most minorities in the news appear as individuals, 'rioters', or youths (each in about 200 items). Institutional presence of minority groups is much less pronounced, appearing in a few dozen items only. Most minority group members are men (if only because they predominate in the crime and 'riot' news). Women appear only in a few dozen of items. Minorities as workers or employers are virtually invisible. Because of the Black Sections subject, they appear more often as members of political groups. In sum, if minorities appear at all in the news, then it is mostly as individuals and in stereotypical roles (criminals, 'rioters'), or as members of controversial organizations or groups (such as anti-racist groups, religious organizations, churches, etc.). They seldom appear in 'normal' roles, such as workers, students, employers, union members, etc.

Further analysis of the overall actor-perspective of the news reports shows that a third of the stories have mixed majority–minority presence in their topics (that is, both majority group members and minority group members are main actors), another third of the stories have primarily majority actors, whereas only a seventh of the news stories primarily have minority actors. Nearly a fifth of all stories do not have topical presence of minorities at all, but an exclusive presence of majority group actors. In other words, as we shall see in more detail in our analysis of quotations in Chapter six, whereas majority actors appear in more than 85 per cent of the stories (and are the main or exclusive actors in 50 per cent of the news items), minority groups are topical actors in fewer than 50 per cent of the news items. Hence, in news about ethnic affairs too, white groups, institutions, and individuals play a dominant role as actors.

The differences between the newspapers are not dramatic, although the *Guardian* has comparatively more general news stories with primarily minority actors than the conservative Press (especially in the *Telegraph*, which has less than the average number of exclusive minority stories). *The Times* has a higher than average number of items without minority actors, and the *Guardian* a much higher than average number of stories with primarily majority actors. The tabloids tend to have a mixed presence of minority and majority actors. These figures are interesting, because they suggest that when the presence of news actors is concerned, there is no obvious distinction between liberal and conservative, or between the quality and the popular Press. Thus, the *Guardian* may have somewhat more stories with the main presence of minority groups, but at the same time it has many fewer news items with a mixed presence of majority and minority actors. Thus, a liberal view on ethnic affairs does not guarantee that minority groups are portrayed more prominently. Another tendency is that the quality Press pays more extensive attention to 'policy' news, which primarily involves the white authorities.

## The subjects of 1989

By way of comparison, let us briefly analyse the subject frequencies for the 1,184 articles that appeared on ethnic affairs during the first six months of 1989 in the major national papers, this time including the *Independent* (see Table 4.3). Recall that the total number of ethnic affairs reports in 1989 is drastically lower than in 1985. This is largely due to the vast number of items on the disturbances in 1985. However, even without the 'riot' coverage, 1985 still has more ethnic news than 1989. Further research will have to show whether reduced reporting on ethnic affairs is a more general trend. As before, the *Guardian* has most items (337), followed at a distance by the three other quality papers (each about 200 items), whereas the tabloids have about 100 articles on ethnic affairs during this period.

We have the impression that routine reporting on everyday ethnic affairs, which never was very extensive, is further deteriorating in 1989

*Table 4.3* Topic frequencies and size of reports in the British Press, January–July 1989

| Topics | Total | Size (in sq. cm) | Times | Guardian | Tele-graph | Mail | Sun | Inde-pend-ent |
|---|---|---|---|---|---|---|---|---|
| Rushdie | 268 | 148 | 59 | 83 | 32 | 17 | 35 | 42 |
| Education, research | 168 | 165 | 33 | 44 | 37 | 17 | 10 | 27 |
| Discrimination | 130 | 138 | 20 | 31 | 28 | 19 | 8 | 24 |
| Party politics | 116 | 160 | 21 | 33 | 22 | 8 | 7 | 25 |
| Religion | 104 | 189 | 29 | 21 | 16 | 14 | 3 | 21 |
| Immigration | 98 | 138 | 7 | 37 | 23 | 7 | 5 | 19 |
| Race relations | 94 | 158 | 17 | 25 | 25 | 10 | 7 | 10 |
| Crime, police | 90 | 140 | 13 | 23 | 23 | 8 | 14 | 9 |
| Sanctuary | 84 | 151 | 15 | 23 | 14 | 9 | 6 | 17 |
| Minority attacks | 71 | 132 | 10 | 17 | 10 | 9 | 17 | 8 |
| Refugees | 60 | 177 | 10 | 22 | 11 | 2 | 3 | 12 |
| Black Sections | 62 | 170 | 13 | 14 | 12 | 5 | 3 | 15 |
| Prejudice | 50 | 112 | 7 | 9 | 12 | 5 | 11 | 6 |
| Employment, unemployment | 48 | 166 | 11 | 13 | 9 | 8 | 3 | 4 |
| Arts | 44 | 151 | 3 | 20 | 10 | 3 | 0 | 8 |
| Demonstrations | 42 | 145 | 7 | 14 | 5 | 1 | 5 | 10 |
| Court action | 41 | 129 | 8 | 7 | 9 | 4 | 1 | 12 |
| Repatriation | 38 | 160 | 7 | 8 | 8 | 4 | 5 | 6 |
| Policing | 37 | 136 | 5 | 12 | 5 | 3 | 1 | 11 |
| Racial attacks | 32 | 148 | 5 | 14 | 2 | 1 | 4 | 6 |
| Media | 28 | 197 | 1 | 11 | 4 | 1 | 6 | 5 |
| Health | 28 | 124 | 3 | 7 | 5 | 3 | 0 | 10 |
| Legal matters | 27 | 176 | 5 | 9 | 7 | 1 | 0 | 5 |
| Government | 22 | 187 | 6 | 5 | 5 | 2 | 0 | 4 |
| Housing | 17 | 170 | 1 | 10 | 1 | 0 | 4 | 1 |
| Culture | 17 | 248 | 3 | 3 | 4 | 7 | 0 | 0 |
| Racism, general | 16 | 128 | 2 | 8 | 3 | 0 | 0 | 3 |
| Social affairs | 15 | 231 | 1 | 4 | 0 | 1 | 4 | 5 |
| Illegal stay | 13 | 146 | 0 | 1 | 4 | 2 | 4 | 2 |
| Affirmative action | 10 | 90 | 4 | 2 | 3 | 0 | 0 | 1 |
| Ethnic affairs | 9 | 186 | 2 | 5 | 1 | 0 | 0 | 1 |
| Facilities, help | 9 | 129 | 2 | 3 | 3 | 0 | 1 | 0 |
| Drugs | 8 | 230 | 1 | 1 | 0 | 0 | 2 | 4 |
| Other | 34 | 218 | 1 | 13 | 6 | 5 | 5 | 4 |

towards an 'affair' or 'scandal' approach. That is, if covered at all, ethnic events tend to be covered massively if they are defined as a sudden national panic (Cohen, 1980). In that case, over-reporting precisely defines an issue as a scandal or affair, and this will again spawn further reactions from politicians, and others involved, which again need to be reported, and so on, thus creating what may be called the 'panic circle'.

Table 4.3 shows that the major panic of 1989 is the Rushdie affair, which directly or indirectly appears in about 22 per cent of all news items (in this subject analysis, only the two major subjects of each news item were counted, so that the sum of the totals in the table yield more than the total number of articles). From the earlier burning of *The Satanic Verses* by Muslims in Bradford to the *fatwa* issued by Ayatollah Khomeini in early 1989, and the British and international reactions to this threat, hundreds of news items and letters to the editor deal with what is represented as a fundamental opposition between 'western', liberal values of freedom of expression, on the one hand, and fundamentalist Muslim intolerance and threats, on the other hand.

The second major topic is again education. After the Honeyford affair in 1985, this time the education issue is primarily discussed in relation to the controversy about special arrangements for Muslims (especially girls): should we accept special, religious schools, and how should these be funded? Again, as in the Rushdie affair, Muslim organizations play a prominent role in the topics represented by this subject, which also explains the high percentage of the score (and the length of the reports) on religion, which is nearly exclusively reserved for topics in which Islamic practices are being discussed. This school controversy is reported as an "affair", and not as part of the everyday reporting about education, which is minimal. We see however that multi-cultural education, as was the case in the Honeyford affair, remains a prominent Press issue.

Again in 1989 the subject of discrimination is frequent, although the reports on this issue are not particularly long. Many of the news items on other subjects involve issues that relate to race relations: if we count all these items together, they may again be among the most frequent of all subjects. Racial attacks, however, is a topic that receives little attention in 1989. Because of the threats of Muslims against Rushdie, this time attacks and demonstrations made by minorities are given extra focus, as was the case for black youths in the disturbances of 1985.

As usual, the subject of immigration remains important; in fact, it is more prominent than in 1985. This time, extensive attention is paid to refugees, the possible immigration of people from Hong Kong, and the immigration of Turkish Kurds. The major immigration story of 1989 is the deportation of the Sri Lankan refugee Viraj Mendis, who had sought sanctuary in a church, but was finally arrested in a police raid on the church and put on a plane to Sri Lanka. This story alone accounts for the large number of items on 'sanctuary' and 'refugees' in the frequency list. Again, reporting in this case has all the properties of an "affair", in which this time the church as well, together with anti-racist groups, are pitched against the authorities. Because of the allegedly dubious status of Mendis' refugee claims, virtually the whole Press agrees that he should not stay.

Crime, which is again high on the frequency list, is occasionally combined with drugs, illegal stay (immigration fraud), and other negative issues. The subject of the Black Sections also remains relevant in 1989. This time, the major story, often reported in large background articles, is the local election in Vauxhall, in which the Labour party leadership substituted a white candidate, a woman (who eventually won the election), for a local black candidate. Although the Black Sections in the Labour Party are not always the main issue in this news, we have categorized them as such because the point of the coverage is often whether or not there should be independent black representatives in the Labour Party.

Political news, as is generally the case in Britain, is primarily party politics, for instance the Vauxhall by-election. City politics is hardly present in the 1989 coverage. National politics coverage is almost wholly limited to official reactions to the Rushdie affair, and to immigration cases. The health items are nearly all about blood tests for immigrants. Again, the issues that are immediately relevant for minority groups, and which do not happen to belong to an "affair", are hardly present: there is little coverage of racism, racial attacks, housing, social affairs, culture, affirmative action, and health.

As may be expected, there are differences between the various newspapers in their accounts of ethnic affairs in 1989. We have seen that the *Guardian* in particular has more items on ethnic affairs than the tabloids, as is usually the case for the quality Press. Deviating from the averages on each subject matter for each paper, *The Times* has relatively few items on immigration, the *Guardian* has nearly all articles on housing, the *Independent* has few on crime, the *Mail* has a relatively large number on prejudice, and the *Sun* has many on attacks by minorities (especially Muslims), *The Times* and the tabloids virtually no news about the arts, the tabloids practically no items on refugees, and the *Guardian* many items (83) on the Rushdie affair.

There are also specific groups associated with the respective topics. Thus most subjects, and especially party politics (Black Sections), employment, education, and crime are nearly exclusively related to West Indians. Immigration during this period focuses on immigrating Kurds from Turkey. Muslims are almost exclusively associated with negative topics, such as education (separate schools), religion, and attacks or protests in the Rushdie affair. Discrimination is mostly discussed for the category of minority workers (and focuses on the case of a Rastafarian discriminated against by a government agency). Of the majority groups and institutions, it is remarkable to find that virtually only the Labour Party appears in ethnic affairs news, for instance in the subject of the Black Sections and the Vauxhall election. It is the government, particularly the department of Home Affairs, that is the majority institution, to the exclusion of almost all others, concerned with immigration and refugee news. The schools and teachers are main actors in education news. Race relations issues are often tied to the government, the cities and city councils and of course the Commission for Racial Equality. The main majority actors in the Rushdie affair are white Britons and Christians in general, the government (relations with Iran and protesting Muslims), the police and business companies (booksellers).

In sum, in 1989 the Press has relatively little ethnic affairs news and even these few items are nearly fully overshadowed by a few affairs: Rushdie, Viraj Mendis, the Muslim schools, and the Vauxhall election. Most other subjects (crime, immigration, discrimination) are covered as usual. New is the increasing attention for refugees, who are however covered in ways that are largely similar to earlier immigrant "waves" to the UK. Most striking is the intensive coverage of Islam, and the definition of Muslims as a political, social, and cultural 'threat', a topic that should be placed of course against the general background of stereotypes in the coverage of Islam in the western media (Said, 1981). Although negatively valued cultural differences have always been a prominent feature of ethnic affairs coverage, there seems to be a marked tendency towards a definition of such differences in terms of a threat to the British people and their culture, in particular, and to western values, in general.

## TOPICS IN THE BRITISH PRESS

After the analysis of the overall subjects of the British Press, we now turn to an informal study of the topics, that is, the most prominent themes or meaning structures of the coverage of ethnic affairs in 1985. Since there are more than 3,000 different topics, we have selected some major topic clusters representing the major 'stories' of the second half of 1985. This analysis is intended both as a general introduction to the 'contents' of these stories, of which further details are studied in the following chapters, and as an answer to the important question of which topics are, or are not, being covered and how prominent such coverage is.

**The 'riots'**

As may be expected from the discussion of subject frequencies and headlines, the topics in the British Press of the second half of 1985 are dominated by the urban disorders. The specific questions raised in such a topical analysis are, for example, how are these 'riots' topicalized? What topics typically appear in the account of the urban disturbances in Handsworth, Brixton, and Tottenham? What is the most important topical information in the news reports and background articles and which relevant topics tend to be played down, concealed, or omitted? Who are the major participants in the topics, what are their roles and mutual relationships, and what are the predicates used to describe who they are and what they do? (For earlier analyses, partly about the 1980 urban unrest in the UK, see also Benyon and Solomos, 1987; Hansen, 1982; Kettle and Hodges, 1982; Murdock, 1984; Murray, 1986; Solomos, 1989; Sumner, 1982.)

The topics on the disturbances may be divided into the following clusters, which represent what is now generally known as the typical 'riot' script according to the British Press.

1 The 'events' themselves: what happened?
2 The assumed causes of the disturbances
3 Comments, reactions, and evaluations of the disturbances
4 Police and court actions following the disturbances (for example, arrests, trials)
5 Other actions, for example, of participants, victims, etc. after the disturbances
6 Inquiries into the disturbances
7 Official plans and policies to prevent or contain future disturbances

Whereas the accounts of the events themselves are concentrated on a few days after the urban disorders, the other topic clusters continue to appear for a period of many weeks after the events. Discussions about causes and policies continue for months.

*The events*

It is not surprising that the major topics summarizing the events feature the usual actions and props from the 'riot' script, that is, fighting, attacks, looting, petrol bombs, fires, bricks and other missiles, and the usual actors, such as crowds, "mobs", youths, on the one hand, and the police and fire-fighters on the other hand (for a more detailed account of the events, see for example, Benyon and Solomos, 1987). Where the headlines may still be vague about the ethnic identity of the major actors, the topics are not: The "mobs" involved are primarily identified as black, West Indian youths, despite the fact that, according to later figures, at least 30 per cent of the crowds were white. Thus, the events are mainly summarized in terms of urban warfare taking place in poor inner city neigbourhoods. Typical topics here may be expressed by the following thematic sentences (which for reasons of space and readability, will henceforth not be given for each topic):

Riots break out in Birmingham (*Times*, 10 September)
Firemen are attacked by mob of 100 youths (*Telegraph*, 10 September)
Mobs burn down shops (*Sun*, 2 October)

We see that the prevalent definition of the situation as given in the headlines, studied in the previous chapter, also summarizes the major topics of the news reports, namely violent attacks on fire-fighters and on the police, looting and burning of shops, and similar actions, usually described in highly negative terms (this stylistic aspect of the description will be further examined in Chapter eight). Several conservative newspapers also feature the conspiracy topic: The 'riots' are organized by "outside agitators", a well-known topic in the conservative coverage of social protest and unrest (Cohen, 1980; Halloran, Elliott, and Murdock, 1970; Solomos, 1989). The point of this topic is that it discounts possible explanations of the causes of the disturbances in terms of spontaneous local rage or frustration about miserable social conditions in the inner cities.

Whatever the further explanation of these events (see below), their primary definition in the news is in terms of criminal greed and of a violent disruption of the social order by black youths, and not social protest or the expression of anger and frustration. Even when police raids led to shooting and seriously injuring a black woman (Brixton) or the death of another black woman (Tottenham), these events are topicalized at a lower level than the ensuing disturbances. This means that such alternative definitions appear less in headlines and leads, feature less detailed information, and tend to appear later in each news item. The difference is particularly clear in the coverage of the Tottenham disturbance, in which a police constable is killed, a topic that, especially in the tabloids, fully overshadows the topic of the death of a black woman, which is topicalized, but seldom expressed in the headlines.

Examining the semantic role structures of these 'riot' topics, we arrive at the same result as in our analysis of the headlines: the police are represented in a victim role, and young male blacks in the active role of aggressors. Also represented as victims of young West Indian males are the Indians who died in a fire during the Handsworth disturbances, the Home Secretary Douglas Hurd, pelted with stones when he visited Birmingham, as well as journalists of the *Sun* attacked during these disturbances. For the Press accounts of the disturbances in Brixton and Tottenham, we find essentially the same semantic 'cast', although "outside agitators" have become more prominent than in the Handsworth story.

## The causes

In order to keep the riot story alive, and once the disturbances are over, the riot script requires at least some attention to their causes, which continue to be occasionally discussed, especially in the quality Press, during the weeks that follow. The tone is set by the Prime Minister Thatcher and the Home Secretary Douglas Hurd, who define and explain the disturbances in terms of "criminal greed" and a "cry for loot", definitions gladly adopted by the conservative Press. To back up this 'explanation', the conservative Press adds its own stories about local drugs traffic by "drugs barons" and crime in the inner city. We see that once a social event itself is defined as criminal, its causes must also be defined as criminal. Thus, for the *Telegraph*, the Handsworth disturbance is the first "drug riot" in Britain. For the readers, this explanation is made credible when it is set against the background of prevalent stereotypes that relate drugs primarily with young black males.

The same is true for the accusation of conspiracy by outside "agitators" or even Cubans (*Telegraph*), which adds the missing political link of the left in the construction of the criminal causes of the disturbances. Further explanation of the urban unrest in terms of the social and economic situation of the inner city, and the responsibility of the Thatcher government, is made superfluous in that case. Instead, the pervasive tactic of blaming the victims, that is, the minority community, or searching for other villains, is consistently applied in the conservative Press. The same attribution to the minority community takes place when the *Daily Mail* explains the disturbances and the death of two Asian men with the familiar terms of a 'race war' between the (jealous, and apparently 'lazy') West Indians and the (hard-working) Asians. The consistent denials by the Asian community of this alleged rivalry are topicalized only in the *Guardian*.

On the other hand, the other major news actor, the police, while presented as victim in the primary definitions of the disturbances, has no role in the explanation of its causes. Racist policing and harassment (found by Lord Scarman to be a major cause of the 1981 Brixton disorders; see Scarman, 1981; Institute of Race Relations, 1985; Gordon,

1983), is consistently non-topicalized in the present coverage. At most, the police are accused of having indulged in the "softly softly" approach of so-called 'community policing', which the right-wing Press sees as the major cause of what they continue to describe as "no go areas". Other accusations against the police are ignored or carefully put in disqualifying quotes.

Thus the social explanations of the disorders are systematically denied or discredited by the right-wing Press (Hall, 1987; Solomos, 1989). If mentioned at all, they seldom reach topic status, except in a few editorials, but in that case only in order to be rejected. However, *The Times* and especially the *Guardian* do topicalize the social conditions in the inner cities: unemployment, bad housing, lack of community services and, occasionally, discrimination. The standard argument, to which we return in the next chapter when we examine the argumentation structures of the Press, is that deprivation is "no excuse" for rioting. After all, so the argument goes, many poor people are law-abiding citizens and do not riot. The fact that the disturbances always occur in poor inner-city areas, is not seen as an indication of the deeper causes of the disturbances. Rather, it is the black community of these inner cities that is blamed, not the poor conditions, thereby disregarding the fact that riots have a long white history in Britain's inner cities (see, for example, Benyon, 1987). Similarly conspicuous is the absence of the topics of discrimination and racism as possible causes of the disturbances. Incidental discrimination in employment is sometimes briefly mentioned, but systematic, structural forms of racism are never topicalized, even in the liberal Press, except in an occasional, moderate letter or opinion article.

## The consequences

After the disturbances, the major topics soon shift to the consequences of the 'riot script', that is, policing, containment of future riots, police inquiries, and trials. Another consequence of the 'riot script' is the topic of a serious ("Scarman-style") enquiry into their social causes, which is advocated only by the *Guardian* but forcefully rejected by the conservative Press with the argument that "we already know the social situation of the inner cities". Indeed, once urban disturbances are defined as criminal in their nature as well as their causes, the continued relevance of the social reasons for them is as unwelcome for the conservative Press as it is for the Thatcher administration. Most other news about the consequences of the urban unrest is about verbal activities, for instance, during political party meetings of the Tories and Labour, or by the authorities, that is, the criticism, accusations, and discussions about 'what should be done'. Most of these discussions do not address the causes of the disturbances, but the future of tough policing (such as, whether or not rubber bullets or water cannons should be used in the future). Thus, prevention through social measures is overshadowed as a topic by the focus on law and order and the future containment of the 'ethnic problem'.

In sum, the topicalization of the various elements of the 'riot script' is carefully managed by a number of strategies that make sure that the nature, the causes, and the consequences of the 'riots' are firmly blamed upon the West Indian community, and especially black youths. The description of the disturbances in terms of criminal greed, aggression, or blood-lust, their explanation in terms of similarly criminal causes (drugs) or political agitation, and their future containment as a practical problem of law and order, not only confirms prevailing prejudices about blacks or the radical left, but also exonerates the police and the Thatcher government. All other possible definitions and explanations (rage and frustration about socio-economic conditions and discrimination) are similarly ignored or under-topicalized.

## Immigration

Although less than in previous decades, immigration is still among the most prominent Press subjects in 1985. Its topic clusters deal with immigration policies, decisions of non-admission and expulsion, repatriation, family reunion, illegal entry and residence, and the treatment of immigrants. Again, we notice that Press accounts seem to follow some kind of ideologically framed 'immigration script', in which these topic clusters appear as main categories.

### Policies

The topics on immigration policies focus on the major conflicts that divide Tory and Labour positions on immigration, on the one hand, and the government or authorities and the immigrant communities, on the other hand. The Thatcher government and the Tories generally favour restrictions on immigration, a stand also supported by most of the conservative Press, whereas their opponents criticize the current policies, and demand fair immigration rules (despite the fact that previous Labour governments also enacted stricter immigration rules). Critical Labour officials sometimes qualify government policies as racist, whereas the radical right-wing Monday Club, following in Enoch Powell's footsteps, is reported by the *Telegraph* to have again called for a ban on black immigrants.

Most topics organized around these policy conflicts deal with proposals and discussions about stricter visa requirements, extra border checks, and general conditions on admission. The *Mail* specifically focuses on alleged abuses of British 'hospitality', and calls for stricter immigration rules. It does not hesitate to publish, with apparent approval, overtly racist statements by right-wing politicians who claim that without further curbs on immigration Britain may become the world's "dustbin". One issue particularly resented by the right-wing Press is the decision of the European Court that equal rights of immigrant women are violated when they, unlike men, are not allowed to bring in the spouses they married abroad (that is, mainly in South Asia). As usual, the right-wing Press fears large scale fraud – "brides for sale" – when women are allowed to bring in their husbands.

The major immigration story in the autumn of 1985 is a row in Parliament between the Home Office and Labour MPs accused of abusing their right to 'represent' immigrants. For the right-wing Press this row is of course most welcome in a bid to associate Labour not only with illegal immigrants, but also with vast amounts of money. One tabloid claims that such immigrants cost the taxpayer billions of pounds!

The predicates of the topical propositions about immigration policies are concepts such as 'curb', 'control', 'restrict' and similar notions, which are correctly descriptive of the practices of immigration control (see also Gordon, 1985). The main topical agents of these propositions are invariably the white authorities: the government, Parliament, political parties, and occasionally organizations that provide help to immigrants. Immigrants themselves are usually only passive actors in such topics, unless they are presented as involved in various kinds of immigration fraud.

## Admission and expulsion

Besides these general policy topics, the concrete everyday stories of individual admissions and expulsions are the next instalment of the scripted immigration stories. During this autumn, we again find an illustration of the well-known "luxury immigrants" myth, this time about a rich Nigerian family temporarily housed by a (left-wing!) city council in an expensive hotel, and which wants to fly home only on a first class ticket. Such stories are ideal to discredit black immigrants and to make a case against further immigration, thereby confirming well-known prejudices about the costs for the 'ratepayer'. Harassment of immigrants by the immigration authorities is seldom topicalized by the conservative Press.

Other immigration stories are also set in a negative framework. Thus, the case of whether or not second wives of (Muslim) immigrants from South Asia will be allowed to enter the UK not only draws attention to 'numbers', but also associates such immigrants with dubious cultural practices (second wives, arranged marriages), if not with fraud. The same is true for the "brides for sale" story, in which Asian girls are alleged to be sold to men who want to immigrate to the UK.

## Repatriation

The topic cluster of immigration in the British Press is typically related to the issue of repatriation, a favoured topic of the new right, and prominently topicalized by Enoch Powell. The conservative Press has an ambiguous stand on repatriation. On the one hand, it rejects forced repatriation of established immigrants as "unpractical" (*Mail*), but on the other hand, it is also made clear that any 'illegal' immigrant should be expelled. Similarly, the right-wing threat of repatriation may be strategically used to warn the black community to behave, as we shall see in an analysis of tabloid editorials in the following chapter. Despite its formal rejection of Powell's ideas, the conservative Press seldom misses the opportunity to publicize his racist views, so that millions of readers will know them. *The Times* even publishes another recent diatribe of Powell against immigrants, thereby legitimating his racist views as part of the public debate, even when it distances itself from such views. A 'reassuring' *Sun* poll shows that the majority of the British people do not support Powell's "astonishing 'Blacks go home'" call. That white public opinion (or the methods by which it is assessed) is fickle, is shown a few weeks later, after the Brixton and Tottenham disturbances, when the *Mail* reports that most white Britons want to stop further immigration and favour repatriation.

In sum, also the topicalization of immigration is largely set in a framework of negative associations, such as political rows, numbers, luxury immigrants, costs to the 'ratepayer', fraud, illegal residence, and 'strange' customs. As in earlier decades, the topics of immigration focus on problems, if not on threats against white Britons. It is not surprising that although forced repatration is not advocated, it remains a legitimate option. It is not surprising either that the racist nature of many immigration restrictions and laws, as well as the treatment of new immigrants by the authorities, are seldom topicalized.

## Social affairs and employment

The cluster of social affairs topics is primarily discussed here because of its noteworthy under-topicalization. Except for occasional background articles, especially in the quality Press, about the socio-economic causes of the 'riots', topics that deal with housing, city development, welfare, health care, facilities, or other issues that are important for minority groups, are rare. Liberal voices (Labour, the churches) are reported to advocate energetic measures for the inner cities, but the conservative Press agrees with the Thatcher government that enough money has been invested in them, and that the only way minority groups, and especially blacks, can solve their problems is to take the initiative into their own hands, and to start their own businesses (see, for example, Smith, 1989). In other words, the solution is Thatcher's ideology of popular capitalism. When Prince Charles is reported to take special interest in the inner cities and observes a rift between the haves and the have-nots, this develops into a carefully managed mini-scandal.

We see that the most prominent strategy of the topicalization of social affairs in the conservative Press is similar to that for the disturbances, namely, to define the situation in such a way that the government is not responsible and that the minorities are largely blamed for their own situation. Those who have an alternative definition of the situation, as does the Church of England in its report *Faith in the City*, are consequently branded as "Marxists".

Similar remarks hold for the topicalization of unemployment, which during this period is extensively covered in a series of articles only in *The Times*, in which occasionally even the views of black people are being quoted. Discrimination in hiring practices and on the job are briefly mentioned when the social causes of the 'riots' are discussed, but usually presented in terms of an agent-less, regrettable phenomenon, instead of as a specific, illegal act of employers. Rather, West Indian blacks tend to be blamed themselves and, in tactical comparisons with the diligent Asians, accused of not trying hard enough. Even moderate proposals for affirmative action are resolutely rejected as an attack on the freedom of enterprise if not defined as reverse discrimination. This is one of the topics that show how the conservative Press defends both the interests of employers as well as those of the white group in general. It is not surprising, therefore, that these newspapers are furious about the very few cases in which a black worker is thought to be given preference over a white applicant.

## Law and order

Crime is a major subject of ethnic reporting. We saw in Chapter one that much earlier research found that it is usually among the most prominent issues in the coverage of minorities. As soon as black people are somehow associated with a breach of the law, such events become newsworthy, although the same crime committed by whites would be ignored or played down. This is especially the case when such crimes, real or alleged, can be construed as a 'threat' to white people (indeed, 'black on black' crime is usually ignored). Such crime is no longer just 'crime', but 'black crime'. Moreover, minorities and especially black males are often associated with specific kinds of crime and deviance, for example, violence, rioting, drugs, mugging, and prostitution (Hall *et al.*, 1978), and seldom white collar crimes, although fraud with subsidies is a quite common topic as well. It is therefore in line with prevalent prejudices about black criminality that much of the coverage on the disturbances is primarily associated with such specific forms of 'black crime' (see also Chibnall, 1977; Graber, 1980).

Besides the riot-related crimes and their later treatment in court cases, we find such topics as general law and order discussions (for instance during the Tory party conferences), projects for new laws of criminal evidence and public order, worries about increasing crime (especially in the inner cities), and the recruitment of new black police officers. But even these topics are often related to the prevention or containment of future disorders (see also Benyon and Solomos, 1987). The same is true for the recurring topic of styles and modes of policing, which the tabloids want to be tough, instead of the 'softly softly' community policing. To legitimate its views, and to avoid obvious accusations of racism, the *Mail* even publishes a series of very long articles on tough policing in the Caribbean, thereby implying that when the black police there behave like this against blacks, it is ridiculous to criticize white police harassment of young blacks in Britain.

One major crime highlighted by the right-wing Press is the case of the blonde, white girl, daughter of a Tory MP, raped by a group of young men, who are duly identified as 'black' by the right-wing Press, despite the rule of the code of conduct of the NUJ which proscribes irrelevant mentioning of ethnic or racial identity of news actors (see Appendix, pp. 255–6). In this case, however, the right-wing Press is particularly intent on adding this identification, because the rape took place during the disturbances, which allows them to criminalize further the urban revolt as well as blacks. It is not surprising that these newspapers are far from happy with the "light sentences" given to the perpetrators, and generally resent that the courts are "too soft".

The other crimes routinely reported are those associated with drugs, mugging, and assaults. Even the mugging of headmaster Honeyford's wife in Jamaica is covered (*Mail*), on the one hand because Honeyford is newsworthy, and on the other hand, it seems, because he is thereby portrayed as a double victim of black people. More important, reporting about such a crime in Jamaica further contributes to the criminal stereotype about Jamaicans and other West Indians in Britain. Similarly, if a black policeman breaks the law (reselling confiscated drugs), this will also hit the headlines.

Against the criminalization of blacks, we find concealment or playing down of unlawful or immoral police behaviour. Indeed, as we have seen before, police harassment, and discrimination and racism in the police force, are barely covered. When it ever happens that the racist officers are fired the Press briefly reports such an extraordinary event, without discussing the event and still using quotes around 'racist' after the police management itself has found proof for such an accusation! One single article, published in *The Times*, discusses discrimination in the courts.

In sum, law and order reporting in the British Press during the mid-1980s continues a long tradition of media criminalization of the black community. As always, the perspective and evaluation of the white authorities, and especially of the police, continue to prevail over minority views. The focus is on those crimes that may be interpreted as confirming prejudices about black people, and that may be seen as a threat to white people. In other words, crime is not covered as involving black individuals, but as a form of 'group crime', for which the whole black community tends to be blamed, if only for condoning it. The common slogan "We are not safe in our own cities anymore", therefore expresses not only a characteristic right-wing concern, but is also a particularly prominent proposition in a racist ideology.

## Education

If there is one field of ethnic conflict in British race relations, as seen by the right-wing Press, it is education. In this view, 'multi-cultural', and especially anti-racist education, is interpreted as an attack against white British values, if not as a form of 'reverse racism'. It is therefore routinely stated that immigrant children should adapt to the dominant culture and learn English, whereas white British children should not be forced to learn anything about minority cultures, let alone about the power structures involved in ethnic relations. Right-wing wrath is directed against even the most moderate forms of anti-racism in the schools. Critical evaluations of children's books, textbooks and curricula are branded as intolerance if not as censorship, as we shall see repeatedly in the following chapters. Whereas such education topics may be expected in the quality Press, some major conflicts are also debated in the tabloid Press, which however is not so much interested in good education, as in alleged left-wing and anti-racist "indoctrination" in the schools.

*Honeyford*

As we have seen in the study of the headlines in the last chapter and in the analysis of the subjects given above, the Honeyford case is one of the major 'ethnic' stories of 1985, in which the irate reactions in the conservative Press in particular play an important role. The topics of the hundreds of Press accounts of this story are rather straightforward. The legal battle about this case features topics such as the decision of the court that Honeyford was wrongfully suspended, and that the Bradford council was thinking of appealing against the verdict. Most reports in the tabloid Press, however, focused on the protests of the parents and the school boycott that followed Honeyford's return in the autumn of 1985. As may be expected, and as we have seen in the headlines, the tabloids represent picketing parents as "mobs" who are engaged in violence and obstruction. Despite its intention to appeal against the court verdict, the city council is reported to threaten the boycotters with legal action on account of truancy. We see that when Asians are no longer meek shopkeepers who believe in the Thatcherite dream, but resist racist schooling, they are no longer portrayed so positively.

The conceptual structure of these topics is ambiguous. That is, on the one hand, the basic topic 'Parents protest against Honeyford' clearly emerges, and represents a correct reconstruction of the facts. On the other hand, however, the parents are associated with the well-known right-wing evaluation of protests in terms of deviance, disruption, irrationality, radicality and lack of tolerance. As was the case in the Press coverage of the miners' strike and other industrial disputes (Glasgow University Media Group, 1976, 1980), parental protests are localized on the streets and in picket lines. Parents are portrayed as keeping children out of school, and responsible for the victimization of their own children as well as for the "hate campaign" against the headmaster. It is not primarily Honeyford, the courts or his colleagues who are problematized in this way. On the contrary, in most topics Honeyford plays the double role of victim and hero. Similarly, the conservative Press does not topicalize Honeyford's writings as a threat to good education or to race relations. Neither does it focus on his problematization of minority children.

The *Sun* and the *Mail* have made the Honeyford case their *cause célèbre*, and unambiguously support his "heroic battle" against what they see as the "black racists" who relentlessly vilified him in a two-year hate campaign. The tabloids present themselves as the defenders of freedom of speech and can only agree with Honeyford who finally told the 'truth' about multiracial schools. We shall come back to the deatils of this ideological dimension of the Honeyford coverage later.

*Multi-cultural education*

The events of the Honeyford affair are the most prominent illustration of a more general issue – multi-cultural education, which is associated with problems and conflicts in many other ways: Muslims who want their own schools, language problems of immigrant children and anti-racist guide-lines that "indoctrinate" children. When schools ban police officers on account of what they see as racist policing, the *Mail* topicalizes the event as 'anti-police – or even as anti-English – propaganda' in a barrage of articles examining relevant teaching materials that allegedly incite children to "race hate". Thus the tabloids find evidence of a 'race war' in the schools between white and black.

Not topicalized are the various forms of racism in education, such as the consequences of 'streaming' and the undervaluation of black pupils in the classroom and in counselling, depite the recurrent complaints of Asian and West Indian parents and findings of much research (Brandt, 1986; Troyna and Williams, 1986). A large study done by Professor Eggleston, which finds extensive evidence of discrimination in schools, is, however, briefly covered. If some attention is given to racism in children's books and textbooks, the right-wing Press portrays such criticism of racist learning materials as a form of censorship, intolerance, or inverse racism. In particular, the proposed banning of *Little Black Sambo* from school libraries is found to be ridiculous, and a form of terror tactic by the anti-racists.

## Culture

The topicalization of culture is limited to only a few issues. The major dimensions of Press reporting about culture are cultural differences and conflicts, in which other customs, habits, or philosophies are often made to look silly or strange, if not as a threat against 'our' culture. Religion is a prominent case. During the second half of 1985, for instance, there is a long debate, carried most fully in *The Times*, about Jewish rituals for slaughtering animals. Dozens of reports and letters deal with whether or not ritual slaughter is hurtful for animals, a topic that is of course never dealt with for 'normal' slaughter. Indeed, during these months, there are more reports in *The Times* about how animals may suffer from ritual slaughtering than about racial attacks against Asian families.

Other topics deal with the controversial plans for the building of a Hindu temple, and with some questions of Islam, such as the position of Asian girls. Generally, then, culture is newsworthy when it can be defined as problematic and as an illustration of stereotypes or prejudices. If the

*Mail* discusses Rastafarianism, it will typically focus on drugs (ganja smoking), and on drug abuse as an excuse for rioting. The same is true for the other cultural topics, such as whether Asian children should be taught Bengali and, in 1989, the long debate about independent Muslim schools and of course the Rushdie affair. Typical socio-cultural topics are polygamy or arranged marriages, which are newsworthy because they are 'strange' and a typical example of the 'threat' of multi-culturalism. In the few items on the role of the media, there is some discussion on whether or not certain television programmes, notably the one featuring Alf Garnett, are racist or not. The *Sun*, as may be expected, rejects such an accusation as ludicrous. Finally, there is a small scandal about the BBC, accused of having advertised for racists for a television debate.

In sum, culture is not a prominent topic cluster of the Press. The main focus is on problematic cultural differences and deviance, and on those practices of other ethnic groups that are thought to cause difficulties for the dominant group. The dominant culture is never problematized or challenged, nor is it explicitly discussed at all; typically, it is presupposed. There is not a single news report, not even in the quality Press, on cultural discrimination.

## Politics

Most political topics in the second half of 1985 directly or indirectly deal with political reactions to the disturbances, and have been discussed before. Part of these 'riot-aftermath' topics are about a new public order (or policing) Bill, and about opposition to it.

Most other political items are about Black Sections in the Labour Party, a controversy that pitches the Labour leaders against black politicians and the black community (Solomos, 1989). The structure of these topics is straightforward: 'X wants Black Sections, and Y does not'. The major fear of the Labour leadership is not only that separate Black Sections are against party unity, but also that they may cause a loss of votes from anti-black constituents. The details of the argumentation reported in the Press are more important here, since they reveal something about the opinions within the Labour party regarding black political revendications and autonomy (Hall, 1988; Reeves, 1983; Solomos, 1989). We return to such details later. The majority of these political items appear in the quality Press.

The political topics of the right-wing Press focus on Labour and the left, usually in a critical vein. Thus, if Labour, or a leftist council is seen to 'waste taxpayers' money' on anti-racist 'nonsense', this will be a preferred topic. Similarly, the few black politicians are always closely watched, and if failing for whatever reason, they will become a major target for Press attacks.

## Race relations

If we disregard the exceptional events of the disorders, there is one topic that clearly dominates the coverage of ethnic affairs in the British Press: race relations. Hundreds of news reports and background articles deal with the "problems" of a multi-cultural society, both in the liberal and in the conservative Press. Indeed, most of the topic clusters discussed above have important race relations dimensions, which therefore need not be analysed again.

The qualitative differences between the newspapers, however, are considerable. We have already found that in the right-wing tabloids, race relations are generally covered as some kind of 'race war', as a deep conflict between the white majority and the West Indian or Asian minorities or immigrants. In this 'race war', further exacerbated by the 'riots', white British society is portrayed as threatened by the social and cultural implications of a multiracial or multi-ethnic society. The *Telegraph* even speaks of the white British as the "lost tribe" of race relations (21 November 1985).

Any changes, however small, proposed for white British laws, rights, habits, politics, or culture, thus tend to be resolutely resented and rejected by the right-wing Press. Accusations of white prejudice, intolerance, discrimination, or racism are categorically denied or at least found exaggerated. It is not surprising, therefore, that those who advocate socio-cultural and political equal rights for minority groups or who struggle against racism and discrimination in many sectors of British society, are the main target for the tabloids' crusade.

These groups or organizations are commonly described with the term "the race relations industry", which is first of all portrayed as preventing "free speech" (*Mail*, 18 October). Ironically, the 'race relations industry' is the only industry not supported by the Right. Its leaders are called the "pundits" of race relations, whereas the *Sun* simply calls them "snoopers", that is, people who "imagine racism where none exists" (2 August). We return to the analysis of this anti-anti-racist style in Chapter eight. Whether the moderate Commission for Racial Equality (CRE) or more radical anti-racist groups, they all are aggressively attacked because of their purportedly unreasonable demands.

For the conservative quality Press, that is, for *The Times* and the *Telegraph*, this attitude is more attenuated and indirect. Of course, radical changes and anti-racist proposals are not endorsed, and racism is also usually denied or understated, except for some clear cases of discrimination. The liberal view, defended in the *Guardian*, comes closer to the minority points of view, or rather to that advocated by the moderate, Labour left, sometimes tinged with paternalistic overtones. Radical anti-racist positions, or their political consequences, are occasionally heard here, but are not dominant, as we have also seen in the case of Black Sections in the Labour party.

Forms of everyday racism are barely covered. There are virtually no reports, whether in the liberal or the conservative Press, of the daily experiences of minority group members with various sorts of discrimination in their lives. More general remarks about discrimination in housing or employment may sometimes be made, for instance in order to explain the urban unrest or the situation in the inner cities, but a detailed coverage of such experiences, and who is responsible for such forms of racism, is rare.

What is covered, then, are the more public cases, often related to a legal battle, official CRE reports, statements by politicians, and of course the harsher or more overt cases of racism, for instance when a club refuses entry to a black musician, or when building societies discriminate against blacks in the allocation of loans. If people go on strike because of the racist behaviour of one of their colleagues, this also will be topicalized and ridiculed by the right-wing Press.

We have seen that extremist right-wing views, for example, the recent repatriation calls by Powell and his followers, are covered more ambiguously. Officially, the conservative and even the tabloid Press reject such "simplistic" solutions to the "problem" of race relations, but right-wing Tories who express such views nevertheless have access to the right-wing Press. In other words, Powellite opinions are not so much rejected in principle, but because they are impractical or at most "heartless". In this respect, the reaction of the conservative Press is similar to that of many conservatives in general, and to that of Thatcher in particular, for whom Powell's ideas are at most politically inopportune.

The topicalization of race relations follows a rather coherent pattern, which may be partly predicted from more general news values and routines. Instead of providing a more structural discussion of race relations in Britain or western Europe, most reports and background articles tend to focus on tensions, conflicts, and scandals. Such reporting is in line with the negative problematization of ethnic affairs, which satisfies the news value of negativity, and which is especially relevant in the portrayal of relations with any political, cultural or social out-group or country. Similarly, conflicts are usually described in terms of deviance of the out-group, and never as the result of power relations or the dominance of the white group. As is the case in storytelling, conflict coverage typically places people or groups against each other as proponents and opponents, which allows rather concrete and dramatic, while personalized, reporting. These are essentially the ingredients of what the Press loves to report: a "row".

For the tabloids such conflict stories involve clearly defined heroes and villains, victims and perpetrators, especially when violence or aggression are involved. We have seen how the right-wing Press distributes such roles over white and black people, for instance in the coverage of the disturbances, the Honeyford case, and multi-cultural education. If white people are not portrayed as heroes, then they tend to be presented as victims, not only of black crime or aggression, but also of black revendications of equal rights, such as those defended by black "racists" or by the "race relations industry".

## Anti-racism

One prominent feature of most ideological topics mentioned above are the repeated attacks by the conservative Press on anti-racism. The prototypical semantic structure of these topics is straightforward: 'Anti-racists NEGATIVE PREDICATE good/innocent British X', where the negative predicate may for instance be 'to attack', 'to fire', 'to protest against', or 'to criticize', and where X may be a white teacher, a textbook, white employees, employers, or simply 'ordinary people', all playing the role of victims. We have also seen that the major strategic move of these right-wing attacks against the anti-racists is that of reversal: 'They are being intolerant' or 'We are being discriminated against', for instance in reports about critical evaluations of racist children's books or toys (such as the 'golliwog'), about affirmative action, or in the few cases in which a black applicant is seen to be favoured above a white one. In other words, the major thrust of these topics in the conservative Press is what may be called anti-anti-racism. Also in order to avoid accusations of racism, these attacks are directed less against West Indians or Asians than against white anti-racist groups and organizations, that is, the "busybodies" of the "race-relations industry".

## Racial attacks

We already suggested that there is one race relations topic involving similar negative attitudes in the liberal and conservative Press: racial attacks, especially against Asian families. The violent and dramatic nature of such attacks is widely condemned, by the liberal Press as a typical manifestation of the extreme right, by the tabloids as a form of hooliganism like all others. That is, the topicalization of these events is quite different, even if the negative opinions about such attacks are rather general. Indeed, the violent extreme right, such as the National Front, is also outside the consensus for conservative politicians and the Press. There are several reasons for this attitude, beside the obvious moral indignation about killing or harassing innocent families. Firstly, they give a bad name to right-wing politics. Secondly, they address popular feelings and therefore may steal votes or win allegiances that the more respectable parties may want to control.

The general racial attack topics describe cases of arson, personal aggression, destruction of property, and other forms of violence against Asian families. Some of these stories, including those about sports events, especially in the *Guardian*, leave no doubt about the deep-seated racism as expressed in the behaviour of some groups of white males. The reaction is that the victims or their organization complain with or about the police, and demand better protection. Indeed, the police are usually found to be too casual about such attacks. On the other hand, several topics are about the police asserting that the problem has their full attention, and that all is being done to find the criminals.

More interesting from our point of view is that the police often tend to deny the 'racial' nature of the attacks. The denial of racism, as we have repeatedly seen, is a major strategy, both among ordinary white people and among the elites. That is, for the police the attacks are primarily a form of illegal violence and harassment, like all others, and only 'racial' when there is explicit proof that the violence was committed with racist intentions, which inevitably cannot always be proven.

Whatever the point of view of the police regarding racial attacks, the conservative Press does report the attacks, though only the most conspicuous and horrific cases: everyday forms of harassment are seldom reported or further investigated. Also, whereas the topic of policing after the 'riots' is prominent for many months, this is not the case for policing against whites who participate in racial attacks. The assurances of the police authorities that the problem has their full attention apparently satisfy most of the media. That the lack of energetic policing or strict goverment measures against racial attacks may partly be explained in terms of covert – or not so covert – racism of large parts of the police force itself is naturally taboo in the Press, though widely accepted as an explanation in the immigrant communities. Indeed, if the racial attacks had any link with political violence, it would consistently have been defined as "terrorism" and dealt with as such.

## SUBJECTS AND TOPICS IN THE DUTCH PRESS

In order to put the results of the analysis of the topics of the English Press in a comparative, international perspective, we briefly summarize the results of a similar study of the topics of some 1,500 items in the Dutch Press during the same period: August 1985 to January 1986. The newspapers studied were the following national dailies: liberal *Volks-krant*, conservative quality newspaper *NRC-Handelsblad*, best-selling (about 750,000) popular conservative *Telegraaf* and *Algemeen Dagblad*, liberal protestant *Trouw*, and very small left-wing *Waarheid*, as well as the Amsterdam city newspaper *Het Parool*. Of these newspapers only left-wing (previously communist) *Waarheid* can be said to have a consistent anti-racist point of view. Details of this study, as well as our earlier work on the Dutch Press, are published elsewhere (van Dijk, 1983, 1988b, 1988c, 1988d).

The smaller number of items in the Dutch Press allowed a topical analysis that was somewhat more sophisticated than for the British Press. For each topic the approximate semantic structure was established, that is, the agents involved, as well as their roles, and the types of predicates used to describe their actions and properties. A more detailed analysis such as this allows us to determine, among other things, how many different topics can be assumed under more abstract categories. For instance, across different subject categories (for example, immigration or education), it may be the case that similar types of actions are being reported and topicalized by the Press, along the lines 'Majority Institution Helps Minority Group'.

### The ethnic situation in the Netherlands

Reporting about ethnic affairs in the Netherlands should of course be understood against the background of race relations in that country, where there are both similarities with and differences from those in Britain or other European countries (Castles, 1984). Topicalized in the Press are the largest immigrant groups: on the one hand the Turkish and Moroccan 'guest workers', most of whom decided to stay after their immigration to the Netherlands in the 1970s, and on the other hand the Surinamese group, which mainly arrived after the independence of Surinam in 1975, and which largely consists of a group of Afro-Surinamese and a group of what are commonly called 'Hindustans', that is, Surinamese of South Asian origin. The third major group are the people who earlier came to the Netherlands, after the independence of Indonesia in 1948, including the group of Moluccans. Except for the

Moluccans, these 'Indos' are often said to have been rather well integrated into Dutch society, and are not even considered as an 'ethnic minority' (the terms 'race' or 'racial minority' are seldom used in the Netherlands, mainly because of their associations with Nazi conceptions of race and racial superiority).

The socio-economic and cultural position of these groups is essentially similar to comparable groups in Britain (especially the West Indians) and in Germany (Turks). That is, they generally have the worst jobs, they live in decrepit inner city areas, and have the highest unemployment rates, although the Dutch welfare state may have softened somewhat these basic forms of inequality. Politically and culturally too, the situation is somewhat comparable to that in the UK in the 1970s. That is, political representation and power of minority groups and organizations are minimal (for an introduction to the subject see, for example, Schumacher, 1987).

Despite the well-known self-myth of the Dutch as a tolerant people (sometimes also voiced in English publications, as in Bagley, 1973), ethnic prejudices and discrimination are widespread, and white resentment generally focuses on various forms of affirmative action, especially in the business community. Indeed, minority unemployment, largely due to bad schooling and especially to discrimination by employers, is the highest in Europe, and may reach more than 50 per cent for young black and Moluccan males. One marked difference with surrounding countries is that blatant forms of discrimination and prejudice are marginal (although in 1989 one representative of a racist party was elected for Parliament). That is, the kind of things that in the UK, Belgium, France or Germany may be said by people like Powell or Le Pen, and also by more 'respectable' right-wing conservatives, are generally outside of the consensus in the Netherlands, and sometimes successfully dealt with in court.

On the whole then, as is generally the case for Dutch social relations and culture, ethnic conflicts are less extreme than in many other countries. This is partly the result of earlier religious conflicts and the particular type of Dutch democracy, managed until today by a complex system of political, social, and cultural pluralism, in which every religious group had its own domain of power (parties, schools, unions, or media). Immigrants soon got their own small niche in that consensual system of power distribution.

However, the more indirect and subtle forms of racism in the Netherlands may be even more insidious, while more difficult to combat and to challenge (Essed, 1984, 1991). As we have seen for Britain, the denial of racism is widespread in the Netherlands, especially among the elites. And, as is also the case for the position of women in the Netherlands, the socio-economic consequences of deep-seated forms of prejudice and discrimination are especially obvious in the domain of employment and legal rights. That is, it is felt that minorities may be 'helped', but they should not defend their rights, let alone make demands, or "force us" to employ them. Therefore, although less openly vilified and socially more 'taken care of' than in other countries, the minority groups in the Netherlands have less social, political, and cultural power than minority groups in the surrounding countries of western Europe.

As may be expected, the Dutch Press fairly faithfully reflects and sustains this socio-cultural framework and this type of consensus of the typical pluralist state. There is no tabloid Press as in the UK or Germany, although the positions of the popular *Telegraaf* are often similar to those of its somewhat more elitist British counterpart of the same name. This means that, compared to the British Press the more strident forms of anti-minority reporting are minimal, and the broad Press consensus denies the prevalence of racism in the country, and generally represents minorities in terms of *having* (in the liberal Press) or *causing* (in the conservative Press) 'problems'. This is particularly the case, again, in reporting about refugees, especially in the conservative Press (*Telegraaf* and *NRC-Handelsblad*). Let us now see how these general features of reporting are exhibited in the subject matters and topicalization of ethnic affairs in the Netherlands.

## Subjects

In many respects the subjects that are discussed in ethnic affairs reporting in the Netherlands are similar to those in the UK (see Table 4.4). If we disregard the rather specific subject of the urban disturbances in England in the autumn of 1985, we see that in both countries, race relations (including discrimination), immigration, and crime are among the most frequent subjects. The ordinary life of ethnic minorities, as reflected in news about work, housing, health, culture, and politics, is relatively little covered, as is generally the case in ethnic affairs news (see Chapter one). Immigration is very prominent during this period in the Netherlands (as it was also in the 1960s as well as in 1989 in the UK), because of the immigration of new refugee groups (first Tamils, later Iranians, and others).

Although the various subjects, especially immigration, are distributed over all ethnic groups in the Netherlands, a topic such as crime is particularly associated with blacks (Surinamese) and Turks. On the other hand there are few articles that deal with discrimination against black

*Table 4.4* Frequencies of general subjects in the Dutch Press, August 1985–January 1986

| Category | Frequency | Responses as % | Cases as % |
|---|---|---|---|
| General | 31 | 1.4 | 2.1 |
| Immigration | 446 | 20.8 | 29.6 |
| Work, unemployment | 109 | 5.1 | 7.2 |
| Housing | 84 | 3.9 | 5.6 |
| Health | 50 | 2.3 | 3.3 |
| Education | 80 | 3.7 | 5.3 |
| Research | 123 | 5.7 | 8.2 |
| Culture | 76 | 3.5 | 5.0 |
| Politics | 98 | 4.6 | 6.5 |
| Social affairs | 152 | 7.1 | 10.1 |
| Crime | 194 | 9.1 | 12.9 |
| Religion | 54 | 2.5 | 3.6 |
| Economic affairs | 6 | 0.3 | 0.4 |
| Race relations | 90 | 4.2 | 6.0 |
| Discrimination | 357 | 16.7 | 23.7 |
| Other | 193 | 9.0 | 12.8 |
| Total | 2,143 | 100.0 | 142.1 |

(1,508 valid cases)

people. There are few differences between the newspapers, although the conservative popular *Telegraaf* pays special attention to crime, as do the British tabloids, whereas liberal *Volkskrant* has relatively more items on discrimination. All newspapers, and especially *NRC-Handelsblad*, pay much attention to immigration.

## Topics: Actors and actions

The analysis of more detailed topics confirms these overall subject frequencies (see Table 4.5): when we categorize the macro-propositions (topics), we again find that immigration, ethnic relations, and crime are the most frequent issues in Dutch reporting about minorities. If we distinguish between top level (often headlined) topics and lower level, secondary topics, we see that some topics (especially ethnic relations) tend to be more frequent as main topics, whereas others (especially social affairs) rather appear at lower levels in the news items. In other words, besides the variable frequencies observed for different topics, there are also differences in the relevance assigned to certain topics.

In our analysis of the Dutch topics, we assigned a 'semantic formula'

*Table 4.5* Frequencies of major topics in the Dutch Press, August 1985–January 1986

|   |   | *Primary topics* | *Secondary topics* | *Total* |
|---|---|---|---|---|
| 1 | Immigration | 426 | 365 | 791 |
| 2 | Social affairs | 161 | 190 | 351 |
| 3 | Justice, police | 361 | 312 | 673 |
| 4 | Education | 64 | 60 | 124 |
| 5 | Culture: media, arts | 213 | 106 | 319 |
| 6 | Employment, unemployment | 132 | 93 | 225 |
| 7 | Politics | 81 | 52 | 133 |
| 8 | Ethnic relations, discrimination | 385 | 212 | 597 |
| Total |   | 1,823 (57%) | 1,390 (43%) | 3,213 |

*Note:* Total analysed (assigned to a category): 3,781
Number of reports analysed: 1,518

to each topic. For instance, the rather general topic 'Minority group protests against discrimination in employment', would be translated as '05B-92A-07', that is, in words: 'Protests Minority Group – Discrimination by Majority Group/Person – Employment'. This allows us to further analyse in what kinds of actions and in what kinds of social domains the white majority and the minority groups are involved, and what their respective roles are.

Examining the frequencies and role of the news actors involved in these topics, we observe first that, unlike in the British Press, the general category of 'ethnic minorities' is very frequent (occurring in 436 topics), followed at a distance by Surinamese (264), Turks (289) and Moroccans (267), as would be expected. It is however striking that in 1985 Tamils, Iranians, and other refugees together appear more often than any other minority group (appearing in 516 topics). Clearly, the latter groups are most prominent in immigration topics. Surinamese, on the other hand, are often associated with the police and the judiciary (in 78 topics), whereas they are actors in only two of all the topics about education!

Of the majority actors, the authorities, such as the government, ministries, and the city administrations, are the most frequent actors, especially in immigration and social topics, closely followed by the police and the judiciary. Various opposition groups, including those that are critical about Dutch immigration and minority policies, such as action groups, unions, and churches, each appear in only a few dozen topics.

Further analysis of topical predicates shows that 'to discriminate' is the most frequent (207) action, followed by 'to expel' and 'to improve', all actions of Dutch majority groups, group members, or institutions. The most frequent minority actions are 'to have problems', 'to commit a crime', and 'to protest', predicates that show in a nutshell how minorities are represented in the Dutch Press.

Note that majority actors (often individuals and business, seldom the authorities) are often negatively characterized by the act of discrimination, but that improving the situation of minorities, help, and similar positive actions are also very prominent, especially in the accounts of the involvement of the national or local authorities. Thus, if the police take Turkish lessons in order to facilitate communication with Turkish minority groups, this is a 'positive' action that will typically be topicalized. Positive actions of minorities are much less prominent, if represented at all.

Most striking are the topics, actors, and actions related to the subject of immigration. Although Surinamese, Turks, and Moroccans continue to be represented in immigration topics, new immigrants, and especially refugees from Sri Lanka, the Middle East, and Africa receive special attention in 1985. We suggested in Chapter one that this coverage had all the features of a media panic, in which the small, overpopulated country, was seen to be "invaded" (*Telegraaf*) by "economic" (read: bogus) refugees. Two series of topics and actions are involved here, pitching the refugees (and some of the action groups that help them) against the authorities, in other words, the dialectic of seeking refuge and being denied it, on the one hand, and the topic of temporary housing in shelters or boarding houses, on the other hand. These groups are also primarily represented as 'making demands' and 'protesting'. These expressions of 'ingratitude' are often resented by large segments of the population, as is also clear from letters to the editors of the popular Press (Dubbelman, 1987). In other words, the political and media panic built up against the refugees indeed had a marked negative influence on the perception of Tamils and other recent refugee groups.

Discrimination is a frequent topic in ethnic affairs news in the Netherlands. Note however that most of these stories are about incidents, that is, about individuals and businesses that have discriminated against minority group members. Such stories presuppose that overt and clear cases of discrimination are outside of the consensus. Contrary to the practices of the right-wing Press in England, cases of discrimination are seldom ridiculed, although they are not reported as major scandals. The conservative popular Press usually ignores discrimination. At the same time, however, there are very few stories in the liberal Press that deal with discrimination and racism in general (except in the small *Waarheid*).

Indeed, as we have suggested earlier, for the Press as well as for many other elites, 'racism' in the Netherlands does not exist – unless as an issue brought up by anti-racists, as is the case in the UK.

The other topics are discussed as may be expected. There is an overall association between minorities or immigrants and illegality. As is the case in the UK, immigration is repeatedly connected with illegal entry and residence, fraud, false papers, trafficking of people, and other forms of deviance. Crime stories, especially in the popular Press, help to confirm the prejudices about 'minority crimes', such as violence, drugs, and mugging. Social affairs topics focus on the many problems minorities are having or causing in welfare, health care, housing, and education. The authorities predominantly play a neutral or positive role here: they regulate and help. Minorities themselves are essentially passive: they are practically never topicalized as being actively engaged in improving their situation. Cultural differences are usually emphasized, and often taken as explanations of various forms of deviant behaviour (for instance, in drugs or other crimes, or even in education). We already have seen earlier that the social and especially the political organization of ethnic minorities in the Netherlands is hardly encouraged and the Press pays little attention to it. Indeed, it very seldom uses minority groups as sources and spokespersons.

## Summary

Topical analysis of the Dutch Press shows that the coverage of ethnic minority groups focuses on a few stereotypical issues (immigration, crime and ethnic relations), while ignoring other relevant ones. The dominant perspective is nearly wholly white and Dutch: the Dutch authorities in particular are prominent in most topics, and represented in neutral and positive roles. Minorities are only active in negative news (illegal entry and residence, crime, protests, and demands), and seldom seen as actively improving their situation. Whereas the liberal Press emphasizes that they have problems, or even represent them as victims (for instance of incidental discrimination), the right-wing Press tends to focus on the problems they allegedly cause, if not on the threat they pose to Dutch society, initially through "massive" immigration, then through their demands for scarce resources (mostly housing, education, and especially jobs), and finally by engaging in drug dealing and other crimes.

We see that despite some differences, the overall topicalization of ethnic affairs in the Netherlands is not very different from what we have found for the British Press. Differences are mostly of degree: less harsh attacks against anti-racism, more neutral attention for discrimination, more interest in social welfare topics and a less aggressive style. On the other hand, the Dutch Press also seems to take minorities less seriously: they are mostly shown to be passive, are not often quoted or used as sources, their social and political organizations, as well as their cultural activities, are virtually ignored. Instead, white organizations or 'experts' tend to appear as 'representatives' for ethnic groups in many topics. Criticism of government policies (such as in expulsion cases) or discrimination exists, but focuses on incidents and individual cases. Serious critical analysis of ethnic policies of the government or the other authorities and institutions (education, the judiciary, health care) are hardly ever topicalized. Perhaps most important, there is no serious discussion of, let alone support for, affirmative action or other policies that implement equal rights in fundamental domains, least of all in their own institutions. Indeed, Dutch newspapers hardly employ minority journalists.

In sum, although the Dutch Press on the whole may be less negative and less aggressive in its ethnic affairs coverage than the British Press (and especially the British right-wing Press), it certainly does not challenge either the fundamental ethnic consensus or the underlying ethnic power relations. For the Press, as for the general ethnic consensus in the Netherlands, ethnic and political pluralism may imply recognition of the presence of ethnic groups, or some allowances for 'their own culture', but definitely not a recognition of equal rights.

## FURTHER COMPARISONS AND OVERALL CONCLUSIONS

To put the analysis of the subjects and topics in the British and Dutch Press coverage in 1985 and 1989 in further perspective, we should briefly compare them with results of other research. Note though that such comparisons are somewhat hazardous because other researchers usually have different categories and different ways of assessing the data, so that only general content tendencies can be compared.

In their analysis of *The Times, Guardian, Express* and *Mirror* coverage of race relations in the 1960s, Hartmann, Husband and Clark (1974) already found that immigration, race relations, and (at some distance) crime were the most frequent subjects, which is similar to the 'structural' (non-affairs, such as 'Rushdie') categories in the 1989 British news, as well as in the Dutch coverage. In the 1960s too, 'social' issues such as housing, health, and employment are not very prominent.

In the USA, the study by Martindale (1986) of the coverage of race relations during the 1950s, 1960s, and 1970s in the *New York Times*, the *Atlanta Constitution*, the *Boston Globe*, and the *Chicago Tribune*, does not make use of similarly detailed categories. However, she found that the coverage of black problems was only a small fragment of the total coverage of blacks, although this percentage increased from about 5 per cent in the 1960s to about 10 per cent in the 1970s. Relevant as a comparison to the 'riot' coverage in the British Press is that she also found (like the Kerner Commission) that most attention in the 1960s is paid to black protests themselves, and very little (between 3 per cent and 11 per cent, depending on the newspaper) to the causes of the urban uprisings. Johnson's analysis of the Boston media (Johnson, 1987) shows first the high frequency of sports items (which are much less prominent in Europe), followed however by crime (appearing in 401 of 2,499 stories), business, state government, and entertainment. In the coverage of blacks in the USA immigration is of course not a relevant topic. The various social topics, as in Europe, score very low. There are no data about discrimination or racism stories.

For the local Canadian Press studied by Indra (1979), the data for the 1960s and 1970s, based on an analysis of the Vancouver *Sun*, show decreasing topicalization of violence and crime, although these issues remain much more prominent than the social issues of housing, education, welfare, or health. As in other countries, ethnic relations are among the most frequent subject categories. Most prominent in the local Canadian Press are however legal and legislative issues (such as claims by North American native peoples). Immigration and immigration restriction also remains a frequent topic.

Merten *et al.* (1986), in their study of the West German Press, also found that – both in the tabloids and the quality Press! – crime, accidents, the judiciary, and catastrophes are the most frequent subjects in ethnic coverage, followed in the tabloids by sports and in the quality Press by political issues. Other major categories, as is the case in the USA, are arts and folklore (because the authors also examined the coverage of visiting foreign artists). When focusing on immigrant workers, the major topics are human interest issues (nearly half of the coverage, especially crime), social affairs, culture, and politics. For refugees, the major subject is politics, followed at a distance by human interest and social affairs.

From these studies as well as from our own research, together based on content analyses of tens of thousands of news items in many newspapers in several countries, covering several decades, we conclude first that the category of crime or violence is always among the five most frequent issues in ethnic coverage. Depending on the specific situation (country, historical period), we further find race relations, including discrimination, and immigration and residence issues to be most prominent, followed at some distance by the stereotypical 'black performance' issues of sports and the arts (including celebrities), especially in North America. Over the years, legal and political issues and controversies are increasing as typical 'conflict' subjects. Cultural (educational, religious, linguistic) differences and conflicts are also increasingly frequent issues in the Press, most prominently illustrated internationally by the Rushdie affair, by the Honeyford case in the UK, and more recently, in France, in the issue of headscarves of Muslim girls. We may summarize these general conclusions by the general rule that events that are seen as most problematic or threatening to the interests of the white majority tend to be most prominent, and vice versa, events and situations that are most problematic and threatening to the interests of minorities are covered less prominently. In other words, ethnic affairs coverage in the Press rather closely reproduces, confirms, and legitimates prevailing ethnic ideologies as well as the power relations based on them.

# 5 News schemata, argumentation and editorials

## A THEORY OF SUPERSTRUCTURES: THE SCHEMA OF NEWS REPORTS

The topics we have examined in the previous chapter are subject to a specific type of organization. They are structured by abstract underlying forms, which we call 'superstructures', or textual 'schemata'. Many discourse genres, including those of the media, have their own characteristic schematic form or superstructure. Such a superstructure consists of a number of conventional categories, which exhibit a special linear order, as well as hierarchical organization. They determine what content typically comes first, second, or last in a text (for details, see van Dijk, 1988a).

Thus, news reports conventionally begin with a *Summary* category, which in turn is sub-divided into a *Headline* category (which itself may be complex), and a *Lead*. As the name suggests, the Summary category summarizes the topics of the news reports, that is, its most important information. The rest of a news reports also features a number of conventional categories, more or less explicitly known and used by news-makers. *Main Event* is the central, obligatory category of this 'body' of the news report, and organizes the information about the prominent, recent event that gave rise to the news reports in the first place. Each news report at least has a Summary and a Main Event category (see Figure 5.1).

However, in longer news reports or features, and especially in the quality Press, the recent event is often reported against a specific background. Hence, we may also introduce a *Background* category in the schema of news reports. Background information may be of two basic types, namely actual *Context* information, and information about the *History* of current events. Context places the event in a broader framework of other current events, sometimes of a more structural, sometimes of an incidental nature. Thus, the visit of the British Home Secretary, Mr Hurd, to Handsworth, is placed within the context of

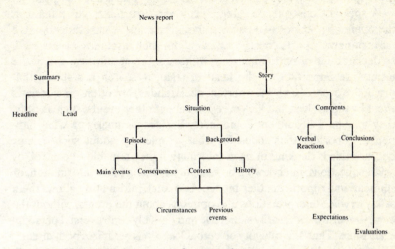

*Figure 5.1* Hypothetical structure of a news schema

information about the local disturbances, whereas – more structurally – the 'riots' themselves are sometimes reported against the background of the socio-economic context of the inner cities, or even broader, in the context of immigration and race relations in contemporary Britain. Historically, the present riots may also be discussed against the backdrop of the earlier disturbances in 1980 and 1981, for example, those in Bristol and Brixton. In other words, contextual and historical backgrounds provide information that allows better understanding of current events.

News events are not only described 'in depth' against such a background, but also as part of a sequence of events. Immediate causes may be mentioned, and these are sometimes reported in previous news reports, of which the information may be summarized in the present report, for instance in a *Previous Events* category, which serves as a reminder for the present report. Similarly, current events may in turn become the immediate conditional or causal events for various types of *Consequences*. If these consequences are newsworthy by themselves they may even become the Main Event because news reports are structured by a recency principle: given two or more events of similar relevance, the most recent information is usually considered to be most important in the Press, and often tends to be most prominent in the report, for instance by occurring in the headline. Thus, if a morning newspaper already brings information about the riots, the evening newspaper may focus on the immediate consequences, such as reactions of the politicians, while presupposing much information of the riots in a Previous Events category.

A special Consequence category is *Verbal Reactions*, which features the opinions of major news actors about the main events. Indeed, large parts of news reports consist of news about such discursive events, such as declarations of participants, eyewitnesses, the authorities, and, if the events are important, of the head of state. Research has shown that discursive events (such as important declarations) are often a major news event by themselves, but also in reports about other events, such as riots, they may be a prominent component. Besides summarizing what happened, reporters thus focus on what people say about such events, because this is the kind of news information they are able to control, by asking questions, interviewing news actors, reading other information, or summarizing reports in other media. Also, such information allows them safely to voice interpretations and opinions about the events, without the need to venture necessarily subjective and possibly controversial personal evaluations. Thus, the category of Verbal Reactions organizes both discursive news events in their own right, and at the same time allows newsmakers to include provisional opinions that also put the events in perspective.

Finally, news reports may also feature a *Comments* category that contains the opinions of the journalists themselves, for instance an evaluation of the main events, or expectations and predictions about what is likely to happen next. This is not an obligatory category, although at least briefly, news reports will often try to draw some conclusions of this type. This will typically be the case, in background articles, and in editorials, which specifically focus on such journalistic opinions about recent events. Below, we shall study in more detail the specific structures of editorials.

These respective categories of news reports together form an abstract 'schema'. Other discourse genres may also have such a schema, each with its own characteristic categories, for instance, in everyday stories, in scholarly papers, or in conversations. This schema, however, is a theoretical construct. In practice, some categories may be missing, and they may often also appear in a different order. For instance, it may happen that Verbal Reactions or Comments come first in the news reports, especially when they contain information or opinions that are important in their own right.

Some categories of the news schema (such as the Summary and the Main Events) are obligatory, that is, they occur in each report, whereas others (for example, Comments) are optional. Also, just like the topics in each schema category, the categories of the text (except of course the initial Summary) are usually delivered 'in instalments', that is, of each category the most important information is expressed first. Similarly, there are other strategies that may be used in the actual realization of topics and the schemata that organize them, such as recency (the most recent events tend to be mentioned first), relevance (the information that is most relevant for the readers tends to come first), and general news-worthiness (information that has the highest news value comes first). In other words, unlike the order of everyday stories, that of a news report is not primarily determined by chronology or causal relations, but by various strategies of importance or relevance. As we have seen before for topical hierarchies, this top-down ordering may also influence the structure of the mental model the readers build of an event they read about in the paper. It is this mental model that is the basis for the ways readers use the information they read in the Press.

Note that the news schema discussed above only applies to proper news reports, and not to other newspaper genres, such as background articles, features, columns, and editorials. The latter genres may be considered as textually independent manifestations of some of the major categories of the news item, such as Background (Context and History), Verbal Reactions (as in detailed interviews with major news actors), and Comments (Expectations and Evaluations). Editorial articles are discussed below. In news about ethnic affairs also, proper news items are the most frequent news discourse genre (usually about 60 per cent of all items). Background and opinion articles, both in the 1985 and the 1989 coverage, each account for about 7 per cent of the items, editorials 4 per cent, and letters about 12 per cent (in 1989, especially in connection with the Rushdie affair, more than 16 per cent of all items are letters).

## NEWS SCHEMATA IN REPORTS ABOUT MINORITIES

Schemata may manipulate the topical organization in news reports, and therefore they may have ideological implications. This is also true for news reports about ethnic affairs. One prominent category of news schemata in ethnic affairs news, the Headline, has already been extensively studied in Chapter three. But what about the Lead, Main Event, Background, Verbal Reaction and Comment categories? How is the topical information discussed in the previous chapter organized in the text? What tends to be given prominence, what information is presented first, and what information last? Which news schema categories are emphasized, and why?

This chapter focuses on the details of a few typical examples of news reports about ethnic affairs in the British Press. First we analyse a news report about the Honeyford affair, then we study editorials about affirmative action and about the urban disorders.

# Empty desks and protesters greet headmaster in race dispute

## From Peter Davenport, Bradford

Mr Ray Honeyford, the headmaster who was suspended six months ago in a dispute over his views on multi-racial education, returned to his school yesterday to find protesters outside the gates and more than half his pupils absent.

Noisy demonstrators called for Mr Honeyford to be dismissed as headmaster of the Drummond Middle School in Bradford, where 95 per cent of the 530 pupils are from ethnic communities.

Protests were expected after Bradford City Council announced Mr Honeyford's reinstatement pending its appeal against the High Court decision that he should go back to his job.

Yesterday dozens of the youngsters joined a crowd of about 100, including some parents, to wave banners and shout slogans calling their headmaster a "racist" and demanding his removal.

They formed up with protesters each holding a white card bearing a single letter to spell out the message: "We have no confidence in Honeyford". Another poster proclaimed: "Honeyford and Botha, they are both the same, they play the racist game".

There were allegations yesterday that some children intending to go into school were persuaded not to do so by some of the demonstrators. Others, more determined, were led through the protesters by police officers into the school yard.

Mr Honeyford, however, avoided the demonstration by arriving at school shortly after 7am when only half a dozen protesters were present. He seemed unperturbed by the chanting and noise outside which echoed around the school.

Speaking in the school library, Mr Honeyford said he was delighted to be back. "I have mised the school and I am looking forward to getting back into the hurly burly of school life. I have missed my colleagues and the pupils very much."

He said he wanted to see the school return to normal as calmly as possible. "The only time we have trouble in this school is when the pressure groups act in a certain way. But I will not give way to bullyboy tactics."

Mr Honeyford was suspended after writing articles which were held to be critical of Bradford's multi-racial education policies. He argued that white children could be disadvantaged if they were in a minority in a class. But he has persistently denied charges of racism.

The demonstration at the school gates yesterday had been carefully organized with children chanting well-rehearsed slogans. It did not get out of hand and the only time it seemed in danger of doing so was when a handful of people supporting the headmaster, including two punks, one a girl with blue hair and another a teenage boy with streaks of vivid red in his long black hair, arrived and unfolded a banner saying: "Welcome back Ray".

Leading the support group was Mrs Christine Marshall, a housewife, whose daughter had attended the school 12 years ago. She said yesterday: "It is a shame the headmaster has been persecuted like this. It has all been blown up out of proportion and I think the people here today are being manipulated. I just wanted to show my support."

Mr Amin Quershi, a former school governor and a member of the Drummond School parents' action group, organized the chanting among the children and encouraged them to run away from the school gates, probably for the benefit of television cameras.

Protestors yesterday said they were planning a long campaign to last several months to put pressure on the council to remove Mr Honeyford from his post permanently.

*Figure 5.2* Article from *The Times*, 17 September 1985
Reproduced by permission of *The Times*

**Example 1: The return of Honeyford** (*The Times*)

On 17 September 1985, *The Times* carries a report about the return of Honeyford to his school (see Figure 5.2), after his court victory against the Bradford council. First, we assign parts of the text to different schematic news categories, and then give some comments about these relations between the topics of the text and its schematic form.

We see that the major part of this news item consists of several instalments of the Main Event category, that is, the category that embodies information about the current event that gave rise to the news report in the first place. Here we find information, also summarized in the Headline and the Lead section, about the return of Honeyford and the protests against his return. This information gets more specific the further 'down' we come in the report. First, protests are mentioned in general terms, later who were protesting and what the protests amounted to. The Lead, and the Previous Events category also briefly put the current event in perspective, by mentioning the fact that Honeyford was suspended because of his criticism of multi-cultural education. The context that makes both the previous events (suspension) and the current events (protests of parents and children) understandable is only mentioned very briefly, in the passage that says that 95 per cent of the pupils are from ethnic communities.

Besides elements of style, such as the more or less negative descriptions of the demonstrators ("noisy"), to which we turn in Chapter

*Table 5.1* Schematic news categories of text

| Text | Category |
| --- | --- |
| EMPTY DESKS AND PROTESTERS GREET HEADMASTER IN RACE DISPUTE | Headline |
| Mr Ray Honeyford . . . absent | Lead |
| Noisy demonstrators . . . Bradford | Main Event 1 |
| Where 95 percent . . . communities | Context 1 |
| Protests were expected . . . job | Previous Events 2 |
| Yesterday . . . removal | Main Event 2 |
| They formed . . . game" | Main Event 3 |
| There were allegations . . . yard | Main Event 4 |
| Mr Honeyford . . . school | Main Event 5 |
| Speaking . . . much" | Verbal Reaction 1 |
| He said . . . tactics" | Verbal Reaction 2 |
| Mr Honeyford . . . racism | Previous Events |
| The demonstration . . . Ray" | Main Event 6 |
| Leading the support group . . . support" | Verbal Reaction 3 |
| Mr Amin Quershi . . . cameras | Main Event 7 |
| Protesters yesterday said . . . permanently | Verbal Reaction 4 |

eight, the interesting point of the organization of the content of this report lies in the order in which the Verbal Reactions category is realized. If we disregard the text on the protest cards of the demonstrators, the first to speak is Honeyford himself, described as "unperturbed". Since he describes the action groups as indulging in "bullyboy tactics", his evaluation gets more prominence than those of the action groups themselves, whose indirect comments are only mentioned towards the end of the report. Even before that, a counter-demonstration of a few people is mentioned, and these are actually quoted although they are much less numerous in number, and can hardly be seen as representative of the parents.

There is no direct quotation of the action group itself, and their reasons for demonstrating against Honeyford. These reasons are earlier summarized by the allegation of "racism", duly put between distancing quotation marks, and by the contents of the cards saying that the parents have no confidence in Honeyford. In other words, most prominent in this news report are the negatively defined ("noisy") protests of demonstrators, the positively defined ("unperturbed") reactions and opinions of Honeyford, followed by opinions of his supporters. The demonstrators are neither asked their opinion, nor their reactions to the allegations of Honeyford and his supporters. They tend to be briefly mentioned only at the end. Structural context information that could explain the protests are kept to a mimimum. There is no explicit Comment category, although some expectations are mentioned indirectly in the last paragraph where the plans of the protesters are mentioned. Evaluation of the events by the reporter are also implicit, and may be inferred from his qualifications of the demonstrators and of Honeyford, respectively. We see however, that this perspective on the events also shows in the schematic ordering and the prominence of the information: acts that are found negative (noisy protests) are foregrounded, whereas possible justifications for such actions are downgraded or entirely ignored.

## ARGUMENTATION

Whereas news reports have their characteristic news schema, other news genres may have their own typical schematic organization. Comments, columns and editorials, for instance, often have a persuasive function, and therefore usually exhibit various kinds of argumentative structure, which they share with many other persuasive genres (see, for example, Huth, 1978). Thus we shall examine below whether editorials also have an organizational schema of their own, besides a more general argumentative structure.

The classic theory of syllogistic argumentation distinguishes between a Premises category and a Conclusion category. Premises may be of different types. They may make statements of particular fact, include generalizations or other information and opinions that may make the conclusion plausible, credible, or otherwise acceptable for the reader (van Eemeren, Grootendorst, and Kruiger, 1984; Cox and Willard, 1982). More than many other kinds of schematic structure, argumentation has an implicit dialogical principle, even in monological texts. That is, the author uses arguments that may implicitly respond to possible objections, or counter-arguments, of a real or imaginary opponent, or simply of the reader.

As we have done for news schemata, it makes sense to distinguish between abstract argumentative schemata, or normative rules, of a discourse, and the actual strategies followed by the participants in an argumentative interaction. Thus, each strategy may be analysed as a series of 'moves', which each have the function to make other moves, and finally the Conclusion, more credible. Part of these strategies may have a more general persuasive nature, and are not properly 'argumentative', for example, smiling at your opponent or making use of non-offensive style. Obviously, the distinction between arguments and style is fuzzy. After all, the very choice of words (see the 'terrorist' versus 'freedom fighter' pair), may be a very important means to express opinions, and such opinions necessarily also play a role in argumentative discourse. Also, strategic principles may change the normative structure of argumentation schemata, again in order to enhance effectiveness. For instance, in many arguments, the category of Conclusion may be realized first, that is, before the arguments that support them. In other words, real argumentation is often messy and incomplete and often does not follow the normative rules of argumentation, or the rules for their schematic organization.

## Example 2: Anti-discrimination proposals by the CRE: the *Telegraph*'s response

As an illustration of these structures of argumentation, let us analyse a concrete example, an editorial published in the *Telegraph*. The occasion for this editorial is a report to the Home Secretary by the Commission for Racial Equality (CRE) calling for more effective laws and regulations against sexual and racist discrimination. The changes advocated by the CRE are intended to improve the 1976 Race Relations Act. The CRE wants more power in making its own investigations and proposes that employers monitor and report on minority employment. The CRE also

# MAKING TOO MUCH OF RACE

THE COMMISSION FOR RACIAL EQUALITY is calling for changes in the 1976 Race Relations Act which would give it greatly enhanced powers. It claims that ethnic minorities continue to suffer high levels of discrimination and disadvantage and that the 1976 act should be altered to challenge more effectively entrenched racial discrimination. The Commission wants general powers to investigate rather than only react to specific allegations, special tribunals to hear race and sex discrimination cases and monitoring of the numbers and progress of ethnic staff.

No one would deny the fragile nature of race relations in Britain today or that there is misunderstanding and distrust between parts of the community. Nor would one challenge the motives of many well-meaning individuals. What one must ask is whether enhancing the powers of the race relations industry will genuinely benefit ethnic minorities or give further opportunities to those who are only too keen to exploit any fears within the minority communities for their own political ends. The Tory MP for Westminster North, Mr John Wheeler, recently alleged that the CRE and the Joint Council for the Welfare of Immigrants were damaging race relations, particularly by perpetrating myths and innuendo about the integrity of immigration officers.

There are some, particularly in local government, who have a vested interest in the politics of race. Wider general powers to investigate could become a snooper's charter while special tribunals would be a threat hanging over the best of managers. Most disturbing of all is the suggestion that there should be "ethnic record keeping" to monitor equal opportunities. The small businessman, already burdened with legislative constraints, is hardly going to welcome this extra form to fill in. Moreover, one must ask who is most appropriate to decide which ethnic minority an individual belongs to? Why should a man be characterised in this way at his place of work? It would be entirely inappropriate if an organisation like the GLC were to get hold of these returns and only award contracts to firms employing what they considered to be an adequate number from ethnic minorities. Already the GLC has stopped its contract for Kit-Kat because the producer, Rowntree Mackintosh, refuses to answer questions about its employment policy. Any moves which make it easier for certain councils to find out this sort of information, will not help race relations.

*Figure 5.3*  Article from the *Daily Telegraph*, 1 August 1985
Reproduced by permission of the *Daily Telegraph*

pleads for the establishment of special discrimination tribunals, replacing the present industrial tribunals, whose effectiveness is found lacking.

We have found in the previous chapters that the right-wing Press generally reacts very negatively against any attempt to introduce forms of affirmative action. In order to find out what such reactions look like, we examine the editorial of the *Telegraph*, published on 1 August 1985, about this CRE proposal. We shall go through this editorial sentence by sentence, and evaluate each move in its argumentative rejection of the CRE plans. It seems as if the *Telegraph* here argues against the CRE. However, since it addresses its readers, the argument is also meant to persuade the readers, including politicians, of the negative implications of the CRE plan. In other words, the argumentation addressee for such editorials is multiple.

If we go through this *Telegraph* editorial sentence by sentence, we may make the following summarizing observations about its argumentative strategies (a full analysis of the text would be vastly more complex). The beginning of a new paragraph is signalled with '¶':

### 1 MAKING TOO MUCH OF RACE

This is the summarizing title, which implies that more than enough has been done to counter discrimination, and which suggests that the 1976 law is more than adequate, and should not be changed. Also, the "too much" suggests that the *Telegraph* shares the more general opinion, also regularly voiced by right-wing politicians and the tabloids, that the issue of 'race' gets too much attention.

*2¶The Commission for Racial Equality is calling for changes in the 1976 Race Relations Act which would give it greatly enhanced powers.*

This summarizing lead sentence has a second evaluative implication ("greatly enhanced powers") about the role of the CRE. Again, it is suggested, but not explicitly stated here, that the CRE would get too much power in enforcing anti-discrimination law.

*3 It claims that ethnic minorities continue to suffer high levels of discrimination and disadvantage and that the 1976 act should be altered to challenge more effectively entrenched racial discrimination.*

This is a continued summary of the CRE plans. The use of "claims" suggests that the CRE's statements about continued high levels of discrimination are not necessarily accepted by the *Telegraph*. Extensive research evidence, also supplied by the CRE, to the effect that discrimination is still prominent is ignored here, and presented as an opinion. Discrediting facts as subjective opinions is a well-known argumentative move to attack the position of an opponent. As we shall see later when we analyse the role of sources and quotations, the use of "claim" by the *Telegraph*, when referring to the findings of the CRE, leads CRE Chairman, Peter Newsam, to write a letter to the editor a few days later, protesting against this kind of expression.

> *4 The Commission wants general powers to investigate rather than only react to specific allegations, special tribunals to hear race and sex discrimination cases and monitoring of the numbers and progress of ethnic staff.*

This sentence continues the summary of the CRE plans. Together with the previous sentences, this part of the editorial may be categorized as the Summary of recent events, which will form the point of departure for the arguments of the newspaper. It is the position of the opponent which the newspaper has set out to comment upon, and eventually aims to refute. Note however that such a Summary is seldom neutral. We have seen that it already embodies, sometimes implicitly, evaluations of the events, that is, the CRE plans.

> *5 No one would deny the fragile nature of race relations in Britain today or that there is misunderstanding and distrust between parts of the community.*

The first move in the *Telegraph*'s own argument is a disclaimer of a very familiar kind, especially in talk and text about race relations (see van Dijk, 1984, 1987a), a so-called Apparent Concession: 'We know that there are problems, but ...' Note however that the editorial does not say something like "No one would deny that discrimination is still rampant in Great Britain". On the contrary, this situation is severely underplayed by the use of understatement. First, the vague notion of "fragile" is used, which does not necessarily imply a negative evaluation. More important, however, the *Telegraph* goes on to say that "there is misunderstanding and distrust between parts of the community". Not only is this concession very vague and unduly restrained about what is at stake – discrimination – but also the responsible actors of the act of discrimination are concealed here, and it is suggested that distrust and misunderstanding are mutual. This also implies that ethnic minority groups are responsible for "fragile" race relations. Thus the *Telegraph* not only reduces the seriousness of white discrimination, but by generalizing the argument to race relations generally, first diverts attention from members of the white dominant group as the responsible agents of discrimination, and secondly attributes part of the blame to the minority groups themselves. We see that the concession is, indeed, only apparent: no real concession of the main point, the seriousness of white discrimination, is made here.

*6 Nor would one challenge the motives of many well-meaning individuals.*

Another concessive move follows in this next sentence. This argumentative step has several functions. Firstly, by recognizing that there are well-meaning individuals with (respectable?) motives, the *Telegraph* emphasizes its own moderation and tolerance: we understand and respect our opponent. Secondly, however, the use of the expression "well-meaning" usually implies that despite their good intentions, people may make mistakes in their actions. Associated with this evaluation is the well-known stereotype of the "bleeding heart" liberals, who have good intentions, but whose actions are hardly to be taken seriously.

*7 What one must ask is whether enhancing the powers of the race relations industry will genuinely benefit ethnic minorities or give further opportunities to those who are only too keen to exploit any fears within the minority communities for their own political end.*

After these disclaimers, which essentially are forms of positive self-presentation ('We are no racists, but...'), the newspaper finally comes up with its own opposition to the CRE plans. Again, the moves of this sentence are complex and have several argumentative, political, and ideological functions. The first counter-argument is stylistically presented with reticence. It is not a categorical statement, but a variant of a rhetorical question ("What one must ask is ..."), suggesting doubt about, instead of rejection of the opponent's view. This opponent is not identified by its name, however, but is associated more generally with a negative collective term, typically used by the right: "the race relations industry", suggesting that the CRE and similar organizations are only in the business of profiting from their anti-discrimination activities. Obviously, such a descriptive term not only contradicts the "well-meaning individuals" used in the previous sentence, but also casts doubts on the moral standards of the opponents. The *ad hominem* argument is a well-known argumentative ploy. This argument is spelled out in a disjunction that both vilifies the opponent, and at the same time positively emphasizes the role of the *Telegraph*: it seems to take the interests of minorities at heart ("genuinely benefit ethnic minorities"), while at the same time implying that anti-discrimination is only a political game, thereby suggesting implicitly that this is typically the aim of the left. The CRE is even accused of "exploiting fears of minorities", so that they may continue to vote Labour. Indeed, as we have seen before, the major attacks by the right-wing Press are generally aimed at whites who show solidarity with minority groups. Thus, the argumentation of the right in the delicate field of race relations aims at a subtle combination of positive self-presentation and negative other-presentation, this time not of minorities themselves, but of those who are seen as their political representatives within their own, dominant group. These are the 'enemy within', who can also be vilified without risk of incurring a 'racist' label.

> *8 The Tory MP for Westminster North, Mr John Wheeler, recently alleged that the CRE and the Joint Council for the Welfare of Immigrants were damaging race relations, particularly by perpetrating myths and innuendo about the integrity of immigration officers.*

To support the argument that the CRE, as part of the "race relations industry", in fact harms minorities, another critic of CRE policies is quoted. The fact that this critic is an MP may give some additional weight to the statement – an often used credibility move. However, that it is a Tory MP is not a powerful aspect of this move, because it could easily be defeated by the same argument of political partisanship, which the *Telegraph* claims to attack in the first place. The allegations brought by the quoted MP are also rather vague ("perpetrating myths and innuendo about immigration officers"). The argument by itself, however, is found strong enough, by the simple fact that whoever accuses officers (such as the police) cannot be a trustworthy, law-abiding citizen, a move that is also repeatedly used in discrediting anybody who criticized the police after the riots. That the accusations of an alleged attack on immigration officers are irrelevant to the present point is apparently found less of a problem here: the coherence is established at a higher level, that of attacks against the authorities generally, that is, against the state.

> *9 ¶There are some, particularly in local government, who have a vested interest in the politics of race.*

The self-interest argument is continued here and apparently begins to take a prominent role in the *Telegraph*'s attack against its opponents. Instead of examining the effectiveness of the CRE plan, which is simply doubted without further argument, it is found more propitious to discredit the integrity of the opponent. Riding its own allegations of political self-interest, the *Telegraph* now shifts its target from the CRE to "local government"; read: left-controlled city councils. If the CRE could still claim to be politically impartial, and therefore command respect, these local governments certainly cannot, and therefore are a more rewarding object of right-wing attack. From the economically tainted allegation of self-interest of the "race relations industry", the argument now focuses on the self-interest of those involved in the "politics of race".

*10 Wider general powers to investigate could become a snooper's charter while special tribunals would be a threat hanging over the best of managers.*

The CRE's plan to investigate cases of discrimination are described as a form of "snooping". Since this negative term is often used by the right-wing Press in matters of race relations, and of course never applied to other law enforcement agencies, it has very specific ideological implications. It not only suggests that the investigations of discrimination are intolerable, but also that they are morally wrong: what employers do is their own business, and nobody should interfere with them. At the same time, the use of "snooping" reflects badly on the "snoopers", and therefore further enhances the negative description of the opponent. It implies the ideological proposition that discrimination is not a question that should be 'policed' in the first place, but a question of morals and opinions, best left to the initiative of the people themselves. In this respect, the right-wing Press has surprisingly little respect for its own celebrated emphasis on law and order. Finally, and perhaps most important, it is especially business that is targeted by the CRE plans; and any form of monitoring or investigation would be an infringement of the basic tenets of capitalistic ideology, that is, the freedom of enterprise.

*11 Most disturbing of all is the suggestion that there should be "ethnic record keeping" to monitor equal opportunities.*

It is not surprising that the *Telegraph* categorically rejects ethnic record keeping as a way to monitor non-discriminatory hiring and promotion. This is one of the main argumentative positions defended in the editorial.

*12 The small businessman, already burdened with legislative constraints, is hardly going to welcome this extra form to fill in.*

To support this rejection, the "small businessman" is called on stage, apparently too busy to fill out so many other forms. By thus defending the 'common man' (when arguing with an anti-discrimination body like the CRE, the newspaper not even has the sensitivity to include women in its argument; indeed, sexism and racism often go together), the *Telegraph* uses a familiar 'popular' argument and further discredits the CRE as not only anti-business, but also as opposed against ordinary people, and especially overburdened, hard-working small businessmen. Wisely the *Telegraph* does not mention where the real effects of the proposed change of law would have to be sought: big business. After all, the small business people, if targeted at all, would also have very few personnel, and it would probably cost them only a few minutes per year to write down how many of their employees belong to minority groups. Also, the *Telegraph* seems to agree with all the other "legislative constraints" on business, but does not further argue why precisely this, relatively light, constraint is unacceptable.

*13    Moreover, one must ask who is most appropriate to decide which ethnic minority an individual belongs to?*

A different, more practical argument, pertaining to the application of the proposed law: "Who is most appropriate to decide" about ethnic membership? Here the bewilderment of whites facing a complex racial and ethnic mixture is translated into a practical objection against the CRE proposal. Such doubts are seldom voiced when ethnic minorities are to be identified as such by the Press when they are seen to be perpetrators of crime, or participants in riots. That the minorities themselves may be best qualified to categorize themselves is not even considered as a possibility.

*14    Why should a man be characterised in this way at his place of work?*

A more forceful argument, pertaining to "a man", is proposed here with a rhetorical question, which might suggest, maybe not wholly without grounds, that ethnic minority groups themselves might, for other reasons, object to 'ethnic' registration.

*15    It would be entirely inappropriate if an organisation like the GLC were to get hold of these returns and only award contracts to firms employing what they considered to be an adequate number from ethnic minorities.*

However, the *Telegraph* is not primarily worried about the possible implications for minority personnel. On the contrary, coming back to the central political argument, the ethnic registration might negatively reflect back on the employer, for instance when local councils (like the GLC) apply rules of contract compliance. In other words, the real fear of the *Telegraph* seems to be that employers might indeed be discriminatory, or at least have no equal opportunity policy, so that they may be lose business from left-wing councils.

*16    Already the GLC has stopped its contract for Kit-Kat because the producer, Rowntree Mackintosh, refuses to answer questions about its employment policy.*

These worries are supported with a specific example. Note though that it is stated that this firm refuses to answer questions about its employment policies. That is, the reader should not draw the conclusion that it lost its contract with the GLC because of discrimination. Also, it is ignored here that many other firms apparently have no objection to ethnic monitoring and so doing good business with the GLC.

17  *Any moves, which make it easier for certain councils to find out this sort of information, will not help race relations.*

The conclusion, therefore, remains political. Not only are further regulations against discrimination opposed, but also the possible implication of contract compliance enforced by leftist local governments is forcefully rejected. The interests of the ethnic minorities, briefly mentioned earlier in the editorial, are not further detailed. A more effective anti-discrimination law that allows investigation, monitoring and maybe even contract compliance, will especially hurt business, and is therefore rejected. New anti-discrimination laws, indeed, are not very effective, from the point of view of the business world, that is. And it is this position that the *Telegraph* defends in its argumentation, in which ethnic white dominance, conservative political power, and business interests mingle in a rejection of moderate anti-discrimination policies.

## EDITORIALS ON THE 'RIOTS': PERSUASIVE RHETORIC AND ARGUMENTATION

In light of this first example of strategic argumentation in a right-wing editorial, we now examine more closely the editorials about the urban disorders (for other studies of right-wing editorials on ethnic affairs, see also Bonnafous and Fiala, 1984; Ebel and Fiala, 1983). Although we have assumed above that there may not be a conventional schema for Press editorials, statements of opinions in the editorials about the disturbances may be of three different kinds. That is, they may be inserted into, or subsumed under, three functional categories, *Definition*, *Explanation* or *Evaluation*, and *Moral*. Further empiricial research will have to show whether these categories are part of a more general, formal schema of editorials. Thus, firstly, opinion statements may define the situation, that is, give a summarizing description of 'what happened'. This information focuses on the present, or very recent past. Secondly, opinion statements may explain the situation, that is, account for causes of events and reasons of action: why did it happen? These statements are often about past events and circumstances, or about a more general current context. Thirdly, many editorials feature a category of *Prediction* or *Recommendation*, which we may subsume under the broader category of a *Conclusion* or *Moral*, and which focuses on the future: what will happen?, or what should or should not be done? To make argumentative positions defensible and acceptable, these opinions must be supported. Like other discourse types, therefore, editorials exhibit argumentative structures and strategies, as we have seen in the *Telegraph* editorial.

The possible effect on the readers of the persuasive goals of editorials can be speculated about only in terms of assumed shared interpretative frameworks of the reading public of the British Press in the mid-1980s, which in turn are acquired through the complex cognitive processes involved in media use, to which we return in Chapter nine. That is, ultimately, a sound analysis of argumentation should also be embedded in a socio-cognitive, socio-cultural, and political framework. Positions defended by the Press are not personal opinions, but manifestations of more complex, socially shared, and dominant ideological frameworks that embody institutional relationships and power. We have earlier stressed that the argumentation of editorials is not only addressed to the reading public as a whole, but also to the social and political elites. This explains why editorials do not merely formulate opinions to be conveyed to the public, but also attack, defend, or give advice to the authorities. The role of editorials in the reproduction of the ethnic consensus is inherently tied to such a broader framework.

## The editorials

In each of the newspapers studied, the disturbances in Handsworth, Brixton, and Tottenham gave rise to one or two editorials, both in the quality Press and in the tabloids, appearing one or two days after the riots. Typically and as may be expected, the editorials in the quality Press are much longer and much more complex. *The Times* editorials have three columns of about 50 lines, and may run up to approximately 750 words, whereas those in the *Guardian* have a similar but more variable length, distributed in one or two columns. *Mail* and *Telegraph* editorials fall in between, and are usually somewhat shorter (about 400 words on average). *Sun* editorials, headlined by the phrase "The Sun Says", are mostly rather brief (100–200 words). Editorials are marked as such by a fixed position in the paper, by the newspaper's logo, and by relatively broad column size (about 7 cm, except in *The Times* which has 5 cm columns). None of the editorials is signed or datelined and all have a brief headline, often summarizing one main opinion.

There is an interesting regularity in the distribution of the editorials. That is, most newspapers have two editorials about the first riot, the one in Handsworth, on 11 and 13 September (the *Guardian* a third one on 18 September), then one about Brixton on 30 September, one about Tottenham on 8 October, and finally one or two on the political aftermath, such as the declarations of black leader Bernie Grant, and the

Tory and Labour conferences during which the riots were discussed, on 10 October and after. In other words, there is an agreement about the importance of the events, and about the relevance of a leading comment on them in these cases. This is not surprising for social disorders of this scale, but the agreement in number, frequency, and publication date of the editorials reveals something about common news values and routines in reporting social unrest.

## Defining the situation

The answer to the question 'What happened?' is of course given primarily in the news reports of the respective newspapers. However, in order to evaluate and explain them, editorials often summarize or recapitulate the events, select relevant dimensions, or focus on specific actions or actors. That is, they briefly define or redefine the situation. However, summarization, selection, and focusing presuppose ideologically framed opinions, which are part of the editor's cognitive model of the situation. That is, what is summarized about the situation in an editorial reveals something about the contents and hierarchical structure of the cognitive model about the riots, for instance, what is important information in the model, and what is not. Also, more than in news reports (especially in the quality Press), the description of events in editorials is not restrained by criteria of assumed 'objectivity'. That is, the facts may be described in evaluative terms, thereby allowing the editor to express an opinion about the events.

The primary definition of the disorders in all newspapers is straightforward, and was already studied in our analysis of headlines and topics: an "orgy" of murder, fights with the police, arson, looting, destruction, petrol bombs, bricks, and barricades are the actions and props of this well-known script of violent urban disturbances. Implicitly or explicitly, this type of disorder is qualified as "criminal" by most editorials. The right-wing Press adds that there is evidence of "vicious" or "malicious" premeditation, despite the spontaneous reactions to the incidents that sparked the disturbances, thereby enhancing the criminal and conspirational nature of the rampage. Some newspapers go beyond such accounts of criminal fact, and see the 'riots' as the "collapse of civil order" (*The Times* about Brixton), or as a "direct challenge to the rule of law" (*Sun* about Handsworth). In other words, not only has a crime been committed, but the foundations of order are threatened. In more contemporary parlance, the *Sun* typically defines the events as a form of "terror".

The protagonists in these clashes are well-known. Rampaging crowds are systematically described as "mobs", thereby enhancing the irrationality of the crime. Otherwise, the participants are characterized as "hooligans", "thugs", and similar evaluative descriptions of the same style register. No newspaper leaves any doubts about the identity of the main perpetrators of the crime: male, Afro-Caribbean youths. The *Guardian* adds that whites were also involved, a fact ignored by other editorials. Some editorials also introduce "outside agitators".

New is the death of Asian shopkeepers in Handsworth, also prominently mentioned and redefined as "murder", which transforms the disorder into a "murderous riot" for most of the right-wing Press. The sympathy for the Asian victims is more pronounced than when they are the victims of racist attacks by young fascists during the same period. The clash between West and East Indians is seen, in other news reports, as evidence of a racial war, if not of "black racism". This is a common strategy of transfer in the general dissimulation and denial of white racism in the right-wing Press.

Besides the black villains and the Asian victims, there is finally the police, "society's guardians", variously described as heroes and as victims, who are said to have behaved with "courage and determination" (*Sun*, 11 September). Especially when a policeman is killed, in the Tottenham riot, the victim interpretation becomes prominent: "Police constable Keith Blakelock was deliberately and savagely hacked to death when he was trying to defend firemen from the mob" (*Mail*, 8 October) or "brutally stabbed to death" (*Sun*, 8 October).

Finally, there are the two black women, victims of the police in Brixton and Tottenham. They are only casually mentioned, namely as the objects of a tragic accident, an "error" (*Times*) which was the result of "flawed judgement" (*Mail*). The death of one of them was her own fault: "Mrs Cynthia Jarrett died of a heart attack. She was grossly overweight and had other medical problems" (*Sun*). Hence the accusation of police 'killing, provocation and brutality' is resolutely rejected in the *Sun*. Only the *Guardian* gives a more personal description of Mrs Jarrett.

We see that the selective summary of the events is hardly ambiguous in most editorials, and leaves little room for other interpretations, for instance in terms of protests, rage, resistance, or other descriptions that would recognize more charitable motives of young black people. Even when a black woman dies, the reaction of the crowd as a form of "vengeance" is rejected by the *Sun*. The dominant reading of the events, thus, remains within the framework of law and order: violence, destruction, crime, lawlessness, anarchy and terror.

## Explanation

The explanations of the events fill most of the editorials. Primed by public debates about the 1980–1 disturbances, the respective positions are clear. Either the riots are primarily evaluated as crimes, or they are evaluated and partly excused as disturbances or protests that are motivated by social "deprivation". All editorials agree that at least the Handsworth disorders were probably a premeditated crime, for some only understandable in light of the Birmingham drugs scene. For the *Telegraph*, indeed, Handsworth is the first British "drug riot", presumably provoked as a reaction to tough police actions against hard-drug dealers. Brixton and Tottenham need some more explanation, since in these cases one woman was shot and another died as a consequence of a police raid on her house, which would allow an explanation in terms of spontaneous anger or of justified violence against police provocation and harassment; this was also the case in the Brixton riot of 1981, according to Lord Scarman's explanation of the situation (Scarman, 1981).

Most editorials do at least briefly mention the facts of social deprivation, of the inner cities in general, and of the black community, in particular: bad housing, unemployment, lack of services and education, and discrimination. However, all newspapers, except the *Guardian*, reject a broad, Scarman-style inquiry, with the argument "We know all this already". This reaction is not surprising, since a repetition of the findings and recommendations of another serious inquiry into the social background of the urban disorders would be politically highly unwelcome. In the right-wing Press, the social situation is mentioned only in order to reject it as a necessary or sufficient cause of the riots. This central position is defended with the standard argument that most other poor people don't riot to express their grievances. The fallaciousness of such an 'argument' is like that of the argument that rejects smoking as a cause of lung cancer because not all people who smoke die of lung cancer. Similarly, the shooting incidents are rejected as an acceptable reason of protest by the routine phrase "No excuses". The law-and-order reading of the riots is consistent: a crime is a crime, and social explanations are either irrelevant or no valid excuses. This is important, since as we shall see below, this also means that no concerted actions need to be taken to alleviate the problems of the inner city: it is not the government that is at fault, nor the police, but the black community itself. While recognizing the criminal nature of the disorders, only the *Guardian*, especially after Brixton and Tottenham, emphasizes the social backgrounds of the riots.

Within this overall framework of explanation and argumentation, there are of course variations and nuances. The main position must be backed up with credible arguments, using 'facts' and 'figures'. Handsworth is easy. The *Telegraph* summarizes the various arguments as the right-wing Press has them: it cannot be poverty, because most other poor people are law-abiding citizens. It cannot be police harassment, because this area was well-known for its soft community policing. And it cannot be the government, because the government just gave them £20 millions' worth of aid. So, it is lawlessness, greed, drugs, or other problems associated with the black community. This is Hurd's position. The same is true, *mutatis mutandis*, for the other riots. Interestingly, the 'criminal' explanation is hardly an explanation at all. It evaluates the events, and the only explanation would be in terms of inherent criminal tendencies of the actors, namely, black youths. Such a position is difficult to maintain explicitly, because of its clear racist implications, so the editorials suggest it only indirectly, such as when they speak of "endemic petty crime" and especially drug abuse in the black community.

In order to support further the 'criminal' explanation of the riots, a safe and expedient strategy is to attack the other position, that is, the social explanation of the riots. *The Times* claims a moderate, and therefore 'wise', middle position, and takes neither explanation as the only explanation. In its later editorials, however, the law-and-order interpretation gradually prevails. Social deprivation may be mentioned, although never as an excuse for the riots, but is not further spelled out, and barely found important enough for further government actions beyond a "review of policies".

The right-wing popular Press is more straightforward. For the *Telegraph*, the *Sun*, and the *Mail*, the main ideological opponents are the sociologists: "In no time, the sociologists will be picking among the debris of Handsworth for evidence of social protest. They will be eager to find signs of resentment over deprivation and unemployment. They will lecture about racial tension between West Indians and Asians" (*Sun*, 11 September). Hence, social conditions are mentioned but rejected, both as a cause and as an excuse. Therefore the professionals who may want to analyse these events, especially from a more social and critical perspective, are also disqualified, if not vilified.

Other explanations better fit the ideological framework: for instance, it is assumed that the police have become too permissive. For the *Mail*, also the "race issue must be discussed with honesty". That is, we should not hesitate to blame the blacks, and not fear to be called 'racist'. Another explanation, that black kids are "stuffed with ethnic education" at school, instead of being taught "to love their country" , so that they become alienated (*Mail*), expresses a fragment of the underlying ideology of white nationalism of the right-wing Press. Finally, it is argued as a further explanation that the black community condones crimes, shelters criminals, and generally does not want to integrate, as the Asians do. Its culture is defective, because "Chinese, Pakistanis and Indians live at peace because of strong family ties and codes" (*Sun*). The black leaders, if they have control at all, are not strict enough with their young, or do not encourage them to join the police.

In other words, the blame for the criminal riots is sought in the black community itself. The government, the police, or any other institution that may be responsible for unemployment, bad housing, or other conditions of the "ghetto", are exonerated. Discrimination is briefly mentioned only in the quality Press. Systematic patterns of racism, in employment, housing, and education are never mentioned, let alone spelled out as possible motives of urban protest by those who are most affected: black youths. No editorial details the actual lives of black people in the inner cities. No editorial quotes or provides the view of the black communities or their leaders. Whereas the 1980–1 urban unrest at least allowed some measure of serious discussion in the media and in politics of the socio-economic backgrounds, most reactions to the 1985 disturbances emphatically deny the relevance of these backgrounds, and therefore take the issue of racism and deprivation in the inner cities off the public and political agendas (see Solomos, 1989).

## Moral

Finally, the Conclusion or Moral category of the editorials features the advice or predictions these definitions and explanations of the riots give rise to. The recommendations are straightforward for most of the right-wing Press, though again with some variation in degree and mode. All newspapers emphasize that the criminals, and especially the killers, must be "brought to justice". They will sometimes admit that limited inquiries are necessary into the immediate causes of the riots, and into the practices and policies of policing where "errors" have been made, like the shooting of an innocent woman. We saw that deeper probing by Scarman-style investigations is emphatically rejected (except by the *Guardian*), with the argument that we already know enough about social deprivation, and because the police have already learned their lesson from Scarman. *The Times* vaguely asks for a "review" of inner-city policies of the government.

The recommendations of the right-wing Press mirror the law-and-order interpretation of the disturbances: the criminals (murderers, looters, agitators) must be "hunted" and brought to trial. Next, sentences for them should be stiffer (the *Sun* casually suggests life stretches). The

*Mail* fears, however, that some judges may not play that game, so that finally these "perversely lenient" judges should also be disciplined, or else the law should be rewritten to allow for minimum sentences for certain crimes. We see that a right-wing law-and-order position does not seem to bother with such matters as the autonomy of the courts.

The major recommendation is that order and faith in the law must be restored. Obviously the instrument for this restoration are the nation's "guardians": the police. A large part of the debate, therefore, focuses on police powers, policies, tactics, autonomy, weaponry and on the advantages of strict or sensitive policing. At this point the politicians are called in and explicitly addressed. In fact, we should read the editorials as primarily addressed to them, through the detour of the reading public (whose votes the politicians need to stay in business). They are the ones who must provide the police with extra powers. Critical opinions about this solution are attacked. The Labour Party, the black communities, and all others of 'the other side', are vigorously reminded of their civic duty either to support (if not love) the police, or else. Thus, first the police should be allowed to act more sternly. Less radical newspapers, such as *The Times*, recommend a more moderate solution: "the ghetto must be policed, sensitively, but with strength and firmness, to ensure that public order is upheld without interruption" (*Times*, 30 Septemeber, after Brixton).

One important topic in the Moral sections of the editorials deals with the police technology for the operationalization of riot containment. For the tabloids this invariably means CS gas, water cannons, and/or plastic bullets (as in Northern Ireland), instruments that are becoming increasingly accepted as a legitimate solution to the nation's social problems. The quality Press is more cautious about such devices and signals their possible dangers.

Another central issue in the Recommendations are the feared "no-go" areas, rejected by all, with a fascinating mixture of arguments. The *Telegraph* takes the most powerful move, and rejects this "American" invention, because it would mean an "abhorred" form of discrimination of the ethnic communities. After all, law-abiding West Indians and Indians have the same right of protection against dealers and muggers. In other words, if the right-wing Press wants to propagate rights for minority communities, it emphasizes the "right" to be firmly policed. It need hardly be stressed that other minority rights are scarcely defended in the editorials of the right-wing Press. The *Sun*, similarly, also claims "justice for all", when recommending a police crackdown on the inner city. The dramatic consequences of similar policing (Operation Swamp) in Brixton four years earlier, i.e. large-scale disturbances, are apparently forgotten.

A second major group of recommendations is addressed to the black community. Since the riots are primarily interpreted as a crime committed by blacks, the solutions are naturally sought in the Afro-Caribbean community itself. The recommendations here take the form of barely concealed threats. Firstly, for the right-wing Press strong leadership, if not authoritarian paternalism, is the solution for the ghetto, so that the leaders can keep a tight control over "their young". Young black kids should be taught love for their country and "not be stuffed with ethnic education", or else the black community will be further alienated from white British society. Secondly, the communities should co-operate with the police to bring the criminals to justice, or else they are accessories after the fact of murder. Thirdly, blacks must join the police, in order to do their own 'tough' policing for the predominantly white police force. That much of the resentment in the black communities has been based on white police behaviour, despite more recent "community policing", is overlooked in this call for co-operation. These calls for black police officers, and for "integration" generally, simply presuppose that blacks are welcome in the white institutions.

Generally, the recommended solution is that blacks should obey the rules and adapt to the mainstream of British society, or else the fascists or racists will move in. This threat is particularly cynical. The right-wing's own (more or less) bad guys, such as Powell or the National Front, may take the opportunity to repeat their calls for repatriation, or worse. The tabloids formally condemn these racist ideas and actions, and emphatically claim that "they have always stood up for the coloured minorities of Britain" (*Sun*), but they go on to suggest that with enough provocation the dark forces of the right may no longer be contained. Even though rejecting Powell, his spectre is nevertheless conjured up as a reminder of what other policies could be developed if the black community doesn't behave.

As may be expected, the *Guardian* is the only newspaper that extensively encourages more government intervention (dubbed "the socialist option" by the *Mail*), whereas *The Times* is prepared to review the current policies for their effectiveness. The other newspapers briefly pay lip service to the need to attend to social problems, but also ignore or reject a solid and serious inner-city intervention by the authorities.

**The actors**

The definition, explanation and recommended consequences of the disorders also feature prominent actors, first of all the black youngsters, pitted against the police, and then Asians, communities, politicians,

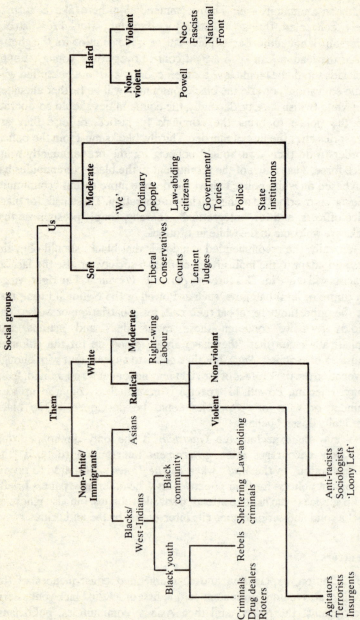

*Figure 5.4* Ideological group schema according to the editorials of the right-wing British Press

government, agitators, fascists, and some others. To understand further the argumentative structures of the editorials, which after all focus on the defence of own positions and the attack of opposed positions, as well as the underlying ideology of the attitudes and opinions expressed in these arguments, we need to have a closer look at this cast. In social and ethnic issues especially, in which opposing opinions are closely associated with attitudes about the main protagonists in the social and ethnic events, these attitudes are organized as belief schemata about social groups (see van Dijk, 1987a, for details). Therefore, we should analyse with whom the newspapers relate, positively or negatively, and why. What is the internal cognitive representation the newspapers have of blacks, Asians, the police, the government, or the other actors involved?

Since there is no space here to detail such an investigation into group representations, a simplified schema is proposed, along the usual dimension of 'us' and 'them'. This dimension is well-known from the study of both everyday and institutional expressions about race relations. The same is true for editorials. Some actors belong to 'us' (British, whites, ordinary people, etc.), and some to 'them' (aliens, criminals, blacks, etc.).

Figure 5.4 gives such a tentative schema for the right-wing Press. Each node in the structure represents a relevant ethnic, social, or political criterion of differentation between the groups below that node. Thus at the highest level, the distinction between 'us' and 'them' is that of "belonging" or not, exemplified in the often expressed criterion of "integration" or "adaptation". Associated with these criteria are certain evaluations. Generally, 'us' is associated with the value *good* or the evaluation or emotion of *like*, and 'them' with *bad* and *dislike*. In other words, in such an ideology, and rather generally in social perception, there is a binary division between in-groups and out-groups, even when such a division may be variable, and flexibly adapted to new situations, or even change under social pressure. For reasons of simplicity I focus on the right-wing ideological framework, because we have four newspapers yielding data for constructing the framework. For the liberal ideology of the *Guardian*, the relationships are more complex, and will not be further examined here.

The schema is an abstract reconstruction of the underlying system of group representations of the right-wing Press. It has been derived from the overall evaluations of the respective groups in the argumentation and the style of the editorials. Consistent negative evaluations place a group under the 'them' category. The more negative the evaluations, the larger the socio-cognitive distance from 'us'. Therefore, each right branch of the 'them' category features a group that is relatively closer to us, and hence less negatively described than those under the left branch of the same node. Whereas the tabloids position themselves at the point we have marked in the schema, *The Times* may be placed somewhat to the left, and might therefore be considered as too 'lenient' by the tabloids. Similarly, the *Guardian* would probably position itself under the white moderates, with the whole left branch under the header 'them'. Finally, for both the moderate conservatives and liberals, the 'radicals' (whether left or right) may all be grouped under the same 'them' category. The major nodes in that case are 'moderate' and 'radical', respectively. In other words, the social group schema may differ for each social group or institution, depending on its own position or perspective, but the basic categories used in such a schema may be the same.

For the tabloids the centre for 'us' is of course the newspaper, or rather the editors. However, as an actor the newspaper seldom intervenes in these editorials, although sometimes it is positively self-presented. The *Sun* for instance makes the well-used disclaimer ('I'm not a racist, but ...'): they have always stood up for the ethnic minorities (see Hollingsworth, 1986, for some evidence against the claim). The editors of the right-wing Press by nature associate with the conservative power structure, that is, with Tory politics, Thatcher, state institutions (primarily the police), private enterprise, and generally the conservative power elites. This association is multiply signalled in the editorials: they are the ones who are never criticized, or only lightly, for example, for regrettable "errors" or misguided policies. Also, given its assumed 'intermediate' function, the Press, and especially the popular Press, is presenting itself as *vox populi*. Hence its recurrent, positive reference to "ordinary people", "law-abiding citizens" or simply the "people of Britain".

However, the picture is somewhat more complex. That is, even among 'us', there are those who are too soft, such as the "lenient" judges who are not harsh enough against rioters, on the one hand, and the ones who are too 'strong' on the radical right, that is, Powell and the neo-fascists. Both are condemned, but certainly not as belonging to 'them'. That is, their ideas or practices may be rejected, but only because they exaggerate or, as in the case of Powell, also because his ideas are not practical. Those of 'us' who are too 'soft' favour the case of 'them', and therefore they need correction (such as firing judges). The same is true for others of 'us' who tend to be too liberal, too understanding, of 'them', such as Scarman, or some liberal-conservative Tory politicians. Interestingly, this rejection of 'hard' and 'soft' groups, associates the 'ideal' position of 'us' ('we, the Press'), with a middle or moderate point of view, which is of course inherently good. Note that this we-core of 'us' may move somewhat. Thus, for *The Times* it is less to the right than that of the *Sun*, or rather closer to 'them' (from the point of view of the *Sun*). Indeed, *The Times* advocates some solutions that are rejected by the *Sun*.

'Them' for the right-wing Press combines vastly different groups. Common to 'them'-groups is that they are in essential ways 'different' from 'us'. They look different, think differently, and act differently. However, again, there is variation here. Even the rather categorical and radical editorials of the *Sun* and the *Mail* make subtle differences in this "demonology" (as the *Guardian*, appropriately, calls it when commenting upon the tabloid coverage of the riots).

A first basic criterion is that between "Coloured" and White, or between Aliens and Non-Aliens. "Coloured" are black or brown people, usually immigrants, often commonwealth citizens, but also Chinese, or Mediter- raneans. Depending on the perspective, either colour (or other aspects of appearance) or origin will be most relevant. Thus, sometimes 'American' or 'Continental' people or ideas may also be rejected as 'alien' to the white insular British.

However, the major division is between Coloured/Immigrant and White/Original Britons. 'Them'-groups are further divided according to whether specific criteria define the others as closer to 'us'. For instance, among the immigrants a major distinction is made between Asians and Afro-Caribbeans. Asian shopkeepers were victims of Afro-Caribbeans, they are 'haves', they have small shops. Like 'us' and white ordinary people they are presented as hard-working, as small enterpreneurs (and hence as good capitalists), and as victims of blacks. They also look more like us, and share in the Indo-European cultural tradition. For the editorials, this holds especially for these riots, however. When Asians are attacked by white fascists, because they are Asian, or discriminated against because they are non-white, the editorials are more confused, ignore the events, or simply deny discrimination or racism. In other words, Asians are close to (if not among) 'us' as long as they are opposed to 'real' blacks, that is, Afro-Caribbeans. Note that in the negative evaluations as well as the recommendations of the editorials, it is always the Afro-Caribbean community that is blamed or advised to better its life (and to take an example from the Asians).

But even the Afro-Caribbeans are not all the same. That is, some distinctions are sometimes made, although also often collapsed for the sake of the argument. Thus there is on the one hand the black Community and on the other hand the criminal black youngsters (drug dealers, thieves, rioters, killers, etc.). And even within the Community, the right-wing Press may still distinguish between the good ones and the less good ones, namely between law-abiding citizens, who help the police and denounce crime, and those who are allegedly sympathetic to the revolting youths, who condone crime, and shelter criminals.

The white section of 'them' is largely there because of political criteria.

For Tory newspapers, Labour is there. That is, the leftists, socialists, and their ilk. Their categorization is complex and multiple. They may be seen as anti-capitalist, as anti-British, and in our case as pro-black. Again, there are distinctions here between 'hard' and 'soft', between 'radicals' and 'moderates', between 'violent' and 'non-violent', or even between young and old. Far out are of course the young, violent, leftist youths, often associated with similar black youths, and variously described as agitators, insurrectionists, rioters, Marxists, Trotskyists, and ultimately of course as terrorists. Among the non-violent radicals, we find the extreme left, but also sociologists and all those who advocate fundamental social change (prototype: Ken Livingstone, one time leader of the leftist Greater London Council). Since they are often also intellectuals and sometimes part of a cultural elite, they are the true opponents of right-wing editors. They are attacked most often and most viciously by the Press. Occasionally in the present editorials but more often in those about other topics, anti-racists also belong to this category, especially since they dare to call the right-wing Press in Britain racist, and because they associate with minority groups (see Murray, 1986; Seidel, 1988b). We come back to these attitudes about the anti-racists in the following chapters. Terrorists may be most different and most despicable, but for the editors there is not even a basis of comparison. They are simply criminals and belong to another species. For them a police "hunt" is in order. Among the moderate left, there are finally more subtle divisions, for instance, between right-wing Labour and those (like Kinnock) who are not strict enough against the radicals, or who have too much understanding for their ideas and actions. They are usually the target of good advice from the Press on keeping their radicals under control.

Finally, combinations are possible, such as radical left-wing blacks. The major prototype here is Bernie Grant. Since he also expressed himself against the police, seemed to condone the riots or even murder, he is for the popular Press the devil himself: he combines all negative criteria: he is black, Labour, leftist if not Marxist, critical of the police, and calls 'us' racists. The *Sun*, indeed, explicitly wishes that he "may rot in hell". Bernie Grant is systematically vilified as "Barmie Bernie" during this season, in a large number of articles as well as in some editorials. And although Kinnock rejected Grant's statement (that the police had received "a good hiding"), the soft socialists are criticized for not removing him as a candidate for a seat in Parliament.

We see that this binary schema of 'us' and 'them' allows us to reconstruct the attitudinal 'positions' of the major actors as they appear in the underlying opinions of the editorials in the right-wing Press. It is this schema that represents an abstraction of part of the social and political worldview of the editors. The distinctions of 'difference' are marked or signalled in the text by the amount, nature, or distribution of evaluative statements or the style and rhetoric of actor descriptions. Note however that each 'node' of the schema is itself a complex 'group schema', featuring sometimes complex structures of beliefs about the respective groups. Some of these propositions have been discussed above in the analysis of the argumentation structures of the editorials, for example, Young male blacks are criminal, use or push drugs, they are violent, don't take jobs, etc. These group schemata form the underlying stereotypes or prejudices of the social cognitions of the editors.

**The ideological value structure**

The way the Press presents and represents social actors is part of a broader ideological structure of values. It is this ideology that explains why specific groups are dealt with positively or negatively and why such value judgements constitute a coherent (though not necessarily psychologically consistent) system of social representation. This system features a hierarchically organized set of norms and values that defines fundamental goals of groups and their members.

In the editorials of the conservative Press, and especially of the tabloids, this ideological framework is straightforward. Complexities, sophistication, subtlety and contradictions, which often characterize ideological positions (for instance as represented by the *Guardian*), are lacking here. Figure 5.5 presents a tentative schematic representation of this system (for details of this right-wing discourse and ideology in Britain, especially in the context of Thatcherism, see for example, Gordon and Klug, 1986; Hall, 1988; Levitas, 1986; Reeves, 1983; Rich, 1986; Seidel, 1987, 1988a; Solomos, 1989).

This schema may be read as follows: the fundamental notion of the ideological system, organizing virtually all its other norms and values, is Order. The maintenance of order requires Authority, which is exercised through various types of Power or Control, both personal and moral, as well as social and political. Hence, in the riots, the major concern of all editorials is that, whatever else may be done, first order must be restored, and respect for Authority (of the state, the police) must be re-established. The subsequent focus on the containment of the riots, by tougher and more sophisticated policing, presupposes this concern for the exercise of authority.

These basic notions may then be applied and differentiated for different domains of society. Along the personal dimension, the black community is criticized for not having "disciplined their young", which

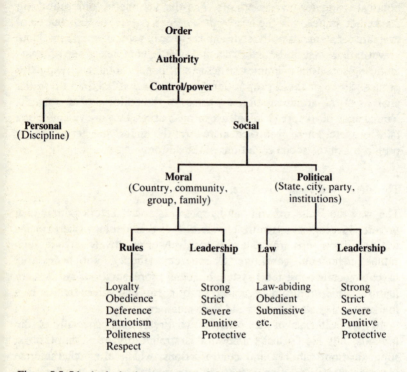

*Figure 5.5* Ideological value structure of the editorials in the right-wing British Press

both presupposes the personal value of self-control as well as the social value of respect or submission. Both in the social or moral realm, as well as in politics, finally, the fundamental values of order and authority are translated as moral rules or as laws, on the one hand, and as characteristics of dominance and leadership, on the other hand. Leaders, whether of the black community, or of the state, must be strong and strict, that is both punitive, internally, with respect to internal infractions of the rules or the law, as well as, externally, protective of the group against other groups. Hence, from the group members, loyalty, obedience, and respect are requested in order to keep intact the system of internal hierarchies and external group dominance.

This well-known system permeates virtually all value statements of the editorials. Indeed, most of the values are actually mentioned explicitly in the accounts and evaluations of the urban disorders, as we have seen above, and as we shall see in even more detail in the next chapters. For our discussion on the reproduction of racism in the Press it is however important to stress that this system is not only a general representation of the kind of moral order that is the goal of conservative ideologies. Rather, this system has important social, political, and cultural implications. Indeed, the Order as defined here presupposes the authority and the power of the white group, and therefore represents a system of racial or ethnic dominance and control, or 'ethnarchy' (see Mullard, 1985a, 1985b, who speaks of 'etharchy'). According to such an ideology, young black males have not merely violated the moral or social order in general (as when their uprising is defined as 'crime'), but more fundamentally, they have shown how to contest the white order, in this case by challenging the authority invested in its "guardians", the police.

Again according to the editorials, the same is true for the ethnic communities as a whole, which have not shown enough respect, deference, obedience or loyalty to the white dominant order. They are accused when seen as not "integrating" (West Indians), or selectively praised when they do "adapt" (Asians). Cultural autonomy, and especially anti-racism in education, are explicitly condemned as examples of this lack of patriotism, if not as an attack on white values, that is, as a challenge to the dominance of white dominant culture and structure in contemporary Britain. However, since conflicting norms of socio-political equality prevent racial or ethnic dominance from being defended in such terms (although this sometimes does happen), the Press presents its evaluations in a moral framework. Since this moral framework is supposed or suggested to be natural and general (indeed, who would be in favour of crime?), it is well suited to conceal the relations of socio-political power and inequality involved. Any explicit reference to such white group power, for instance in accusations against racist policing or discrimination in employment, is resolutely rejected, and returned with a vengeance, as an immoral attack on the white group, and defined as 'black racism'.

Finally, a similar analysis holds for the political implementation of the ideological system. Whereas blacks or other immigrants are thus represented as a threat to white order and hierarchy, the left is first morally attacked as the representative of the forces of disorder, of chaos, and lack of authority. Again, the moral values here are used to defend or legitimate political power structures, in fact those controlled by the right. Hence the obsession, also in ethnic affairs news, with the "loony Left", and with the real or imaginary appearance of urban revolutionaries of various brands (Trotskyites and others). Obviously, at present, and with a minority population of a few per cent, the real power struggle is located here, as we shall also see later when we examine the stylistic details of its formulation in the Press. We shall also see in that case how political aggression may be used, just like the moral attacks described above, as a concealment of ethnic or racial dominance.

## Conclusion

Our analysis has shown how the ideological structures of the right systematically appear in argumentation schemata, rhetorical devices, lexical style, and in the overall organization of editorials, such as the definition and explanation of the situation and the recommendation of future action. Indeed, the editorial is *the* formulation place for newspaper ideologies. We also have seen what role ethnic minorities and especially blacks play in these ideological frameworks, and how such a position gives rise to negative beliefs and evaluations of blacks in the power struggle between order and disorder as it is manifest in the riots as well as in their editorial consequences.

Ethnic prejudices and stereotypes are not innate. They are acquired, largely by text and talk. It is the fundamental thesis of this book that the media play a vital role in this reproduction process. Confronted with fundamental changes in the social and ethnic context, many readers have sought for interpretative frameworks, for definitions and explanations of the new situation and for practical guide-lines for future communication and action. Editorials, even more than the news reports on which they are based, offer precisely such practical, common-sense frameworks for making sense of the social situation. Readers may often reject such proposals, if they read such editorials at all. Fortunately, many do so. Unfortunately, even more readers accept these editorials wholesale, simply because they have no information or occasion to form alternative, anti-racist attitudes and ideologies. Here lies the core of the autonomous contribution of the Press to the reproduction of racism.

# 6 Quotations and sources

## QUOTATION AND NEWS PRODUCTION

Possible biases in the coverage of ethnic affairs not only reside in the selection and prominence of news actors, but also in the ways they are presented as speakers who give their interpretation of, and opinions about news events. Therefore this chapter examines the sources and quotation patterns in news about minorities. It tries to answer questions such as: Who is speaking, how often and how prominently, and about what are quoted news actors allowed to give their opinions? Such questions are embedded in a broader theoretical framework that accounts for the access of minorities to the Press, and for the conditions that control the ways they are being quoted in news reports.

Quotation patterns are a fairly direct function of news production processes, which are essentially a complex form of text processing. Reporters covering news events engage in various strategies to get relevant information about these events. Apart from exceptional events such as riots or demonstrations, in which reporters may sometimes act as direct eyewitnesses, much of this information is indirect and discursive. Eyewitness reports of others, press conferences and press releases, other media texts, wire messages, interviews, telephone calls, hand-outs, official reports and documents, books and many other genres of 'source texts' are forms of discursive material used by journalists to write their news reports. Since these source texts are usually much more extensive than the intended news reports, their information must be severely reduced. Selection and summarization are therefore prominent strategies in the management of the huge amounts of textual information that reaches newspapers every day. We have seen before that such strategies are monitored by the models, knowledge, attitudes, and ideologies of newspapers (for details see van Dijk, 1988a).

Source texts not only feature descriptions, interpretations or announcements of events and actions, but also evaluative statements, that is, opinions. If these are voiced by prominent news actors, they may become newsworthy in their own right. We have shown in the previous chapter that news reports even have a special schematic category, 'Verbal Reaction', reserved for such opinion statements of prominent news actors. This means that the reporter will actively seek such relevant opinions, for instance in interviews, in which questions about the opinions of news actors about the current events are routinized moves of information gathering. Since most statements by sources or news actors are too long or too complex, they are also transformed by selection and summarization, that is, by processes that have an ideological basis.

The actual formulation of interpretation and evaluation statements by sources or news actors is itself a complex discursive process. Fragments of statements may sometimes be quoted verbatim, and marked as such by quotation marks and a set of declarative predicates or other discourse-presentation signals, such as "He said", "She declared", or "According to". These forms of direct discourse do not always imply, however, that this is what the source or news actor actually said or wrote, especially in contexts of oral communication. Most forms of quotation, however, are indirect or a mixture of direct and indirect speech. This allows varying degrees of distance, marked in different linguistic ways, between the quotation and what was actually said (Coulmas, 1986).

Quotations have several news functions. Firstly, statements by prominent news actors may be newsworthy in their own right, simply because they express the interpretation or opinions of important news actors. Secondly, a news story may become more lively by occasionally quoting news participants, which is a typical narrative function. Thirdly, quotations enhance the credibility of the account, since their use suggests what credible news participants say about the events. The credibility is also enhanced by the suggestion that the reporter must have had direct access to a relevant news actor. Fourthly, quotations not only allow interpretations of recent news events, but also predictions of future events and plans for coming actions of news actors. Finally, and most important, quotations allow the insertion of subjective interpretations, explanations, or opinions about current news events, without breaking the ideological rule that requires the separation of facts from opinions. That is, opinion statements of sources or news actors are facts in their own right, even if this allows reporters to insert relevant opinion statements in the news reports for which they cannot be held responsible. In sum, quotations have several functions that make news reports more persuasive.

We say that a person or group has 'ideological' or 'symbolic' access to the Press if their interpretations and evaluations of news events are routinely embedded in the account of these events. On the other hand, access is of course also socio-economically determined. That is, in order to get ideological access, sources first need to 'reach' journalists in the first place, a process that is routinely organized by prominent news actors and organizations by discourse events and genres such as press conferences, press releases, hand-outs, public declarations, granting interviews to selected reporters, reports and other source texts initiated and controlled by sources. Only elite actors, institutions, and organizations have such resources of organized media access (Gans, 1979; Tuchman, 1978).

## The ethnic dimension of news production

In Europe and North America such elite institutions are usually white, which by definition gives prestructured priority of access to white sources or news actors. This priority of access is mutual: elite sources have organizations that routinely and professionally approach journalists, and conversely, journalists will preferably turn to such sources because they are assumed to provide more, more regular, more reliable, and more newsworthy information. The same is true for format and style: professional public relations people also know more or less the format and style of news releases, time of presentation, and other tactics to reach journalists and be quoted as speakers. Conversely, more access will itself reconfirm the newsworthiness and hence the power of the white news sources. In other words, there are many socio-cultural and institutional factors that lead to the prominence of white elites in the definition of the ethnic situation.

Minority institutions, especially in western Europe, are generally less influential, have less or no organized Press contacts, such as press officers or press conferences, and for these reasons alone they have less institutionalized access to the Press in the first place. Secondly, if white journalists actively seek information or opinions from minority organizations or individuals, there may be a culture and communication gap, at least when compared to their dealings with the members of their 'own' group. Even cultural differences of style and rhetoric may be the cause of misunderstanding, if not of negative evaluations by whites, which again hardly enhances credibility and access (Kochman, 1981). Thus, reduced access is also symbolic and cognitive. That is, even if a minority institution were regularly to produce press releases of the required form and content, reporters may still find such institutions less prominent, newsworthy, and especially less credible. Thirdly, minority group speakers or sources are often found less credible because they are seen as partisan, whereas white authorities, such as the police or the government, are simply seen as ethnically 'neutral', even in the definition and evaluation of ethnic events.

This also means that minorities often speak in the Press through mediation, for instance through more credible or more accessible white politicians, lawyers, or action groups who defend their 'case'. This also happens in stories in which minority groups are frequent active or passive actors, for instance in riot, crime, or immigration news, in which they are seldom speakers and definers of their own reality. Consequently, they are also seldom heard as having an opinion about majority actions and policies, especially when negative actions of elite whites are involved, for instance in instances of discrimination and racism. If heard at all in such cases, their opinions will be duly marked as such, for instance by quotation marks or other distance words, such as "accuse" or "allege", and always followed by 'independent' (that is, white) sources that soften or deny these accusations. This suggests that we need not only study who is allowed to say what, but also how such declarations are presented, and who else is asked to comment about the current events. We may expect, then, that not only will minorities be less quoted, but if they are quoted, these quotations will tend to be accompanied more often by opinions of white sources or otherwise be presented with reservation in the Press.

## SOME QUANTITATIVE RESULTS

### Minority versus majority actors as speakers

Table 6.1 shows how often minority or majority actors are quoted in the Press. (The figures in this table are based on a first analysis of our data, which consisted of 2,506 items instead of the 2,764 analysed elsewhere in this book.) In order to get a more reliable calculation of percentages, column A lists the frequencies of those items in which minority and/or majority group members occur as actors in the first place: after all, in order to be quoted, one must be an actor in the news item. That is, minority actors occur in some 82 per cent of all items, whereas majority actors are present in more than 94 per cent of the items (which suggests that in less than 6 per cent of all items on ethnic affairs, minorities appear as sole actors!). Minority and majority actors appear together in 77.6 per cent of all items.

Total frequencies of quotation for all papers are given in column B, which shows in how many of all news items minorities or majorities are quoted. Percentages here are given both for the proportion of quote-items relative to the total number of items (2,506) and with respect

Table 6.1 Frequencies of quotation for minority and majority actors, August 1985–January 1986

| Number of articles | A. Total no. of items with min/maj actors | | B. All papers | | | Times | Guardian | Telegraph | Sun | Mail |
|---|---|---|---|---|---|---|---|---|---|---|
| | | | 2,506 | | | 445 | 660 | 649 | 301 | 451 |
| | % of B | | | % of A | % of B | | | | | |
| Min-quote | 2,065 | (82.4) | 432 | (20.9) | (17.2) | 86 (19.3) | 167 (25.3) | 45 ( 6.9) | 25 ( 8.3) | 109 (24.2) |
| Maj-quote | 2,362 | (94.3) | 1,291 | (54.7) | (51.5) | 263 (59.1) | 473 (71.7) | 213 (32.8) | 81 (26.9) | 259 (57.4) |
| Min+Maj-quote | 1,945 | (77.6) | 275 | (14.1) | (11.0) | 48 (10.8) | 116 (17.6) | 34 ( 5.2) | 11 ( 3.7) | 66 (14.6) |
| Min-only-quote | 1,945 | (77.6) | 157 | ( 8.1) | ( 6.3) | 38 ( 8.5) | 51 ( 7.7) | 11 ( 1.7) | 14 ( 4.7) | 43 ( 9.5) |
| Maj-only-quote | 1,945 | (77.6) | 1,015 | (52.2) | (40.5) | 214 (48.1) | 357 (54.1) | 179 (27.6) | 70 (23.3) | 195 (43.2) |
| Min+Maj-quote in news | 1,139 | (45.5) | 175 | (15.4) | ( 7.0) | 40 ( 9.0) | 66 (10.0) | 14 ( 2.2) | 7 ( 2.3) | 48 (10.6) |
| Min-only-quote in news | 1,190 | (47.5) | 95 | ( 8.3) | ( 3.8) | 18 ( 4.0) | 27 ( 4.1) | 7 ( 1.1) | 11 ( 3.7) | 32 ( 6.7) |
| Maj-only-quote in news | 1,372 | (54.7) | 619 | (54.3) | (24.7) | 154 (34.6) | 193 (29.2) | 59 ( 9.1) | 60 (19.9) | 153 (33.9) |

to the number of items (listed in column A) in which speakers are also actors. As might be expected, we see that minority group members are quoted much less often than majority group actors: *minorities appear as speakers only in a fifth of all items in which they appear as actors, whereas majority group actors are shown in speaking roles in more than half of all items*. Together they appear as speakers in only a seventh of all items in which they are actors. In other words, when both appear as actors, the majority group representatives will mostly be the ones that comment upon ethnic events. Indeed, as we show in the second layer of Table 6.1, minorities seldom (8.1 per cent) appear as the only speakers in those items in which both minorities and majorities appear as actors (that is in 6.3 per cent of all news items), whereas majorities are the only speakers in more than 40 per cent of all items in which they are acting with minority groups. Separate analysis of quotation patterns of proper news reports (as differentiated from less prominent background or other articles) shows that minorities are similarly less quoted in these important 'first definitions' of ethnic events. They will even be more rare as single speakers in such cases: *only in 3.8 per cent of all news items, is a quoted minority perspective given*. In other words, our theoretical predictions on news access of minorities seem to be confirmed by these figures on quotation frequencies.

Table 6.1 also shows that there are considerable differences between the newspapers. The *Guardian* generally quotes minorities (and majority groups!) much more often than the conservative Press, especially the *Telegraph* and the *Sun*, which generally have fewer quotes. The *Mail* not only has a rather high number of minority quotes, but also allows them to speak alone relatively often, which practically never happens (in 11 of 649 items!) in the *Telegraph*. The interpretation of these figures is difficult, however. Although there are some quality/popular and liberal/conservative effects, quotation patterns seem to be less directly related to these Press dimensions.

## Speakers and topics

The next question pertains to the topics majority and minority group actors are quoted about. Table 6.2 gives the frequencies of newspaper items about a specific topic. Since the items may be about more than one topic, these figures do not differentiate between quotes about different topics in one item, a problem that needs to be further examined in a more qualitative analysis.

In order to evaluate the frequency distributions, it is useful to keep in mind the overall proportions mentioned above: generally, majorities are

*Table 6.2* Quotation patterns per subject in five newspapers, August 1985–January 1986

| | | | | | | | |
|---|---|---|---|---|---|---|---|
| Min: | Number of items with minority quote | | | | | | |
| Maj: | Number of items with majority quote | | | | | | |
| Min+Maj: | Number of items with minority and majority quote | | | | | | |
| Min-: | Number of items with minority-only quote | | | | | | |
| Maj-: | Number of items with majority-only quote | | | | | | |
| Min-N: | Number of items with minority-only quote in news | | | | | | |
| Maj-N: | Number of items with majority-only quote in news | | | | | | |

| | Min | Maj | Min+Maj | Min- | Maj- | Min-N | Maj-N |
|---|---|---|---|---|---|---|---|
| Ethnic affairs | 13 | 28 | 1 | 12 | 27 | 8 | 18 |
| National policies, laws | 16 | 86 | 9 | 7 | 77 | 5 | 41 |
| Local policies | 23 | 59 | 16 | 7 | 43 | 6 | 28 |
| Politics, elections | 51 | 110 | 33 | 18 | 77 | 11 | 46 |
| Immigration, 'numbers' | 14 | 83 | 8 | 6 | 74 | 4 | 41 |
| 'Remigration' | 10 | 22 | 3 | 7 | 19 | 2 | 9 |
| Housing, first reception | 9 | 25 | 7 | 2 | 18 | 1 | 13 |
| Social affairs, dole | 0 | 10 | 0 | 0 | 9 | 0 | 6 |
| General facilities | 4 | 27 | 2 | 2 | 25 | 2 | 15 |
| Work, (un)employment | 15 | 42 | 8 | 7 | 34 | 5 | 25 |
| Education and schooling | 24 | 134 | 18 | 6 | 116 | 4 | 70 |
| Scientific research | 3 | 24 | 3 | 0 | 21 | 0 | 14 |
| Crime, police, justice | 72 | 237 | 61 | 11 | 176 | 5 | 107 |
| Illegality (of residence) | 2 | 6 | 1 | 1 | 5 | 1 | 4 |
| Drugs | 7 | 16 | 5 | 2 | 11 | 1 | 6 |
| Health | 1 | 3 | 1 | 0 | 2 | 0 | 1 |
| Religion, church | 19 | 18 | 10 | 9 | 8 | 3 | 4 |
| Media | 5 | 21 | 3 | 2 | 18 | 2 | 9 |
| Information, PR | 2 | 16 | 2 | 0 | 14 | 0 | 8 |
| Race relations (general) | 27 | 86 | 20 | 7 | 66 | 3 | 42 |
| Racism (general) | 26 | 67 | 20 | 6 | 47 | 3 | 25 |
| Discrimination | 25 | 64 | 17 | 8 | 47 | 6 | 35 |
| Prejudice(d) discourse | 20 | 115 | 19 | 1 | 96 | 1 | 57 |
| White racial attacks | 26 | 52 | 17 | 9 | 35 | 8 | 29 |
| Attacks by EM | 17 | 35 | 11 | 6 | 24 | 6 | 20 |
| Demonstration, protest | 36 | 54 | 25 | 11 | 29 | 7 | 23 |
| 'Riots', disturbances | 111 | 392 | 74 | 37 | 318 | 26 | 174 |
| Arts, literature, culture | 10 | 17 | 5 | 5 | 12 | 1 | 8 |
| Social–cultural differences | 12 | 16 | 3 | 9 | 12 | 1 | 3 |
| Sports | 10 | 19 | 5 | 5 | 14 | 3 | 10 |
| Human affairs, celebrities | 29 | 44 | 16 | 13 | 28 | 8 | 16 |
| Other | 16 | 39 | 13 | 3 | 26 | 2 | 16 |

speaking in about three times as many items as minority group members, whereas they appear as single speakers in about seven times as many items. Since for many topics the numbers are rather low, the differences here have no statistical significance, but only suggest tendencies that may be explored in further research.

Topics that seem to invite somewhat more frequent minority speakers are: ethnic affairs (where both groups seldom are quoted together!), politics (though seldom as single speakers), emigration, religion, discrimination (though much less as single speakers), racial attacks, demonstrations, the arts, cultural differences, and human affairs. For these topics minorities speak 'only' about half as much as majority group members. The cultural topics (religion, the arts, cultural differences) are the domain (politically relatively marginal) where minority voices are comparatively more prominent. Note however that most of these speaking occasions are relegated to less prominent background articles, and that the total number of items about culture is rather low.

Besides these cultural topics, we may expect to hear minorities especially in racial attacks, in which they are allowed to tell their experiences, and in various forms of social protest, in which they may occasionally tell about their grievances. Note though that they are permitted to speak alone in only seven news items about social protests. Although minorities sometimes appear as speakers in items about discrimination and racism, they will seldom appear as the only speakers in such cases. Finally, minority group members often speak in political news, for instance about the Black Sections in the Labour Party, a topic which is broadly covered by the media, and where Black Section representatives are probably quoted rather often because of their opposition to the Labour leaders. Indeed, this is not so much an 'ethnic' news topic, as a political one.

In absolute terms, minorities speak most often about the disturbances, but this is mainly due to the number of items about that topic. As single speakers, they appear less than an eighth of the times majority speakers do commenting upon the urban disorders. The same is true for minority speaking roles in crime and police affairs, where minorities however seldom speak alone, especially in the news, where majorities speak more than twenty times as often.

For most topics, majority group members also have a vast majority of speaking occasions. Since minority speakers are especially relegated to the realm of culture, protest, and racial attacks, we may expect the prominent news topics to be heavily biased towards white speakers, as is indeed the case. That is, we here find even larger discrepancies than above for such topics as national policies, immigration, housing, social affairs, education, general facilities, media, race relations, and prejudice.

In other words, these subjects are mostly the realm of white actors and speakers in the Press. Some of these differences are even more pronounced for single speaking roles, and for proper news items. Thus, of the many items about education (most of which are about the Honeyford affair), there are few (6) that show single minority speakers, as opposed to the number of items with only majority speakers (116). The same is true for items about crime and the police. Note that the proportion becomes truly dramatic for a topic such as prejudice, where we find *one single* minority speaker against nearly a *hundred* majority speakers! And although minorities often speak in (the few) arts items, as soon as such items become more prominent, that is current events news items, only a single minority speaker is left. In sum, ethnic minority groups are not only quoted much less often than whites, but also on less important topics, with the exception of the political topic of the Black Sections in the Labour Party. This discrepancy is especially remarkable for those topics for which minority groups may, by definition, be seen as experts, such as prejudice, racism and ethnic social affairs. In other words, if they are quoted at all, then it is mostly on 'safe' and marginal topics.

The frequencies for the different topics are too low to differentiate them further for the respective newspapers. *The Times* tends to have relatively more black speakers on politics, the *Mail* on the 'riots', and the *Guardian* on social and cultural affairs, as well as on racism (though seldom as single speakers).

## Minority speakers

Who of the minority groups is speaking most often? Instead of the number of items, we this time calculated the number of speaking events, so that one item may have several minority speakers. We saw that in 2,506 items there are 2,065 appearances of minority group members, of which most are West Indians (46 per cent) and South Asians (25 per cent), and minorities in general (39 per cent). Other groups appear as speakers in only a handful of events. Minorities in general are also speakers in about a seventh (103) of the events (703) in which they appear as actors. West Indians speak more often, that is, in under a third (207) of the events in which they appear as actors (755), whereas South Asians speak in about a fourth of the events (113 of 438 events), although Indians are quoted somewhat more often than Bangladeshis. It is striking that when Jews appear as ethnic actors, they are relatively more frequent speakers than other ethnic groups.

Again, there is a rather heterogeneous pattern of differences between the newspapers, which future research with larger bodies of data needs to detail and explain. Each newspaper appears to have its own preferred minority group as speaker. Thus, West Indians speak relatively more often in the *Guardian* and in the *Mail*, which however quote all groups more often. Despite its preference for Asians as news actors, the *Sun* quotes Asians less than West Indians, and the reverse is true for the *Telegraph*. If West Indians appear as actors in the news at all, the *Mail* and *The Times* will quote them more often than the other conservative papers. The few Jewish actors nearly always speak in the *Guardian* and never in the *Telegraph*. Other ethnic groups and new immigrants are seldom quoted in any newspaper.

Summarizing this quantitative study of quotation in the British Press, we thus find that in general minorities have less to say than majority group members, are seldom allowed to speak alone, speak on less prominent topics and in less prominent news genres such as current affairs reports. Below, we shall further examine these quotation patterns for a number of specific issues.


## THE DUTCH PRESS

Analysis of quotation patterns in the Dutch Press may provide some comparative data. Thus, we found that minorities appear as speakers in 481 (32 per cent), and majority groups in 1,135 (75 per cent) of the 1,513 ethnic news items we studied, figures that are similar to those of the British Press. Hence, in the Netherlands too the comments of minority groups on ethnic affairs are much less frequent than those of majority groups. As may be expected, there is a direct correlation between the frequency of specific issues and the number of speakers about these topics. That is, both minority and majority groups are quoted most often on immigration and discrimination. In both countries minority groups are allowed to speak relatively more often on cultural affairs. An interesting difference with the British Press, however, is that minorities in the Netherlands are also quoted quite often on discrimination issues (in more than 100 articles).

Blacks (Surinamese) are generally quoted more often than Turkish or Moroccan speakers: they account for 30 per cent of all quotes. Other ethnic minority groups are quoted very little, with the exception of Jews, as is also the case in the UK. As in Britain, there are interesting but erratic differences between the newspapers. Thus, the liberal *Volkskrant* clearly favours Surinamese over Turkish and Moroccan speakers, whereas leftist *Waarheid* has a preference for Turkish speakers. Like the tabloids in Britain, the right-wing *Telegraaf* quotes minorities even less than we might expect from its (low) percentage of news items about minorities, whereas the converse is true for the Amsterdam city newspaper *Parool*. Of the majority speakers, the authorities (government, judiciary, local government) are clearly by far the most frequent speakers. The government and ministries alone appear in 44 per cent of all items. White action groups are quoted only in 10 per cent of all items.

## SPECIAL TOPICS

The figures given above are very general, and characterize overall quotation patterns. In this last part of this chapter, therefore, we pay closer attention to the ways news actors appear as speakers in a number of specific cases reported in the British Press, namely, the Handsworth disturbance (156 items), the Honeyford affair (116), racial attacks (37), the Black Sections in the Labour Party (28), and affirmative action (21).

This focus on a few selected issues allows a more detailed quantitative and especially a qualitative analysis. For instance, for these issues we were also able to calculate the size of quotations. After all, minority and majority groups may get a different amount of space when they are quoted. Also, we examined whether speakers were identified by name or not, whether they are quoted in direct, indirect, or mixed direct-indirect mode, and what political background they had.

A first result of this analysis confirms earlier findings on the role of quotation in news reports: a large part of the news report appears to be about what people say, even for typical 'action news' such as that about racial attacks and the Handsworth disturbance.

Tables 6.3 and 6.4 give a first, quantitative, impression of the quotation patterns in the items on these issues. These figures first show again that minorities speak much less often (29 per cent) and less extensively (23 per cent) than majority speakers (71 and 77 per cent). As may be expected, the quality Press has more and longer quotes than the popular Press. The relatively high figures for the *Mail* are largely due to a series of opinion articles by Honeyford. Rather unexpected is the fact that liberal *Guardian* has few quotes on affirmative action, none of which by minority speakers. For most topics the *Sun* does not quote a single minority speaker.

Handsworth gives rise to many more quotes, also by minorities (the Asian shopkeepers), than the other issues. The items on affirmative action are virtually completely dominated by white (individual or institutional) speakers, with the exception of a long article in *The Times*. Although blacks speak more often than whites in the items on the Black Sections, the size of their intervention is still smaller than that of the quotes of whites. Although most quotes are direct, and most speakers are identified, minority speakers are more often anonymous, especially in the tabloids.

There are few differences among minority group speakers. Since most

Table 6.3 Frequency and size (in sq. cm) of quotes of minorities, per newspaper and topic

| | Times | | Guardian | | Telegraph | | Mail | | Sun | | All Papers | | Mean |
|---|---|---|---|---|---|---|---|---|---|---|---|---|---|
| | N | Size | N | Size | N | Size | N | Size | N | Size | N | Size | |
| Handsworth | 21 | 290 | 45 | 1,019 | 16 | 495 | 14 | 288 | 13 | 305 | 109 | 2,397 | 22.0 |
| Honeyford | 6 | 85 | 7 | 101 | 4 | 65 | 4 | 64 | 3 | 35 | 24 | 350 | 14.6 |
| Attacks | 5 | 128 | 15 | 421 | 6 | 108 | 2 | 38 | 0 | 0 | 28 | 695 | 24.8 |
| Affirmative action | 1 | 314 | 0 | 0 | 1 | 17 | 0 | 0 | 0 | 0 | 2 | 331 | 165.5 |
| Black Sections | 10 | 133 | 8 | 179 | 8 | 176 | 5 | 60 | 0 | 0 | 31 | 548 | 17.7 |
| All topics | 43 | 950 | 75 | 1,720 | 35 | 861 | 25 | 450 | 16 | 340 | 194 | 4,321 | 22.3 |

Table 6.4 Frequency and size (in sq. cm) of quotes of majorities, per newspaper and topic

| | Times | | Guardian | | Telegraph | | Mail | | Sun | | All Papers | | Mean |
|---|---|---|---|---|---|---|---|---|---|---|---|---|---|
| | N | Size | N | Size | N | Size | N | Size | N | Size | N | Size | |
| Handsworth | 57 | 2,092 | 46 | 1,676 | 54 | 1,827 | 38 | 1,060 | 30 | 403 | 225 | 7,958 | 35.4 |
| Honeyford | 36 | 621 | 39 | 531 | 32 | 477 | 23 | 2,066 | 12 | 228 | 142 | 3,923 | 27.6 |
| Attacks | 13 | 171 | 22 | 437 | 11 | 234 | 4 | 20 | 0 | 0 | 50 | 862 | 17.2 |
| Affirmative action | 14 | 267 | 8 | 267 | 9 | 181 | 2 | 28 | 6 | 49 | 39 | 792 | 20.3 |
| Black Sections | 4 | 97 | 3 | 249 | 7 | 305 | 3 | 36 | 1 | 21 | 18 | 708 | 39.3 |
| All topics | 124 | 3,248 | 118 | 3,160 | 113 | 3,024 | 70 | 3,210 | 49 | 701 | 474 | 14,243 | 30.0 |

minority actors in British news are men, it is not surprising that they are quoted most often: black leaders, politicians, and businessmen. Female speakers are heard occasionally in personalized background reports on racial attacks.

The majority quotation patterns are much more varied. Most of the categories we have discussed earlier do not appear as speakers for these five isssues. Most prominent as direct (literally quoted) speakers about these four issues are the police, Members of Parliament, teachers (Honeyford), the ministries, city administrations, city councils, and Labour representatives. As may be expected, the longest quotes come from the authorities (police, ministers). Again, most of these speakers are men.

We might expect political variation in the frequencies and sizes of (white) speakers among the different newspapers. However, in most (66 per cent) quotations the political background of the speakers is either irrelevant or unknown. Tories are quoted in 15.4 per cent of the quotes and Labour members in 13.5 per cent of the quotes. The conservative speakers are slightly more frequent in the conservative Press (especially in the *Sun*) and Labour somewhat more prominent in the *Guardian*.

## Some qualitative observations

With the general observation in mind that minorities are generally quoted less often and less extensively on the topics selected, we should finally ask ourselves *how* various groups or actors are being quoted for different topics in different newspapers. After all, a paper may quote an actor in many different ways, for instance by describing the person in a negative, neutral, or positive way, and especially by presenting the words of the speakers in a more or less favourable or credible way. Who exactly is quoted from minority or majority groups, and are their statements pitched against each other, or independent? What, indeed, are the speakers allowed to say, and do such quotation contents support the general evaluation of the newspaper of the events or issues? Let us examine some of these properties for the respective special topics and newspapers.

### *Affirmative action*

Affirmative action, the issue which is probably most relevant for ethnic minority groups and future race relations, is dealt with in only 21 articles, mostly in *The Times* and *Telegraph*. Usually only white politicians and representatives of employers' organizations are allowed to speak on this topic, which mostly deals with a mild form of contract compliance. Only *The Times*, in a series of articles on employment for blacks, quotes the point of view of the Jamaican Chief of Project Fullemploy, Linbert Spencer, about this issue. The rest of the discussion is between employment and interior ministers, and Tory MPs, on the one hand, and a few quotes of CRE chairman Peter Newsam, on the other hand. The tentative idea of contract compliance is ventured in a speech by Home Secretary David Waddington, after an earlier report by the CRE, but most reactions, including those of the employment ministers, are very negative about this idea, and the ministry hastens to withdraw the plan.

The *Guardian*, though expressing its support for contract compliance in an outspoken editorial, has only a few articles about the topic. It is the only newspaper that, besides quoting the negative reactions of the Building Employers Conferation (BEC) and the Confederation of British Industry (CBI), also quotes positive experiences with the code of practice of the Greater London Council with contract compliance.

The *Mail*, in a single small article briefly mentions a split among Tories about affirmative action. It only quotes two negative reactions, including that by junior employment minister Alan Clark, which confirms the general position of the right-wing Press: "Our commitment is to equal opportunities, regardless of race. This means equal treatment but not special or preferential treatment." (*Mail*, 15 October). That is, in the usual disclaimer, equal opportunities are of course favoured, but concrete measures to remedy past inequality and to urge employers to employ blacks, are described as unacceptable "preferential treatment".

The *Sun*, in an editorial, is adamant in its rejection of any kind of affirmative action, and calls the ministry's tentative plan a "massive blunder", using, for example, the unfounded argument that affirmative action didn't work in the USA. The *Sun* doesn't want "packs of government snoopers to be put in companies" and implies that only ability, not race, should be used as a criterion for employment. In its short report about the issue, it quotes, in emphasizing italics, right-wing Tory Harvey Proctor, banned from giving a controversial speech on the topic, as saying: "People are sick and tired of all this race relations mumbo-jumbo", as well as the opposing employment minister (Clarke) and the industry bosses. Neither the *Sun*, nor the *Mail*, has a single voice (let alone a black voice) speaking in favour of government compliance, not even the official CRE. In other words, quotes are here selected according to the view of the newspaper, which as we have seen before, means that any form of positive action must be rejected.

The *Telegraph* has more about this issue (5 articles). It refers first to an SDP report favouring contract compliance, and only quotes SDP leaders Owen and Williams in favour of this measure. The same is true for a later article about a CRE report which is critical about employers, also quoting a critical passage from the report. When the plans of the Home Office are launched around mid-October, the *Telegraph* quotes the arguments by David Waddington in favour of contract compliance – and no opposed voices. However, a few weeks later, after another mild plan for affirmative action by the Ministry of Employment, it extensively quotes Tory MPs and captains of industry against these ideas – also using the argument that "the best person should get the job". In the previous chapter, we have already analysed in detail the argumentation in the *Telegraph*'s editorial of 1 August about a discrimination report by the CRE, in which this newspaper firmly rejects any kind of monitoring ("no snoopers").

*The Times* has most about affirmative action (11 articles). The Home Office "controversial" plans are briefly presented by David Waddington, who, however, at the same time is quoted as saying: "I don't think we can have reverse discrimination in this country." The Thatcher government doesn't want anything to do with fixed quotas, nor with other constraints on employers. The Ministry of Employment, represented by Alan Clark, rejects the plans and is reported to call them "degrading to blacks" – a common ploy in the rejection of affirmative action – and an unacceptable "burden" and "intrusion" for business. In other words, the quotations and speakers selected by *The Times* mainly undermine the idea of contract compliance or fully reject it. There are no speakers in favour of this kind of affirmative action in these early reports, let alone leaders of the black community. One day later, on 17 October, however, proponents of contract compliance, a GLC representative and CRE chair Peter Newsam, are quoted in a background report, emphasizing that the code of practice conforms to earlier legislation of the Tory government. Parts of these quotations are also defensive, and stress that there is no question of "reverse discrimination" or quotas: only proper records are to be kept. The race relations correspondent of *The Times* adds that the "more aggressive contract policies" in the USA have certainly worked (a point simply denied by the *Sun*, as we saw above), and that most US companies now fully endorse them. The fact of persistent discrimination in employment in the UK is also stressed by this correspondent.

In mid-November *The Times* publishes a series of special reports about black unemployment and various training and employment schemes. These reports extensively quote proponents of affirmative action, after an earlier opinion article by Labour MP Jack Straw, who provides counter-arguments against those who oppose contract compliance. Besides other topics, the issue of discrimination is dealt with. Several young people are presented who tell about their work experiences. Also presented is the "radical philosphy", as defended by the director of Project Fullemploy, who is interviewed at length. A black journalist, Syd Burke, finally, is allowed to give his opinion in a separate article. In another article, reporting the reactions to such special training schemes in the business community, only positive experiences are quoted. In other words, more than the other papers during this period, *The Times* pays extensive attention to black employment, and also quotes proponents of "radical" or "controversial" measures such as affirmative action. The main thrust and focus, however, is on practical schemes that are attractive to the business community. Daily discrimination experienced by minorities on the job or while looking for employment are hardly detailed.

## Racial attacks

The quotation patterns in the 37 reports about racial attacks are rather uniform. Again, the quality Press, and especially the *Guardian* (with 14 items), has most on this topic, which is only briefly reported in the tabloids. On the whole, as we have observed before, racial attacks, mostly against Asian families, are condemned by all newspapers, although the right-wing Press is less critical of the lack or inadequacy of police protection about which most Asian speakers complain. There are four groups of speakers here: the Asian victims, representatives of minority organizations, the police, and national or local politicians. Majority group members, however, speak on 50 occasions, and minority group members on only 28 occasions.

We have seen that the *Guardian* publishes most on racial attacks, and also quotes the victims most often. However, this newspaper also allows the police to give their own opinion: "[The] officers have made strenuous efforts to stamp out racially-inspired offences", and quotes the police claim that such attacks are difficult to "target" (a point denied in a quote from CRE chairman Peter Newsam). Also the positive role of the police is sometimes emphasized, for example, in the headline "POLICE SAVE ASIANS". In another report it quotes the president of the local Pakistan Welfare Society, criticizing the police, and a Labour MP urging the introduction of new laws against racial harassment. The chair of the Commons Select Committee on Race Relations, John Wheeler, is quoted on what he calls "these so-called racial attacks", reassuring a visiting Pakistani minister. At the same time, Wheeler lashes out at the "extremism of the left wing of the Labour Party in London which preached aggression against the police", which he found "equally evil" as the extremism of the far right, thereby reducing the seriousness of extremist attacks. Thus, although the *Guardian* is the only paper which occasionally lets the victims detail the gruesome nature of racial attacks in the UK, such quotations are usually limited to background articles and often balanced by the views of the police and the politicians who provide the primary definitions of the attacks in the proper news reports.

The tabloids do report racial attacks, but only very briefly. The *Mail* has a handful of items, in two of which an Indian family is allowed to report about its experiences, all in 10 sq. cm of column space. The *Sun* has one single article, and doesn't quote anybody. Its critical editorial on racial attacks does not seem to be reflected in extensive reporting about these attacks, as is generally the case for right-wing racial crime.

The *Telegraph* has several (10) items on racial attacks, of which the first features community leaders or other Asian spokesmen, as well as the police. The later articles are all about the political implications of the attacks, and only quote the police and various national and local politicians. There are only two Asian speakers, a community spokesman, and a restaurant owner, who are briefly quoted in direct mode. There are no extensive interviews with the victims. Note that the ambivalent position of the police also shows up in the reports. The attacks are said to "increase the fears that racial extremists are behind the recent spate of fires" (12 August), and the statement by community leaders is presented as a "claim that there have been at least 20 attacks on Asian families". After so many attacks against Asian families, Scotland Yard is reported as saying "We have an open mind as to the motives, but so far there is nothing to suggest that it was racist." We see that the general strategy of the denial of racism, which we have encountered many times in our analysis of reporting about race, is even extended to these cases of violent right-wing crime. For the police and the right-wing Press, the victims' race was probably only a coincidence.

*The Times* has only a few items on the attacks. As with the rest of the conservative Press, most of these articles are fairly short, and do not seem to signal that these attacks are a serious threat and a national scandal. There is one, slightly longer, background article by race relations correspondent Pat Healy (13 August), in which a Bangladeshi man and a Bengali girl are briefly quoted, besides Home Office and CRE officials and a white action group. Two days later a call by 50 Asian community leaders and the Black Sections of the Labour Party is reported in indirect statements, also accompanied by a direct police statement saying that the Asians "had been unwilling to listen to the police point of view" – which was that the attacks are very difficult to tackle. Again, there are no extensive background interviews with victims, and few descriptions of the viciousness of the attacks.

Concluding, we find that even in the case of racial attacks, where the experiences and the opinions of a large group of Asians are obvious, most of the conservative Press either does not pay extensive attention to these forms of racial crimes, or tends to limit its reporting to "police and politics" reporting, which emphasizes the viewpoints and the actions of the authorities. The accusations of the victims about lack of serious police action are occasionally mentioned, but not detailed further or investigated. There are virtually no reports which only present the views or experiences of Asian people. If such opinions or experiences are described they are mostly accompanied by comments of the police or the authorities. Only the *Guardian*, which also reports the police position, presents several larger background accounts of the experiences and views of the victims. After the racial attacks during the summer of 1985, there is virtually no follow-up. Apparently, as is the case for the Thatcher government and the police, the issue has no priority for the Press. Indeed, the victims are 'only Asians', and the attackers white.

## Black Sections

The issue of the Black Sections in the Labour Party is the only one that has more black (31) than white (18) speakers in 28 articles. However, white speakers are given more space to state their opinions, mostly in direct statements, whereas blacks are usually reported in an indirect mode. The tabloids hardly report about this political issue, and most items can be found in *The Times* and the *Guardian*, although the *Telegraph*'s reports are usually longer.

These political reports have many fewer quotes than those about other topics. Even in the *Guardian*, Black Section representatives seldom get the occasion to explain their position in detail. Together, they get two dozen column centimetres in a series of news items. BS chair Sharon Atkin is quoted (in indirect and mixed mode) only twice with a few lines of text. Labour leader Hattersley, however, opposed to Black Sections, gets 41 column centimetres in a single article wholly devoted to his opinion (24 September).

Whereas Hattersley is also prominent in the handful of reports in the *Mail* about the BS, there are also two reports that – briefly – quote black "activists", such as Sharma, Profitt, Beloff, and Atkin. However, they are never allowed to speak alone: there is always an official Labour reaction in the same article. We have found only one article in the *Sun* about Black Sections, in which only Hattersley is quoted. The *Telegraph* is more varied, like the *Mail*, and on the one hand publishes a long interview with Hattersley, but also has a few reports with opinions of BS leaders, most of which are quoted indirectly and very briefly, except in a longer report of 1 October about the Labour Conference, at which the BS proposals were defeated. In that report, black and and Asian women delegates, who remain anonymous, are presented as "shouting 'rubbish'" at Hattersley defending his position. Among the several minority speakers at that conference, Sharon Atkin, delegate from Streatham, is quoted most extensively, criticizing Roy Hattersley and the general Labour refusal to recognize Black Sections. Most of these quotes, as is usual in conference reports, are direct. Except for the long article on Hattersley's position, then, the *Telegraph's* reporting about the Black Sections gives predominant space to Black Section representatives.

The same is true for reporting in *The Times*, which quotes Hattersley and Kinnock only once, and black "leaders", "activists", or "organizers" more often, though succinctly, and in rather brief reports. A long earlier report on 21 August on the "Black Power Battle Facing Labour", focuses on "handsome" BS leader Russell Profitt (picture added). Much of this report, however, does only deal indirectly with the Black Sections, and only three other blacks are briefly quoted in it.

Comparing the quotation patterns in the respective newspapers, we find that the conservative Press gives more voice to Black Section representatives than the *Guardian*, which favours official Labour statements. Most of the Press, however, tends to single out Hattersley as the main speaker for Labour, and may give him a full-length interview. Black Section representatives are quoted briefly, and in rather short reports. The detailed position of the Black Section movement hardly comes across. Only in a *Telegraph* report on the Labour Conference, some BS representatives are quoted in a more direct and extensive manner. We have interpreted these results before as a consequence of the general anti-Labour position of the conservative Press (and hence of the Labour orientation of the *Guardian*), which sees the BS not so much as an interesting and serious contribution to racial equality in the political arena, but rather as a source of conflict in the Labour Party. In other words, quotation patterns do seem to have a clear political implication in this case. However, the overall result is that most of the Press is much less negative about the Black Sections than about other minority movements. The *Sun* is an exception: it hardly reports about the issue, and is furious when a black woman (Diane Abbott) unseats an older, white, Labour candidate. With three other black candidates (Grant, Vaz, and Boateng) she was elected to Parliament in 1987.

## Handsworth

With 334 quotes in 156 articles, the Handsworth events produce most 'words' for the Press. We have seen that even in such typically non-verbal conflicts as civil disturbances, discourse soon overrides descriptions of events, which soon lose their interest for the Press, also because these visual images are extensively shown on television (for the role of television in the 1981 disturbances, see Tumber, 1982; Wren-Lewis, 1981–2). Talk after Handsworth essentially involves three groups of speakers: primarily the police, then the national and local politicians, and finally the Asian victims of the disorders, the shop-owners. Occasionally, black leaders and some participants in the disturbances are heard, but their opinion, for instance about the causes of the urban disorders, does not count: they might support the view, emphatically rejected by the conservative Press, that social policy of the Thatcher regime, the situation in the ghetto, and racist policing are the real causes and contexts of the disturbances. Such views, as well as those of "soft-headed" sociologists supporting them, may not be heard, let alone legitimated by quotation, being outside of the conservative consensus. Even including the voices of the Asian shopkeepers, presented as victims of the blacks, and therefore interesting witnesses of "black violence", whites have more than twice as many speaking events (225) in the Handsworth coverage than minority group members (109), and get more than three times as much space to give their opinions.

As is the case in the other newspapers, the *Guardian* quotes many people in its coverage of the Handsworth disturbances, first of all the police and the politicians, such as Geoffrey Dear, Chief Constable of the West Midlands, Home Secretary Hurd, Labour leaders Kinnock and Kaufman, SPD chair Shirley Williams, and Prime Minister Thatcher. The message of both the police and the conservative politicians is clear and quoted accordingly. Hurd defines the disturbances as "not a social phenomenon but [as] crimes", and Dear speaks of "a bloodlust orgy of thieving", evaluations that are rejected by community leaders. Thatcher and conservative MPs expectedly deny unemployment to be a cause of the disturbances, whereas Labour and SPD leaders emphasize that unemployment and urban deprivation, exacerbated by conservative policies, are among its major causes. However, the *Guardian* also talks to more direct participants, such as black youths, including "self-confessed" drug dealers, who on the whole blame a change in policing policy, a claim immediately denied by Geoffrey Dear, who at the same time rejects any social causes for the disturbances. That the *Guardian* also favours a more social explanation of the disturbances shows in its choice of employment specialists, community leaders and others who – albeit briefly – explain their opinions about the local situation.

A day later, the *Guardian* talks with the Asian shopkeepers, who in this interview do not accuse black youths or other rioters, but the police tactics in responding to the disorders. The myth of rivalry between West Indians and Asians, created by the right-wing Press, is prominently denied in the headlines and quotations of a report with interviews conducted by race relations correspondent David Rose. Even the shopkeepers whose shops were destroyed by fire or violence are named and quoted as saying "There has never been any hatred between the communities ... We have always regarded ourselves as brothers here" (12 September). Rather unusual, finally, is a *Guardian* commentary about the coverage of the disturbances by the tabloids, which supports the conservative definition of the disturbances in terms of crime, while spreading the story about why "the West Indians hate the Asians". A long report by Leslie Anthony Goffe, in which he quotes many local people, both West Indian and Asian, shows again that these allegations by the right-wing Press are based on statements of only a few Asian shopkeepers, and that among the – often participating – youths, who are extensively quoted, this "rivalry" is categorically denied. We conclude that the *Guardian* on the one hand clearly provides access to the authorities, including the police, to make their point, especially in the proper news stories, but that it also tries to make the voices heard of blacks, Indians, youths, and others directly involved in the local situation.

In *The Times*, we find primarily the authorities as speakers (the police, Tory politicians, fire officers, coroners, judges, and scholars) and virtually no detailed statements by black leaders, immediate participants, or even the Asian shopkeepers. If their opinions are represented at all, it is through the mouths of white representatives. In the initial reports there are some unnamed witnesses and the same Muslim community leader quoted as in the other papers. When *The Times* investigates the causes of the disturbances it displays conflicting evidence as is also shown in its title "DRUGS AND POOR POLICING BLAMED FOR VIOLENCE IN BIRMINGHAM" (11 September). If occasionally the critical opinion of a black leader (for example, Gus Williams) is quoted, it is soon 'balanced' by another view. As in the other papers, Rastafarian Nigel Heath is quoted in an item on Rastafarian co-operation with the police. The only article with a critical opinion, dealing with the social background of the disturbance, is by Labour MP Clare Short, soon balanced again by professor of sociology Laurie Taylor, who presents a less political, academic, view of the nature of urban violence.

The *Telegraph* has the most extensive coverage of the Handsworth events (43 articles). Essentially the same speakers are again on the scene, first the police, then the local and national politicians, and finally some more direct participants. In a longer report on the "nightmare" with statements of local people, we primarily hear shopkeepers and an occasional black youth. The next day, further interviews with shopkeepers and other local business people excludes blacks altogether. When the police seem to make a deal (which they denied) with Rastafarians to cool the situation, Nigel Heath is interviewed at length, thus providing one of the few statements from those directly involved. Like *The Times*, the *Telegraph* emphasizes the views of the white authorities, but unlike *The Times* it occasionally also lets Asian shopkeepers speak. With a few exceptions, black people are virtually absent as speakers.

Like the other newspapers, the *Mail* interviews the chair of of the Muslim Welfare Defence Council (Mr Zaman) and later, even more extensively, Mr Heath, the Rastafarian. Most other articles have few or no quotes and, if so, will tend to have as speakers the authorities, such as Dear, and politicians. There are however some quotes from shopkeepers. In a typical 'sphere' piece of the local Rastafarian scene, Rastas are quoted when patrolling the streets, but their presentation in that report is hardly serious and is clearly intended to ridicule their activities. Black leaders are hardly heard.

The *Sun* quotes even less, while also beginning with the generally quoted local Muslim leader. Again, as in the *Mail*, Rastafarian Heath is interviewed at length, but in the rest of the coverage black people, usually unnamed, tend to be quoted in a single line. The short reports of the *Sun* hardly leave room for much commentary. Only a few politicians are quoted in a few articles, and it is generally the police that are being heard. A few shopkeepers, in a single report, are speakers and are given exactly 1 centimetre of (3.5 cm wide) *Sun* columns.

Concluding, we see that the British Press publishes dozens of reports on the Handsworth events, but that, with the exception of the *Guardian*, these events are virtually only seen, described, and explained by the white authorities, most of whom defend the criminal interpretation of the cause of the disturbances. Occasionally, local people are being interviewed, but these are mostly shopkeepers, and their comments are mostly limited to their concrete experiences during the disorders. Authoritative black leaders or scholars are virtually absent as speakers. With the exception of the *Guardian*, there is no attempt even to investigate alternative, social interpretations of the disturbances, although *The Times* allows more variation in expressed opinions and publishes a comment by a Labour MP.

## Honeyford

The quotation patterns of the Honeyford conflict are rather different. On the whole, and rather unexpectedly for such a typical 'opinion event', there is not so much talk in these reports. Declarations are predominantly made by white officials, such as city representatives, teachers, lawyers or judges, and of course by Honeyford himself. The participating minority groups, such as the protesting Asian parents, are described as protesters, but seldom interviewed and quoted. Only their slogans or leaflets make it to the papers. In the 166 speaking events, only 24 show non-white speakers, who have a tenth of the speaking space of whites, although the main opposition figure, Jenny Woodward, who is white and heading the action committee against Honeyford, is among those most often quoted. The reports are generally brief, as are also the quotes, which are seldom longer than 5 column centimetres. Few interventions deal with the substance of the controversy, Honeyford's racist statements on multi-cultural education, but focus on the immediate actions in the controversy, such as court proceedings and the administrative aspects of firing the controversial headmaster.

The *Guardian* focuses on these legal and administrative aspects of the conflict, quoting lawyers, Honeyford's union (NAHT) representatives, and several representatives of the Bradford administration and city council. However, on several occasions it also quotes members of the action committee, especially Ms Woodward and protesting governor and Labour councillor Mr Goldberg, at least on a dozen speaking occasions. These speaking events typically take place "on the street", and are seldom longer statements of principle as would be made in in-depth interviews. Honeyford himself is only quoted a few times, as is generally the case in these reports.

A similar pattern can be found in *The Times*: most quotes are by officials, such as those of the Bradford administration and city council and lawyers. Honeyford's opponents, the parents' group and Jenny Woodward, are quoted only a few times. In a longer background article, in which *The Times* leaves no doubt about its position in the Honeyford case, there is a passage with quotes from a more formal interview with parents and other opponents of Honeyford. One of those is black researcher Olivia Foster Carter, who is presented as "having no children at the school", and who is first quoted as denouncing Third World education at the school, as well as rejecting Shakespeare as being racist before she is allowed to summarize her objections against Honeyford. There are no further detailed quotes of those who oppose Honeyford, beyond this fragment of a clearly negative background article about the protest movement ("Honeyford is not a racist unless the word is defined to mean only 'someone of whom an anti-racist disapproves'".)

The *Telegraph* quotes the opponents of Honeyford even less: a few lines for Asian leaders, Jenny Woodward, and councillor Goldberg; the other (few) lines of quotes are for the officials already mentioned above.

The *Mail* is among the staunchest defenders of Honeyford. It is not surprising, therefore, that it quotes him most often and most extensively.

Honeyford even has the extraordinary opportunity to state his case in three page-long articles, which also are the reason that the *Mail* has the highest average length of articles on the Honeyford affair. The relatively few other quotes are from the Bradford city officials mentioned above. Honeyford's opponents are barely quoted. A single article, in which these opponents are headlined as a "mob of Left-Wing crazies", presents Jenny Woodward as the "white leader of a mob of Asian activists", and quotes an anonymous bystander about her as saying "There was just a cold viciousness about her", whereas Asian protesters are described as "chattering noisily". We see that quotation and description here go hand-in-hand in an attempt to discredit Honeyford's opponents. There is not even a semblance of journalistic balance and objectivity here.

The *Sun*, finally, quotes even less, not more than a dozen speakers. Honeyford is hardly quoted, but a – for the *Sun* – fairly long article extensively quotes, without further comments, "single parent" Jenny Woodward and her ideas, though hardly presenting her in a favourable light: "She is the woman fomenting the bitter race row at a Bradford school". An inserted article, summarizing what Honeyford wrote, speaks however of Honeyford's "thoughtful piece" in the *Salisbury Review*. Later the *Sun* proposes its readers "make up their own mind" about Honeyford, by quoting, again without further comment, the major charges against Honeyford, and quoting, of course rather selectively, "what he had really said". In other words, the readers of the *Sun* will have no doubt about the position of this newspaper, also advocated in several editorials, but on the other hand, at least they are able to read the opinions of Honeyford's opponents, who have little opportunity to talk in the rest of the right-wing Press.

## Conclusions

This chapter has shown that minority group members are quoted less often and less extensively than majority group members, even when the topics directly concern them, and even if there are minority experts available to give an opinion. That is, this chapter further confirms the general thesis that the media tend to marginalize ethnic minorities. The quotation patterns show that they have literally little to say. The white authorities, especially the police and the politicians, are the major speakers defining the ethnic siutuation. Most conspicuously absent as speakers are representatives of important minority organisations and black leaders, except when they are critical of the political opponent, as is the case in the conservative Press in its reporting of the Black Sections. If minorities are quoted at all, then it is mostly on 'safe' or marginal subjects, for example, on culture, and much less on topics that are negative for whites, such as prejudice and discrimination. Ordinary people are briefly quoted, especially when they are victims, and only when they tell about personal experiences: they are seldom allowed to voice fundamental criticism of the authorities. A closer analysis of the quotation patterns of some major stories showed finally that in general the selection of speakers is partisan: journalists tend to quote those speakers who voice the position of the newspaper. Newsworthy ideological opponents may also occasionally be quoted, however, although in that case with the usual 'scare' quotes or other distance markers. Despite these strategies of journalistic 'distancing', we also found that even in biased reports speakers are generally presented in a rather neutral way, that is, without positive or negative comments. We assume that professional routines in that case may override ideological positions of the journalists.

# 7    Meanings and ideologies

## RACISM AND MEANING: AN EXAMPLE

The previous chapters dealt with the global meanings (topics) and global forms (schemata) of news reports about ethnic affairs. In this and the next chapter we focus on the 'local' or 'micro' levels of news discourse, that is, the meaning, style, and rhetoric of its actual words and sentences. This chapter deals with the structures and strategies of the local meaning of news discourses and their underlying ideological framework. To get a first impression of the many dimensions of meaning and ideology involved, consider the following passage from an editorial about immigration in a British tabloid newspaper:

> That is why we have to be more brisk in saying no, and showing the door to those who are not British citizens and would abuse our hospitality and tolerance. To do that is not to give way to prejudice, but to lessen the provocation on which it feeds. (*Mail*, 28 November 1985)

In this defence and legitimation of strict immigration laws and practices, the *Mail* uses meaning structures and strategies that are quite frequent in right-wing discourse on ethnic affairs. A first major feature of this passage is that it *presupposes* that 'we [British] are hospitable and tolerant'. That is, the editorial does not assert this to be the case, but simply assumes that this is true. Presuppositions used in this way are an often-used strategic means to conceal controversial claims and are less easy to challenge by an uncritical reader than a straightforward assertion. Also, such presuppositions are often an expression of an underlying ideology, in this case about the characteristics of the white British.

The second prominent meaning strategy appears in the next sentence, which *denies* an implicit accusation, that is, that "showing the door to those who are not British" could be seen as a form of prejudice. Such denials, which are usually followed by *but*, as is also the case here, are one of the most typical disclaimers that characterize the meaning structure of racist discourse. Their aim is to combine a positive self-presentation of the speaker or writer ('I'm no racist'), with a negative presentation of another group. Note that this same sentence also features a presupposition, that is, the claim that prejudice is 'provoked'. This use of 'provoked' *implies* that white British are not naturally prejudiced, but that their prejudice is due to immigrants 'who abuse [British] tolerance'. Apart from *denying* or *doubting* that the British are prejudiced, this claim at the same time *blames the victim* of prejudice, the immigrants.

Thirdly, immigrants are further portrayed in a *negative* way by the use of the verb "to abuse", which also indirectly presupposes that immigrants do indeed abuse British tolerance. At the same time, this use of 'abuse' establishes a *contrast* between the negative properties of the abuser and the good ones of the 'tolerant' British.

Fourthly, consider the use of "those who are not British citizens". This description of foreigners or immigrants *suggests* that the *Mail* only advocates strict immigration rules for people without a British passport, which would be an 'objective' criterion. However, since the notions of 'tolerance' and 'prejudice' are used, it is more likely, given the rest of the coverage in the *Mail*, that this tabloid actually means *non-white* immigrants, since it never speaks out against immigrating EC or US citizens. Conversely, the *Mail* would (and actually does) object to the immigration of non- white Commonwealth citizens, even if they do have (or had) British passports. In other words, the suggestion of an objective criterion 'conceals' the true meanings intended by this tabloid, meanings which may be *inferred* from other words in this passage as well as from other *Mail* coverage.

Finally, throughout this passage we find several other examples of *euphemism*, such as "brisk", "showing the door" and "prejudice", all applied to the British. Within a more critical perspective, these properties could also be described as 'hard' (or 'harsh'), 'throwing out', and 'racism', respectively. However, the choice of such words would hardly be flattering for the self-image of the British as represented by the *Mail*.

We see that an informal discussion of such a short passage already uncovers many different aspects of meaning, such as presuppositions, implications, inferences, concealments, euphemisms, disclaiming denials, blaming the victim, negativization, and in general the combined strategy of positive self-presentation and negative other-presentation. Many of these semantic features involve various forms of implicitness or indirectness. At the same time, these structures and strategies appear to be rather directly related to the ideological opinions and attitudes of this right-wing newspaper about white British and non-white immigrants. It is the aim of this chapter to systematically examine these and other structures and strategies of meaning and to relate these to the ethnic opinions, attitudes, or ideologies of journalists, for instance by making explicit what they leave implicit.

## Semantics and discourse

There is a vast literature in linguistics, philosophy, logic, psychology, and the social sciences about the rather elusive notion of meaning (Lyons, 1977). The kind of theory in these disciplines that deals with meaning is called a 'semantic' theory. For our informal analysis only a few semantic notions will be relevant, however. First, we make a distinction between an abstract and a more empirical account of the concept of meaning. The abstract description, which is typical for linguistics and philosophy, deals with meaning in terms of 'propositions'. A proposition is a conceptual structure which consists of a predicate and one or more arguments. Thus the predicate 'clashed with' may be combined with the arguments 'the police' and 'West Indian youths' to form the proposition 'The police clashed with black youths.' Each sentence of a text may express one or more of such propositions. The more empirical account of meaning focuses on the actual cognitive processes of understanding of the readers: how do readers 'assign' a meaning to a sentence? What is the result of such a process of 'interpretation', and what mental strategies do readers use to arrive at such an interpretation?

The semantics of discourse is not limited to the meanings of isolated words and sentences, however, but also focuses on the ways such meanings are combined with each other (van Dijk, 1977, 1985d). Thus, if meaningful sentences are combined with each other in a meaningful sequence, we say that this sequence is 'coherent'. Whereas the notion of topic discussed in Chapter four deals with the global, or macro-coherence of a text, we here find its counterpart at the micro-level of the text: local coherence. Basically, a text is locally coherent if its propositions are about situations, events, or actions that have specific relations among each other, for instance a temporal or causal relation. Thus, the proposition 'Many people were wounded' is coherent with the previous proposition 'The police clashed with the demonstrators', simply because getting hurt is a possible consequence of a clash with the police.

For our discussion these coherence relations are particularly interesting because local coherence depends on our knowledge and other beliefs about society. What for a journalist is a coherent sequence may be less coherent for some readers. For instance, we have seen earlier that for the conservative Press one of the causes of the riots was the 'criminal greed' of the rioters, a causal explanation that may be rejected by others.

Thus, an analysis of the meanings and coherence relations in discourse allows us to infer the beliefs of the speaker or writer about causal or other relations in society, beliefs which in turn are based on general knowledge, attitudes, and ideologies.

Another aspect of the analysis of meanings is not directly based on such references to the 'facts' or the conditional relations between these facts, but on relations between the propositions themselves. For instance, one proposition may be an implication, a specification, a generalization, or a contrast with respect to a previous proposition.

## PERSPECTIVE

An important feature of discourse meaning is perspective: from which point of view are events and actions described? Does the speaker or writer sympathize with one news actor or rather with another? Theoretically, perspective is not easy to characterize, especially since there are many ways in which writers may be more or less identifying themselves with the position or opinions of the people they write about. Much earlier work on perspective or point of view has been done in literary scholarship (see, for example, Prince, 1982). Perspective in discourse is expressed by various textual signals. Thus, to express a spatial point of view, we may use different verbs, as in 'He *came* into the office' as against 'He *went* into the office', where the observer is in or outside the office. As the double meaning of the word 'point of view' suggests, the choice of a specific perspective may however also imply an opinion, as is often the case in press reporting about ethnic affairs, for instance in the following example that could be applied to the Honeyford case: "The teacher was suspended because of his racist writings" as against 'The teacher was suspended because he was telling the truth about ethnic difficulties at school.'

Perspective is both a local and a global feature of semantics. That is, it is not just expressed by a single word or sentence, but rather by the ways people and their actions (or talk) are described throughout a whole text. Many of the other semantic structures and strategies to be discussed below also imply a specific perspective.

The examples chosen to illustrate the semantics of perspective are chosen from one of the most prominent cases of biased perspective, at least in the conservative Press, that is, the attitudes in the Honeyford affair. The point of view in the description is very clearly that of Honeyford and his supporters, and massively against those who oppose him. There is not even an attempt at objectivity here, and the beliefs or goals of his opponents are never presented in a neutral way, if at all.

In order to provide the necessary interpretation context for each example given below, the text fragments are preceded by a short summary of the topic or event. Text fragments that are omitted are signaled by '...'. Generally, comments between parentheses are our summaries or explanations of context. The part of the fragment that is focused on is in italics. Only in the editorials of the *Sun*, which is replete with italics, bold type, and capitals, is there a potential for conflict with the original text, but we here ignore the 'graphics' of the original, and focus on content.

(Honeyford) *Noisy* demonstrators called for Mr Honeyford to be dismissed. (*Times*, 17 September)

(Honeyford's article in the *Salisbury Review*) This article created a furore and, despite other headteachers in Bradford holding similar opinions, it was Mr Honeyford who was singled out for *alleged racism*. (*Telegraph*, 6 September)

(Reaction of "race lobby" against Honeyford) Why is it that this *lobby* have chosen to *persecute* this man ... It is not because he is a racist; it is precisely because he is not a racist, yet has dared to challenge the attitudes, behaviour and approach of the ethnic minority professionals. (*Telegraph*, 6 September)

These examples show quite clearly the partisan point of view of the journalists writing about the events in the Honeyford affair. The demonstrators are described as 'noisy' and as a 'lobby' that 'persecutes'. The accusations against 'this man' are merely allegations, and their basis even explicitly denied, and Honeyford has 'dared' to challenge the attitudes of minority professionals. In other words, his position is positively evaluated, whereas that of his opponents is characterized negatively. We shall see that also in the other examples we examine, perspective plays an important role.

Such biased descriptions are not limited to the Honeyford affair. Quite generally, acts of "radical" blacks, "loony" leftists and those "anti-racist busybodies" tend to be described in this negative way, as we shall see in more detail below:

(Meeting in Brixton) was plunged into chaos. (Members) were drowned by a series of *noisy* and angry interruptions ... by a handful of *extreme agitators* (*Telegraph* 2 October).

## IMPLICIT MEANINGS

In the example discussed at the beginning of this chapter, we have already found that one of the most powerful instruments in the critical study of discourse is the systematic analysis of implicitness. Because of the knowledge, beliefs, and mental models journalists and media users already have (and partly share) about the world, a large part of the information that plays a role in communication and mutual understanding remains implicit. The text is like an iceberg of information of which only the tip is actually expressed in words and sentences. The rest is assumed to be supplied by the knowledge scripts and models of the media users, and therefore usually left unsaid.

At the same time, however, this general feature of discursive communication also allows the journalist to leave implicit more controversial types of information, for instance, evaluative propositions or beliefs, as when the conservative Press and politicians generally assume that riots are primarily a form of crime or when right-wing editors assume that the Dutch or the British are not prejudiced. The Press need not explicitly say this, but may more subtly presuppose, imply, or merely 'suggest' this belief, and such implicit information may only show 'at the surface' of the text in seemingly innocuous connectives such as 'because', 'therefore', and 'so'.

The analysis of the implicit, then, is very useful in the study of underlying ideologies of journalists. This is particularly relevant in the study of ethnic news reporting, since ideologies and other tacit beliefs play a vital role here. Social norms against prejudice and discrimination, which are known by people who express racist opinions, force them to be careful in what they say and write, so that many meanings tend to remain implicit or are expressed indirectly. We shall see that this contradiction between fundamental social norms and what journalists would like to (or actually do) write or report about minorities is one of the major semantic features of race reporting in the Press.

## Implications

Words, sentences or propositions may have different types of implicitness and indirectness; that is, information that may be *inferred* by language users from their previous knowledge and beliefs is combined with information actually expressed in the text. If a news report says that 'The West Indian women claimed that they were being discriminated against', the use of 'claimed' implies the usual belief-suspension by the journalist. Its use may also suggest that the women were perhaps lying, as is even more strongly the case in the use of verbs such as 'allege'. As we have seen in the previous chapter, the credibility status of quoted speakers, may thus be enhanced or lowered by the strategic use of verbs or adverbs with different presuppositions or other forms of implicitness or indirectness.

We begin our analysis with a study of implications and examine a number of examples from our data to illustrate these sometimes subtle forms of the non-said. The following examples are again chosen from the reports about the Honeyford affair:

[A] member of the parents' action group organized the chanting among the children and encouraged them to run away from the school gates, *probably for the benefit of television cameras*. (*Times*, 17 September)

There is something decidedly rotten about education when a mob of adults *pretending* to be caring parents picket a school. (*Telegraph*, 21 October)

Now, why would the journalist add the phrase "probably for the benefit of the television cameras"? The phrase first presupposes that there actually *are* such cameras. Second, we know that when people do something for the benefit of the camera, it is meant to be publicly seen and recorded, but "for the benefit of" additionally implies that such action is not spontaneous, as is also suggested by the verb "encouraged". In other words, at least some actions of the pupils are not spontaneous, but manipulated. This is consistent with the definition in the conservative Press of the Honeyford case: Asian parents are influenced by white anti-racists, who want to make a *cause célèbre* of the Honeyford affair. This is often also said, especially in the tabloids, but in this passage of *The Times* such an evaluation is merely indirectly implied. Similarly, the use of "pretending" in the second example implies that – according to the journalists – the Asian parents are not 'caring' parents at all, an implication that is part of the overall vilification of the opponents of Honeyford. The conservative Press thus resorts to precisely those tactics of which it accuses Honeyford's critics.

Such implications may sometimes be derived from the use of a single word. Thus, in the following example, the use of "branded", instead of "accused" not only implies that a negative property (racist) is involved, but also and more importantly, that the accusation may be unfounded:

(Strike organized by the Nalgo union) colleagues who walked out over the employment of a supervisor, *branded by them as a 'racist'*. (*Telegraph*, 8 August)

This implication is consistent with the general point of view of the *Telegraph* and other right-wing papers that accusations of racism are usually unfounded or a form of censorship. We return to this central local topic of ethnic news reporting below. Note that the use of the verb "to brand" is mostly used only by the targets of the accusation, or by those who sympathize with them. Its use therefore often implies a counter-accusation, that is, that the accuser acted immorally. One would never say, for instance, 'I branded him as a racist'. We see that the use of a single word may reveal the perspective, allegiances, as well as the opinions of the speaker or writer.

## Presupposition

Presuppositions are a special case of implications. In formal terms, a presupposition is often defined as a proposition that is semantically implied (entailed) by a statement as well as by the denial of that statement (for a more explicit discussion, see Seuren, 1985). The statement "The police have stopped the 'softly softly' approach", and the denial of that sentence, '"The police have *not* stopped the 'softly softly' approach" both imply that the police in fact had a 'softly softly' approach to policing the inner cities. Thus, presuppositions convey information that is supposed to be known and shared by the writer and the reader, and which therefore need not be stated. In this way, the Press may indirectly and sometimes rather subtly state things that are not 'known' by the readers at all, but which are simply suggested to be common knowledge.

In the polarized reporting about race in the right-wing Press, presuppositions will generally focus on negative properties of 'them' (black youths, anti-racists) and positive properties of 'us'. As we have seen in our earlier example, British tolerance is a case in point:

(Racial attacks and policing) If the ordinary *British taste for decency and tolerance* is to come through, it will need positive and unmistakable action. (*Telegraph*, editorial, 13 August)

This passage does not state, but presupposes that British tolerance and decency exists – a presupposition which should be interpreted against the backdrop of anti-racist accusations to the contrary.

Similarly, in the following example the *Telegraph* does not state but presupposes that there are tensions between Asians and West Indians, an assumption which according to most people concerned is false:

(About a speech by Enoch Powell) Open and constructive discussion, for example, of very real difficulties which have arisen in some of our schools becomes taboo, as Mr Honeyford at Bradford has found to his cost. Thoughtful analysis of why in some areas *there is rising tension between Asian and Caribbean populations is rendered dangerous*. (*Telegraph*, 6 September)

Note that the same fragment also presupposes that 'very real difficulties' *have* in fact 'arisen in some of our schools'. We see that presuppositions are a powerful instrument in the implicit assertion of debatable propositions. Their analysis allows us to examine the tacit assumptions of journalists as well as the ideological framework that controls their reporting about ethnic affairs. In the analysis of more specific cases of semantic structures and strategies below, we shall see that presuppositions are at play in many examples of race reporting.

## Vagueness

Implicitness and indirectness may also take the form of various types of vagueness. Typically, this semantic property of texts is used when it is essential to conceal responsibility for negative actions. In the conservative Press this is for instance the case when the actions of the police are described. One way of concealing responsibility is the use of sentences in the passive voice, or the use of nominalizations, syntactic properties of style to which we return in the next chapter. Here, we focus on the meaning implications of this form of vagueness. Take for instance the following example:

> (Brixton) On Saturday, police were petrol-bombed, shops looted and cars burned *after the shooting* of a West Indian woman. (*Times*, 30 September)

In the initial context of this article it is abundantly clear who does the petrol-bombing and looting, but whereas the police in this example are explicitly mentioned as the victims of the petrol-bombs, it is *not* explicitly mentioned that they were the ones who shot the West Indian woman, which becomes clear only in the rest of the text.

Similarly, a 'mob' of Asians is explicitly identified and negatively described as the responsible agent of smashing up a pub, but the white agents that were responsible for the attacks on Asians have disappeared from the sentence:

> (Four Asians acquitted) They were among a mob of 50 Asians who smashed up an East London pub after a series of hammer *attacks* on other Asians. (*Sun*, 14 August)

Biased reporting, thus, generally draws attention to the agency of out-groups when their acts are negative, while playing down or concealing similar acts by in-group members. More generally, the heavy use of nominalizations (for example, 'shooting' instead of '*x* shot *y*') in the Press often obscures the fact of who exactly is responsible for a negative act.

This is typically the case in the descriptions of the social backgrounds of the riots and of the situation in the ghettos:

> (Brixton) Parts of Brixton have become a ghetto. The explanation for that lies in the job market, housing policies, racial discrimination, and within the Afro-Caribbean population. (*Times*, 30 September)

In this example it seems as if the blame is equally distributed: the Afro-Caribbean population is seen as responsible for the situation in the ghetto, but the job market, housing policies, and discrimination are also mentioned. However, the latter causes are only mentioned in general terms. It is not mentioned *who* are responsible for not hiring blacks, giving them bad housing, or for discriminating against them. Obviously, the style of all sentences in news reports cannot always be transformed into active forms in which agents are mentioned. However, the high incidence of passives and nominal constructions such as 'unemployment' or 'discrimination' do tend to conceal the responsible, white, agents.

## Overcompleteness: irrelevance

In these examples of biased perspective, we see that events may be described in many different ways. Two other modes of description are what we call 'the level of abstraction' and the 'relative degree of completeness' (van Dijk, 1977). That is, the same episode may be described in global terms or may be described by referring to the action as a whole, as we typically do in summaries ('I took the train to Paris, and had a nice holiday there'), but we may also describe the small details of all relevant actions ('I went to the station, bought a ticket ...'). Thus, stories may vary between higher level and lower, more detailed, levels of description. Similarly, at each of these levels, we may be more or less complete in our description, that is we may describe many details, but also make a selection and only focus on a few details. These different modes of description may also be relevant in news stories, and may be used to convey different perspectives, evaluations, and especially different weights of relevance to information.

Level of abstraction and degree of completeness may also vary in news reports about ethnic affairs, and in this case overcompleteness often takes the form of functional irrelevance. That is, a description may add an 'irrelevant' detail, but this detail is relevant within a more general negative portrayal of a person or group. It may be the case, for instance, that the actions or appearance of blacks are described differently from those of whites. This would not be surprising if the journalist is white, and therefore, according to insights of the theory of social cognition, would focus on, remember, and find more relevant certain properties of the person who is different from 'us'. Women in the news are more often be described – by male journalists especially – in terms of their clothes and appearance than are male news actors (Tuchman, Kaplan Daniels and Benét, 1978). The same may very well be true for minority actors, who first of all tend to be categorized as members of another group, even if such information would be irrelevant for the story. Often such differences will be rather innocent, or simply reflect general news values, perhaps of cultural interest. On other occasions, however, the different description may signal underlying stereotypes and prejudice, and convey negative opinions or a partisan point of view to the reader:

(Tottenham riots) It was during the search that Mrs Jarrett, *who weighed about 20 stone*, collapsed. (*Telegraph*, 7 October)

(Rastafarians patrolling Handsworth) The man behind the deal appeared to be a 31-year-old *unemployed* Rastafarian. (*Mail*, 12 September)

(TV programme on Hattersley, Sparkbrook) The programme produced interviews with a number of Sparkbrook's Asian citizens, *some unable to speak English,* who claimed to have been signed up more or less without their knowledge. (*Telegraph*, 27 September)

(Comments of Mayor Ajeeb on CRE and Race Relations Act) Mr Ajeeb, *former peasant farmer from Pakistan*, was speaking to ... (*Telegraph*, 16 October)

These are only a few typical examples out of many. In the first the weight of Mrs Jarrett would normally be a completely irrelevant piece of information. However, in this case the journalist adds this information because the weight of Mrs Jarrett is supposed to be a possible cause of her death during the police search. This again implies that the police search itself cannot be seen as the main cause of her death.

The description of a Rastafarian in the second example as being "unemployed" also makes use of information that is irrelevant for the report. However, categorizing a young black man, and especially a Rastafarian, as 'unemployed' contributes to the stereotypical view white people may have of young blacks. Of course, this need not be negative in all contexts, especially when the high unemployment among young blacks is being criticized or used as an explanation for the riots. In this case, however, there is no question of using unemployment in a critical sense, or as an explanation for rioting.

Similar points may be made for the other examples. It is quite irrelevant to the story that Lord Mayor Ajeeb of Bradford used to be a farmer in his homeland. Yet the probable inference that 'he is only a farmer' may for some readers lead to the further inference that 'he is probably stupid, backward, or uncultivated', according to prevailing prejudices about farmers (especially from the Third World), which may implicitly be meant to disqualify Mr Ajeeb.

The most serious and systematic form of overcompleteness is the categorization of news actors by their colour, even when such information is irrelevant. The code of the British Union of Journalists explicitly prohibits such uses of irrelevant ethnic categorization (see Appendix, p. 255–6). The Press Council and, in a recent decision about a code of conduct, a number of British newspapers, have also determined that irrelevance is a criterion for evaluating Press reports. That there is good reason for such a decision is shown in examples like the following headline:

MP'S DAUGHTER RAPED BY BLACK GANG (*Mail*, 30 September)

## SEMANTIC STRATEGIES

Besides the local semantic structures described above, texts may exhibit what may be called various 'strategies'. A strategy is a goal-directed property of discourse, and usually accomplished through various functional 'moves'. Thus we may adequately tell a story or argue about a specific point, but we may do so more or less effectively. We may play a game simply by the rules, but in order to win, we must follow a strategy that will effectively give us the upper hand over our opponent. The same is true in the Press in the explicit or implicit argumentation of opinion articles, and sometimes even in news reports. In order to show that $x$ is the case, we may go through the strategy of arguing the points $y1, y2 \dots yn$, which may each seem to be undeniable by our opponent or reader. Similarly, in the Press, if a newspaper wants to discredit an opponent, it may systematically focus on real or alleged negative properties of such a person or group, as we have seen expressed above in biased and irrelevant descriptions.

Discourse about delicate topics such as ethnic relations is replete with such strategies (van Dijk, 1984, 1987a). We have argued above that one major strategy in many types of discourse about minorities is positive self-presentation. In this strategy white people try to convey the opinion that they are not racist or prejudiced, and will typically make statements like 'I have nothing against blacks, *but* ...', or 'Of course there are also hardworking (peace-loving, law-abiding ...) blacks, *but* ...'. We see that the goal of this strategy is the management of impressions readers or listeners may have both about the speaker or writer and about their targets (blacks). Whereas speakers or writers in this way try to make an impression of tolerance, at the same they time will try to convey a negative impression of the people they speak or write about.

## Denial of racism

In a society where the official norm is that racism or prejudice is immoral or illegal, such a strategy of positive self-presentation is essential. In the case of the examples just given, we find a *Denial* as the relevant functional move in the strategy of positive self-presentation. That this is not the same as a simple assertion may be seen from the invariably following 'but': after the denial of racism, we will usually find a negative statement about an ethnic minority group. For this reason, such strategic moves are usually called 'disclaimers'. In other words, the denial has the strategic function of being able to say something negative about others without running the risk of being categorized as racist. Of course, a reader or listener may disregard such a move and nevertheless think that the speaker or writer is prejudiced.

In the Press too, journalists or other writers need to make a good impression on the readers. Even quite prejudiced articles may therefore strategically avoid the impression that they are racist. Denials of racism, therefore, are a common move in such articles. Similarly, writers who want to say something negative about blacks may add that there are of course exceptions, or that of course "most blacks are OK", a move we may call an *Apparent Admission*. The reverse is true for the description of whites: racism may be generally denied, but it may be admitted that some whites, typically members of an extremist group like the National Front, or even Enoch Powell, are of course 'wrong' (the word 'racist' will even then often be avoided). Another move is *Contrast*, in which properties, usually negative, of 'them' are contrasted with positive properties of 'us', for instance in moves such as 'We are not intolerant, they are!', a move which in this case may also be called *Reversal*, typically so when blame is being shifted to the opponent. Let us examine some examples, and see whether other strategic moves can be found in the Press.

The denial of racism is the most common strategic move we find in the right-wing Press. First, it may take the form of the usual distance or doubt about acts of discrimination, for instance by putting quotes or words like "alleged" in well-known accusation contexts:

WALKOUT OVER 'RACIST' COUNCIL EMPLOYEE.

The woman was recently found guilty of racial harassment by a council disciplinary tribunal because she *allegedly* 'caused offence' to a black member of the union. (*Times*, 6 August)

(Black man sues club for discrimination) *claiming* his performance was cancelled because of his colour. (*Telegraph*, 16 August)

(Anti-fascist rally) The evening combined emotive reminders of the rise of Nazism with *diatribes against racial discrimination and prejudice today*. (*Telegraph*, 1 October)

Even in cases where the racism is obvious or proved, such as when policemen are fired or demoted by their own chief because of racial abuse, the newspapers still write that "racist" police were sacked. (*Sun*, 27 November). And in a *Telegraph* report (19 September) about the Honeyford conflict, the credibility of Honeyford's Asian opponents is even lowered so much that the journalist writes that the Asian demonstrators "claimed" to be the parents of the children! Similarly, even when a court has determined that someone was discriminated against, some newspapers may still speak of "alleged discrimination". We see that the journalistic routine of doubting accusations of racism is stronger than the facts.

An interesting example of the use of "claim" may be found in the following fragment of the news item in the *Telegraph* about a recent CRE report which we analysed in Chapter five:

In its report which follows a detailed review of the operation of the 1976 Race Relations Act, the Commission *claims* that ethnic minorities continue to suffer high levels of discrimination and disadvantage. (*Telegraph*, 1 August)

Along the lines of our own earlier remarks, CRE chairman Peter Newsam reacts as follows to this use of "claim" in a letter to the editor:

Of the Commission you say 'it claims that ethnic minorities continue to suffer high levels of discrimination and disadvantage'. This is like saying that someone 'claims' that July was wet. It was. And it is also a fact supported by the weight of independent research evidence that discrimination on racial grounds, in employment, housing and services, remains at a disconcertingly high level. (*Telegraph*, 7 August)

In other examples, the denial of racism is more explicit:

(Immigration) From the end of the Fifties it was clear that if immigration continued on the same scale, it would lead to great social tensions, not least when there was serious unemployment. *There was little racialism, but* public opinion wanted a brake on immigration before it reached a point at which the absorption which had characterized previous immigrations became difficult ... Anyone who stressed that the objection was not to the presence of immigrants of a different 'race' but to the size of the number of people from sharply different cultural backgrounds coming here for work was derided as 'playing the numbers game'. (*Times*, 17 October, opinion article by Ronald Butt)

(Black Sections) In the more ideologically-blinkered sections of his [Kinnock's] party ... they seem to *gain pleasure from identifying all difficulties experienced by immigrant groups, particularly Afro-Caribbeans, as the result of racism* ... Special sections claiming positions and plum jobs on account of blackness alone will hardly please members of an egalitarian party. (*Telegraph*, 14 September, editorial)

Again, these are only two examples chosen from a list of many. Whereas some reports simply bracket accusations of racism by the use of verbs like 'accuse' or 'allege', the *Telegraph*, in its editorial of 14 September, is much more aggressive, and violently rejects the accusations of the anti-racists, which it systematically links with Labour and especially the radical left. This link established between anti-racists and the "blinkered" or "loony" left is characteristic for the whole right-wing Press, and shows how anti-anti-racism (that is, racism) and right-wing political conservatism are often related.

Journalistic doubt about instances of discrimination is an example of the widely shared prejudice, even among more liberal whites, that blacks are 'too sensitive' about discrimination, and often see bias where there is none. Research shows that the reverse is true: black people for many reasons tend to ignore or explain away discrimination simply as unpleasant behaviour as long as they can, and will only conclude that an action was discriminatory when they have 'tested' it against various types of evidence (Essed, 1991).

## Mitigation and excuse

If blame can hardly be denied, the best strategy is to mitigate the negative action, or to use excuses, as in "the police were *forced* to act in this harsh way". Indeed, the general defence of the police in the right-wing Press typically invites such playing down of or excuses for guilt:

(Brixton) A policeman at the head of one detachment *lost his temper* with a man who had been shouting at him and hit him in the face with his shield. (*Times*, 30 September)

(Brixton) One can see why they [ministers] wish to resist the Left-wing deterministic argument that unemployment plus *a little police harassment* equals riots ...(A government minister, looking at the inner cities) He will see racial tensions – between white and black and, in some areas between Asians and blacks. (*Telegraph*, 30 September)

Similarly, the shooting of Mrs Groce in Brixton is also done by a "nervous" policeman (POLICEMAN'S FEAR THAT LED TO A RIOT, *Mail*, 30 September), and we have seen earlier that the Press suggests that Mrs Jarrett died because of a heart condition due to her weight, not because of a police raid. In the same way, in the first example given above, the reference to a policeman who "lost his temper" functions as an excuse for aggressive police behaviour, since it is also explicitly said that someone else was the cause of this loss of temper.

Allegations of police harassment against young blacks, one of the incontrovertible findings in the Scarman report on the causes of the Brixton disturbances in 1981, as well as in much other literature and documentation, are usually ignored and practically never detailed in the right-wing Press. Only *The Times* prints a critical opinion article by Bernard Levin in which an example of serious police harassment against a black disabled man in a wheelchair is detailed and criticized (later to be extensively responded to by the commissioner of police; such allegations never go unchallenged). In the example in the *Telegraph* quoted here, the possible reason of police harassment is duly mitigated by the use of "a little".

Excuses for cases of discrimination, proven in court and hence undeniable, may subtly be inserted in news reports, as in the following rather obvious example from the *Mail*:

(Discrimination) A club manager banned a coloured singer *after he had been mugged three times by blacks*, an industrial tribunal heard yesterday. (*Mail*, 16 August)

That is, we assume that the *Mail* means that is the club manager who was mugged and not the "coloured" singer!

Deceptive or euphemistic terms may be used describing miserable ethnic relations in Britain, where the *Telegraph* uses the soft term "fragile", in a passage we already studied in Chapter five:

(CRE report) No one would deny the *fragile* nature of race relations in Britain today or that there is *misunderstanding* and *distrust* between parts of the community. (*Telegraph*, 1 August, editorial)

In our earlier analysis of this editorial, we found that in this passage the rather soft terms "misunderstanding" and "distrust" are used to characterize "parts of the community". First, this is a euphemistic way of referring to prejudice and racism (if that is meant), and second, it seems to distribute the blame equally between different "parts of the community". As we have seen in the analysis of concealed agency, the white group is not explicitly mentioned in this case.

Similarly, racism, discrimination, and social inequality are played down in terms of "some disadvantages" in the following fragment from *The Times*:

> (Immigration) Any new immigration population will encounter *some disadvantages* if only in the sense that most will have to work their way up in an unfamiliar society ... For the young, there are *difficulties of employability* as well as of employment. (*Times*, 17 October, opinion article by Ronald Butt)

Note in this last example that unemployment, or discrimination in employment, is subtly attributed to young blacks, who are not simply not hired but 'difficult to employ', which blames them for their own unemployment. Again, employers remain out of the picture. Indeed, *we have not found a single example in the right-wing Press that explicitly blames white employers for even part of the unemployment of young blacks*. In its series of articles on black unemployment, *The Times* only occasionally refers to discrimination and the role of employers. Detailed reports of daily experiences of blacks with job discrimination are wholly absent, even from liberal newspapers such as the *Guardian*.

## Hyperbole

The reverse is also true: if *our* negative actions are to be softened, *theirs* will of course need to be exaggerated. Both as a semantic move and as a rhetorical operation (which we further analyse in the next chapter), hyperboles are known to be frequent in the right-wing Press. Of the hundreds of examples, we offer only the following fragment:

> (HIGH PRICE OF TELLING TRUTH) (About anti-racists) We have tyranny in Britain. (*Sun*, 24 October)

## Ridicule

If arguments fail, ridicule is a potent strategic move to discredit one's opponent. The right-wing Press often resorts to ridicule when discussing anti-racist activities, such as anti-racist teaching for the under-fives, or building an African village for children to play in. Two "funny" examples:

(Anti-racist training) Today the [race relations] industry uses highly sophisticated equipment such as electronic prejudometers which can calculate a person's degree of racial prejudice to one millionth of a prejudon (the recognised international unit of prejudice). (*Telegraph*, 1 October)

(Scarman inquiry) Research scientists at its laboratories ... have already produced a semi-automated Scarman type Inquiry Mk I equipped with thousands of words about community policing, unemployment, alienation and other relevant topics. An ingenious inbuilt safety device ensures that the word 'race' cannot be uttered. (*Telegraph*, 10 October)

Behind the forced laughs, however, the business of this newspaper is dead serious, and there is no doubt about the real message: anti-racism is not just ridiculous, it is dangerous.

### Attribution and reversal: blaming the victim

Besides the denial, mitigation of or excuses for discrimination and racism, the right-wing Press frequently also has recourse to the move of reversing the blame by attributing it to the opponent, part of a well-used strategy of 'blaming the victim'. One element in this strategy is to assert that the blacks themselves act in such a way that prejudice or unequal treatment is justified (there are usually quotation marks around 'prejudice'):

(After two reports about the causes of the riots) While the whites were being scolded once more for their 'prejudice', *the blacks were doing their best to prove it justified. (Telegraph*, 19 October)

Racial attacks are generally condemned, by the right-wing Press included. However, it does not hurt to lift the blame generally put on the police by the Asian victims for their (officially highly denied) lack of zeal in handling such attacks, and apportion some of the blame to the left. This happens in the following quote from the Chair of the Commons Committee on Race Relations, (endorsed by the paper, as is clear from the rest of this article and other reports):

LEFT 'HINDERING POLICE WAR ON RACE FIRE ATTACKERS'. Left-wing sniping at the police is helping to frustrate the fight against racist fire attacks, a senior Conservative MP claimed yesterday. (*Mail*, 13 August)

Complete reversal takes place when blacks and other anti-racists are finally accused themselves of intolerance and racism. Indeed, in this way, the right-wing Press introduces the new phenomenon of black racism against whites, who are now portrayed as the victims. Accusations of black racism as well as victim reversal are particularly frequent in the Honeyford affair, where the controversial headmaster is primarily portrayed as a victim. In other cases of discrimination, prejudice, and racism, the tabloids will try to reverse the charges:

(Review of money for black organisations) Teams from the Home Office and the Environment Department are discussing whether the grants are being wasted or, worse, being used by unscrupulous local leaders to stir up racial hatred and riots. (*Mail*, 25 October)

(Honeyford and other cases) Nobody is less able to face the truth than the hysterical 'anti-racist' brigade. Their intolerance is such that they try to silence or sack anyone who doesn't toe their party-line. (*Sun*, 23 October, column by John Vincent)

(Honeyford quits) Now we know who the true racists are. (*Sun*, 30 November, editorial)

Below, we shall analyse such allegations of 'black racism' in more detail. To complete this reversal, negative other-description must be accompanied by further positive self-presentation. Against the accusations of the anti-racists, the right-wing Press therefore repeatedly claims that the British are tolerant, as we have seen in an earlier example. The following examples are hardly unique:

(Handsworth) Contrary to much doctrine, and acknowledging a small malevolent fascist fringe, *this is a remarkably tolerant society*. But tolerance would be stretched were it to be seen that enforcement of law adopted the principle of reverse discrimination. (*Telegraph*, 11 September, editorial)

(Racial attacks against Asians) *Britain's record for absorbing people from different backgrounds, peacefully and with tolerance, is second to none*. The descendants of Irish and Jewish immigrants will testify to that. It would be tragic to see that splendid reputation tarnished now. (*Sun*, 14 August, editorial)

These and other examples not quoted here also show that tolerance is conditional and should not be confused with weakness. Our tolerance must not be abused, and it does not mean that we will allow 'reverse discrimination'. In statistics about racial attitudes, the *Sun* admits that if there is an intolerant "fringe" (an admission move we analyse below), this is "only" 15 per cent of the white population (NB: 30 per cent for older people!), and if there is prejudice, it is "provoked". Ironically, one month later, the *Mail on Sunday*, on 27 October, reports that 67 per cent of the (white?) British support a proposal to stop all immigration into Britain. Incidentally, these figures in the *Mail* are followed by an irrelevant, isolated quote from a fireman who tells that his black workmate is a "lovely fellow but lazy". So much for British tolerance and the papers that report it.

We have seen before that right-wing newspapers may occasionally reject Enoch Powell's blatantly racist talk as 'unpractical', but at the same time they will also categorically deny that he is a racist. Indeed, sometimes, they will fully agree with him, as in the following *Telegraph* column, which we quote in full, because it is so significant:

> Mr Enoch Powell has again forecast that more than a third of the population of inner London and other large cities will before long be of immigrant stock. Will he get any reponse to his statement? Or will he meet with the same silence he met with when he dealt with this matter in a Commons debate on the recent riots in London and Birmingham. 'It is not judicial inquiries which we require. It is truthfulness and honesty from those who sit in the seats of power. That is what the people of this country want. That is what they have been cheated of so far, but they will have it.' But when they have it, may it not be too late? Hypnotised, so long lectured, browbeaten, brainwashed, injected with enormous doses of of racial guilt, threatened by laws hitherto unheard of, taught to believe, by politicians of all parties, by public men, teachers, clergymen, 'media' people and innumerable others that the very idea of belonging to their own particular country, their own 'nation', is morally wrong, may they not have lost the power of action? (*Telegraph*, 8 November)

How contradictory the frequent calls for law and order of this extremist right-wing writing are, may be concluded from the passage in which laws that prohibit discrimination are represented as a threat, and moderate consensus against blatant racism as an attack against our nationalist morality. Indeed, the ideological distance between the right-wing Press and Powell or the National Front is often hair-thin, and more a question of practical considerations than a matter of principle.

## Comparisons

Talk and writing about ethnic groups frequently resort to comparisons, not only between 'us' and 'them', but also between different ethnic groups or different situations. Such comparisons often have a number of implications that are not spelled out in the text. Thus, the right-wing Press sometimes publishes reports about the situation in the West Indies, not so much to inform the readers about the West Indies, but rather in order to say something about West Indians in Britain. The same is true in the following passage about Rastafarianism in the West Indies:

> (Rastas are involved in the riots in Handsworth) In countries like Trinidad and Barbados, cults like Rastafarianism are roundly condemned by the Press, politicians and church leaders. There are far fewer Rastafarian 'dreads' in Trinidad or Barbados, than in Brixton or Liverpool. (*Telegraph*, 12 September)

By stating that in the West Indies Rastafarianism is widely condemned (by the elites), this passage implies that 'Rastas are condemned even by their own people', which again implies that making negative remarks about Rastas is not a question of white racism, but based on an objective evaluation of their activities or creed, an implication which may be used as a justification of negative reporting about Rastas. This is indeed the case, given the frequent association of Rastas with strange hairstyles, dress, creed, and smoking of ganja (marijuana).

Similarly, the *Mail* publishes a series of unusually long articles about the police in the West Indies, highlighting the fact that the Caribbean police are quite strict and much more aggressive than in Britain, for instance when drugs are involved. This implies that it is quite all right for the British police to be tough with black youths and that they can hardly be accused of racist harassment when black West Indian policemen also act that way against black youths. In other words, the comparisons serve to legitimate harsh policing, while at the same time strategically arguing against accusations of discrimination.

Even more aggressive are the frequent comparisons, especially of the anti-racists and the "loony left", with well-known demons of history:

> (Worker accused of racism) The really alarming thing is that some of these *pocket Hitlers* of local government are moving into national politics. It's time we set about exposing their antics while we can. Forewarned is forearmed. (*Mail*, 26 October, editorial)

Other passages speak of Goebbels or the Nazis, and of communist tyrants, such as Stalin, to vilify their opponents, safely ignoring that, compared with the anti-fascist groups, the tabloids do not exactly have humanitarian reputations.

## Contrast and division

Rhetorically even more powerful is the further extension of comparisons to full-blown contrast. In nearly all examples analysed in this chapter there is the implicit contrast between (good) 'us' and (bad) 'them', as is generally the case in biased discourse about out-groups. Sometimes this contrast is actually spelled out in the form of a strategic move, for instance when Asians and West Indians are compared:

> (Black "lawlessness") By blacks I mean those principally of West Indian origin rather than the quieter, gentler people from the Indian sub-continent who are as law-abiding as the rest of the population. (*Times*, 12 October, column by Woodrow Wyatt)

There are many such passages, especially after the riots, in which semantic contrast is used in order to create the illusion of ethnic rivalry – a well-known divide and conquer strategy. Repeated denials from the Asian community, and even demonstrations in front of the *Sun*'s offices, are ignored. Here is the beginning of the report that sparked this demonstration:

> BLACKS 'ENVY RICH ASIANS'. West Indian jealousy of Asian immigrants' success could have sparked the Birmingham riots, a Tory MP claimed yesterday ... Mr Stanbrook said: 'Indians and Asians have adapted better than West Indians. Many of them work very hard. (*Sun*, 11 September)

But even small incidents may be used to convey this rivalry, in which the West Indians are portrayed as the bad guys:

> 'RACE PEACE' BLACK HIT AN ASIAN. Britain's first black council chief viciously attacked an Asian official during a crowded meeting. (*Sun*, 29 August)

The "vicious attack" in this case consisted in forcing someone to the ground with a walking stick. Even the judge found the event too insignificant to waste expensive legal costs on, and the black council chief was reprimanded but acquitted.

## Admission

Admission is another common strategic move in the description of ethnic minority groups and their members. In order to avoid being accused of making racist generalizations, the conservative Press will make sure occasionally to insert clauses such as "most of them are of course law-abiding citizens, but ..." and other variants of the classic disclaimer 'Some of my best friends are ...':

> (Rastas in Birmingham) These young men with dreadlocked hair – who regard marijuana as a 'holy herb' – know the language of the Left. And *despite the many ordinary, law-abiding Rastas in Birmingham*, the Villa Road variety seem a law to themselves – as I discovered when I visited the area last week. (*Mail*, 15 September)

> (Tottenham, Blacks) There is no doubt that the great majority of West Indians would like to behave and be accepted as normal British citizens: they would be if they were not stirred up by those among them who peddle evil and hatred and by those extreme socialists who aim for revolution on the streets and an anarchy that would make parts of Britain ungovernable. (*Times*, 12 October, column by Woodrow Wyatt)

Such admissions are expectedly frequent in editorials, in which the editors, while saying many negative things about blacks (or black youths) or about the causes of the riots, must make sure to avoid the blame that their newspaper is expressing or confirming prejudices:

> (After the Tottenham riots) Despite the difficulties of bad housing and high unemployment, most men and women in these districts are peaceable and want to make a go of it ... But ... it is in the final resort the blacks of Britain who must decide their own destiny. They must do more to discipline their young. They must find themselves community leaders who preach co-operation, not confrontation. (*Mail*, 8 October)

## Conclusion

From these examples, we see that that the semantics of race reporting is a rich field of analysis, allowing us to examine how the Press describes events, actions, and people involved in race relations. We have found that there are many structures and strategies that are used to deny, mitigate, excuse, or otherwise conceal prejudice, discrimination, or racism, to blame the victims, and to accuse the left, anti-racists, or other opponents. These are typically described in a negative way, sometimes subtly by irrelevant side remarks, and their accusations of racism doubted or otherwise discredited. This need not always be done in an explicit way – although the right-wing Press is not exactly subtle with its accusations. Implications, suggestions, presuppositions and other implicit, indirect or vague means of expressing underlying meanings or opinions may be used to persuade readers to the point of view of the newspaper.

## NORMS AND VALUES

The description of the semantics of race reporting given above, though rather illuminating by itself, needs further analysis and explanation. Therefore, in the last part of this chapter, we turn to a more coherent framework of explanation in which the local meanings and topics encountered above can be mutually related and understood.

Writing about a typical opinion topic such as race relations involves a complex framework of ideological norms and values, which we briefly discussed at the end of the previous chapter. We have found before that the official norm of tolerance and non-discrimination, even in an informally racist society, is rather powerful. One of the ways strategically to avoid the problem of norm or value contradiction, is to have recourse to other norms and values. Thus, it is against the dominant norm (and against the law) publicly to call all black people criminals. However, if it could be shown that many black people show criminal behaviour, norms of law and order will allow a writer to avoid the non-discrimination norm, and make 'safe' assertions about 'black crime'. In that case, the fundamental value of defending the 'truth' can be powerfully applied as a strategic defence move. In the reports about the riots and their assumed causes, such as drugs or simply criminal "greed", right-wing journalists make frequent use of this strategy. Since, as journalists, they may be expected to 'speak the truth', they may now feel entitled to accuse black people, or at least black youth, of committing crime, and to blame the whole black community for condoning it:

> (Tottenham) The time has come to state the truth without cant and without hypocrisy ... the strength to face the facts without being silenced by the fear of being called racist. (*Mail*, 9 October, column by Linda Lee-Potter)

But this example also shows that journalists may still feel that there is a conflict between the norm of tolerance and their underlying negative attitudes about specific minority groups: there is at least a pretence of 'fear' of being called a racist. Notice also that the frankness or sincerity move ("we will now speak the truth") calls for another move, namely, the 'We-are-not-allowed-to-tell-the-truth' move, which appears so often in opinion articles, columns, and editorials of the right-wing Press that we may speak of a racist cliché:

> (Racism in Europe) If there is one subject on which open debate is not conducted, has never been conducted and perhaps never will be conducted in this country it is the subject of race relations. (*Telegraph*, 13 November)

This moral prohibition calls for the transfer and attribution of guilt: some people are responsible for this situation. Therefore, the right-wing Press specifically accuses the "pundits", "snoopers", or the new "inquisition" of the "race relations industry" of exercising various forms of censorship. That this is no more than a rhetorical strategy may be concluded also from the fact that writers who use this ploy mostly *do* speak their minds, and *do* have access to the mass media to do so. It may of course be the case that without the norm of tolerance, and without the law against discrimination, they would express their racist attitudes even more explicitly. Perhaps it is this mixed feeling of limited self-censorship and moral guilt that gives rise to the frequent reversal stragegy of accusing one's opponents of censorship. As the following examples may testify, alleged censorship is a recurring, and highly emotional issue in the right-wing Press, formulated in the most intensive rhetorical mode. Since this strategy is at the heart of ethnic reporting in the right-wing Press, let us quote at length:

(Honeyford) Should they [headmasters] submit *and fail to speak their minds* because they fear the consequences? (*Telegraph*, 6 September, editorial)

(Honeyford) His court success is a *victory for free speech* and a defeat for the blinkered tyrants who believe that the best way round race problems is to pretend they do not exist. (*Sun*, 6 September, editorial)

(Honeyford will quit) It is a major setback for *reasoned argument* about black, white and brown problems ... It is essential that such talking be done. The problems of language, religion, high achievement and low achievement cannot be abolished. There is, to be plain, a West Indian crime problem; is *its discussion forbidden*? The Thought Policeman ... is alive and prospering in the busy, fervent little covens of protest now everywhere on watch. (*Telegraph*, 30 November, editorial)

(Honeyford) For speaking common sense he's been vilified; for being courageous he's been damned, for refusing to concede defeat his enemies can't forgive him ... I have interviewed him and I am utterly convinced that he hasn't an ounce of racism in his entire being ... [Bradford's councillors] who think that truth should be inviolate ... I suggest they should ask themselves what they are appealing against. In my opinion, they are appealing against the right of any honest man to openly voice his fears in racial matters. They are appealing for their own powerful right *to insist men stay silent* out of fear of intimidation. They are appealing for their right to put Bradford under a totalitarian rule and to demand they themselves are called freedom fighters, not oppressors. (*Mail*, 18 September, column by Lynda Lee-Potter)

THOUGHT CRIME NIGHTMARE In the nightmare world of George Orwell's 1984, those guilty of such things as thoughtcrime were always made to stage a full public confession. From Orwell's 1984 to Islington's 1985 is but a short step. The demand by union militants that a supervisor sign statements confessing her racism reminds us of what life would be like for the rest of us if these people ever came to power. (*Mail*, 3 August, full text of editorial)

HIGH PRICE OF TELLING THE TRUTH For the first time in our long history as a nation, ordinary men and women in Britain must now fear to speak the truth. (Fuller, a headmaster, blaming crime at school on West Indians) He was branded as a wicked racist ... We have tyranny in Britain. We have intimidation. We have a sinister attempt first to curb and then to destroy freedom of speech. We have racism too – and that is what is behind the plot. It is not white racism. It is black racism ... But who is there to protect the white majority? ... Our tolerance is our strength, But we will not allow anyone to turn it into our weakness. (*Sun*, 24 October)

These fragments show a surprising coherence. The same arguments and often the same formulations are used by different authors and different newspapers. This suggests that a very powerful ideology is at work, a unifying framework that is routinely applied when understanding and evaluating ethnic affairs. So, what is it that makes the newspapers so furious against anti-racists, so much so that the "reasoned argument" they want soon degenerates into a stream of invective and exaggeration?

One line of explanation, less ideological and more psychological and psychoanalytical, was briefly hinted at earlier: their barely hidden emotions of rage may be partly explained by guilt and moral conflict between shared social norms and personal prejudices. Such an analysis would also allow us to predict the strategy of guilt transfer when blaming the 'others', that is the anti-racists, and eventually the total reversal of white racism into 'black racism', of which 'we' (white British) are the 'victims'. Another reason for this fury may be frustration, a feeling of powerlessness against a defiant opponent.

While such an approach is partly defensible, we prefer a more structural, political, and socio-cultural analysis, which however also includes an important socio-cognitive dimension. Moral conflict, norms, hate against a group, and feelings of powerlessness extend far beyond the realm of individual emotions or personal experiences. So we need to ask questions about group relations, power, and ideologies, and in particular about the specific role of the Press in their reproduction.

## Freedom

We start this analysis by further examining the crucial ideological notion of 'freedom' that appears in many of the passages quoted above. Characteristically, the *Telegraph*, commenting upon the Honeyford case, headlines its editorial THE REAL ISSUE IS FREEDOM. The notion of 'freedom' is not unexpected in the conservative and right-wing Press, and is associated with uses of "free" and "freedom" in expressions such as the "free (that is, western) world" and "free (or capitalistic) enterprise". We shall see below that these social and economic dimensions also play a role in the furious attacks against anti-racists. In the examples just quoted, however, it is primarily freedom of speech that is at stake, and rhetorically set off against censorship, moral tyranny, and 'thought oppression'. Beyond morality these allegations also have an important ideological and political dimension: the anti-racists are invariably identified with the 'loony left', and easily associated with Communism and other 'unfree' ideologies, an association that can strategically be used in a public campaign that may unite conservatives with a broader public alerted against the dangers of the left. A few fragments may further illustrate this close association of anti-racism with the 'extremist' left:

> (Nalgo strike) ... colleagues who walked out over the employment of a supervisor, *branded by them as a 'racist'* ... Behind the decision to step up the dispute, now in its fourth day, lies a series of conflicting allegations of a sustained campaign of racial harassment in the council's housing department and *far-Left infiltration* of Nalgo. (*Telegraph*, 8 August)

> (Labour) Smarting from minority status, the Labour Party has allowed itself to become a haven for extremist minorities, not least supporters of far-out feminism and anti-British black separatism. (*Telegraph*, 14 October, editorial)

While we here uncover one ideological dimension of the Press campaign against alleged censorship, the underlying social and cognitive structures are more complex. After all, the Press itself is not censored, and journalists hardly seem to have a problem in expressing themselves quite freely. It therefore makes sense to emphasize the link between freedom and power. Indeed, these are closely correlated. Power entails the freedom to do as one wishes, and its exercise usually implies control over the actions of others, which again implies a restriction of their freedom (for the notion of power in more detail, see Lukes, 1986). In the realm of discourse and the media, then, freedom of speech presupposes symbolic power, such as access to or control over the media or generally the other means of symbolic reproduction, as well as the possession of various types of symbolic 'capital' (Bourdieu, 1977; van Dijk, 1989a). Now, if the right-wing Press claims that its opponents are restricting the freedom of speech, this presupposes that their opponents have at least a certain amount of symbolic power, and also that the conservative Press, or the political right generally, has less control than it would like to have. Here we come closer to a socio-political explanation of the frustrated fury directed against the anti-racists.

## Symbolic control

On closer analysis, it is not surprising that many examples we quoted above, as well as those we did not quote, have to do with domains of symbolic reproduction, for instance, education and literature. Usually the right-wing Press pays very little attention to culture. However, although teachers and writers are rarely the main news actors of the tabloids, we now find that Honeyford and other teachers accused of racism, as well as racist children's books, regularly hit the headlines. At the same time, whereas the right-wing Press controls a sizeable sector of the means of symbolic reproduction, it has little control over education, teachers and writers. The same is true for academics, who are seen as other competitors in the symbolic realm of the definition of "truth" and the reproduction of public opinion and morals. Moreover, there are the official institutions, such as the CRE, that also are, by law, supposed to define the ethnic situation and pass judgements on those who infringe upon the moral consensus of tolerance or the legal provisions against discrimination. That is, these institutions also control part of the symbolic realm of public speech and opinion about ethnic affairs. And finally, at the political level, there are the few left-wing councils that are able to challenge the moderate consensus and seek to implement anti-racist policies, such as hiring and firing teachers or civil servants, or forcing contract compliance upon local companies. Reversing possible accusations leveled against its own practices, then, the right-wing Press will tend to accuse its ideological opponents, especially teachers, of indoctrination and manipulation:

> (WHERE TRUTH IS TABOO) ... It is time we discuss the race issue in Britain with honesty. No topic is cotton-woolled by liberal commentators with more pious concern. Nowhere is the truth more taboo. Shouldn't our schools be teaching black children to love their country, rather than stuffing them full of ethnic education, which is only likely to make them feel more alienated? (*Mail*, 30 September)

(ILEA: keeping police out of schools) More to the point, what are they teaching them? If it isn't the three Rs, perhaps it is the three Ss instead: sedition, subversion and sociological hogwash. (*Mail*, 19 October, editorial)

It may be added that while the opponents may not control the larger media of mass communication, they are tacitly supposed to have other forms of symbolic capital that gives them at least some power, such as intellectual dominance and moral superiority. After all, a sociologist may have more knowledge about social phenomena, and the anti-racists a better claim at inter-group tolerance than a tabloid journalist. It is not surprising, therefore, that right-wing ideologies combined with a symbolic inferiority complex, may lead to the vilification of sociologists explaining or excusing the riots, the students preventing right-wing politicians from speaking, the teachers indoctrinating 'our' children, or the anti-racists accusing 'us' of intolerance and prejudice. It is no wonder either, that the style register chosen to discredit their opponents is also borrowed from the symbolic sphere: they are agitators. At the same time, the major accusation mirrors the one used by their opponents: they are intolerant and racist.

Finally, there may be another, perhaps more straightforward, reason for the furious attacks by the right-wing Press on the anti-racists. In the Honeyford case, for instance, the staunch defence of this headmaster should not merely be seen as a defence of a valiant teacher who 'dares to speak the truth', or as a counter-attack against the challenge of symbolic power, but also as a form of self-defence. That is, the defence of Honeyford is a strategic smoke-screen, if we assume that the tabloids are hardly interested in education *per se*. Rather, thinking of its own interests and especially its own views, it is plausible that the right-wing Press recognizes in Honeyford or other conservative teachers precisely their own opinions and attitudes. Attacks on Honeyford, thus, are seen as attacks on the views of the right-wing Press itself. In the name of a good case (education, freedom, the truth), then, Honeyford is an ideal victim-hero for the right-wing Press to use to defend indirectly its own case.

## White power

We see that even more is at stake. The Press may well grant academics, teachers, writers, and political activists some control over the symbolic or moral realm, as long as this control does not interfere with its own interests. When race relations are involved, however, it is not merely the power of the Press, or even that of the political right, which is involved, but white group power generally. Dominance, here, is no longer merely symbolic, but also social, political, and economic. That is, white group interests are at stake. Anti-racist action, whether in the schools, at the universities, in literature, or in the leftist city councils, is also a challenge of this power and these interests of the dominant white group, of which the right-wing Press, together with right-wing politicians, has defined itself as the main protagonist.

In light of this role of the valiant defender of 'British' values and interests, we should understand the similarly aggressive attacks on any form of equal rights, anti-discrimination measures, affirmative action, or what is seen as undeserved 'privileges' to minorities. After all, granting these invariably means a limitation of white interests and privileges, and a general loss of white dominance and control. In this framework, then, we should place the frequent news reports about whites being 'victims' of affirmative action, about 'discrimination' against white workers, or about the 'bureaucratic tyranny' of contract compliance. Whereas the intellectuals and the anti-racists may be attacked on symbolic and moral grounds, the 'loony left' is similarly vilified on such political grounds, because money, resources, positions, and power are involved. Thus, the right-wing Press identifies the left with anti-racism. It is not surprising therefore that it is particularly furious when anti-racist actions are politically enforced in the few cities or boroughs controlled by Labour councils (Ben-Tovim, Gabriel, Law and Stredder, 1986).

Most attacks against anti-racists and the left are directed against predominantly white groups or activists. Indeed, the West Indian and Asian communities, institutions, or groups have little symbolic, political, or economic power, and are therefore hardly threatening. Also, they cannot simply be attacked because of their colour or immigrant status without incurring the moral and legal problems mentioned above. Hence, minority groups and equal rights are tackled instead through their white representatives and protagonists. To be sure, black young men will be constantly criminalized or otherwise marginalized in the right-wing Press, but as socio-political opponents they do not really count. Indeed, they will only hit the headlines when, once in while, they appear to be threatening, namely when they riot, or when whites become victims of the crimes of some of them. Semantic content, strategies, and style of description are quite different in reports about the riots from those about anti-racism. These discourse properties will, momentarily, also be violent and aggressive, but the fury here is not one of frustration but rather of outrage: how dare they!

Even Haringey's councillor Bernie Grant, vilified for many weeks in the tabloids for having defended black 'rioters', is dealt with in another mode and style from the anti-racists. He may be a black devil and an individual challenge to white local power, but he is after all of no consequence. Whereas young blacks are criminalized and marginalized, he is simply put in the pathological and diabolical basket, and further used for political gains (also in Parliament and at Tory conferences) and symbolic whipping in the usual front page stories about scandals. The true opponents of the right-wing Press, then, are the political left and the anti-racists, those who have at least some power to challenge white dominance, if only in some schools, universities, or city councils.

More generally, the attitude towards minorities or immigration that may be derived from the fragments quoted above, as well as from others we have examined before, is that of conditional acceptance. Thus, minorities should be meek (like the hard-working Asians), satisfied with what 'we' give them (and hence not make unreasonable demands), adapt themselves to the dominant white British culture, be self-reliant (they should not cost the taxpayer too much), accept their lower position in all sectors of social life and generally avoid being a 'threat' to 'our' safety, interests, privileges, well-being, and position.

These conditions of paternalistic 'tolerance' and acceptance also suggest that the right-wing Press is not only concerned about power in the symbolic realm. Its violent reactions against any form of affirmative action imply that socio-economic power in particular is also involved: businesses should not be limited by administrative or legal measures that counter discrimination or other forms of inequality on the job market. Thus, the advocacy of 'freedom' of speech is closely linked to 'freedom' of enterprise (which seems to imply 'freedom' to discriminate). That even this kind of conditional tolerance is very fragile, may be concluded from the following passage in the *Mail*:

> (Immigration) Our traditions of fairness and tolerance are being exploited by every terrorist, crook, screwball and scrounger who wants a free ride at our expense ... Then there are the criminals who sneak in as political refugees or as family members visiting a distant relative. (*Mail*, 28 November)

## Popular appeals

The concerns and interests of the popular Press and the conservative politicians may not be those of the public at large. This means that the ideological framework must be strategically 'translated' in such a way that a broader reading public can also accept it. Therefore, news reports, especially in the tabloids, feature a number of popular appeals that are powerfully persuasive for those readers who do not have alternative sources of information or robust counter-ideologies. These appeals essentially embody references to various types of threat, to territory, income/money, jobs, housing, safety, welfare, and values. Thus, immigration may be translated as a perceived threat to 'our' territory, with arguments such as: Because of the 'invasion' of thousands of foreigners, we are 'swamped', and 'we do not feel at home anymore'. Similarly, these immigrants may be presented as taking away our jobs or houses, and cheap immigrant labour may be denounced as unfair competition for the wages of ordinary white British workers. Similarly, 'black crime' is represented as a threat to our safety, the dole as a waste of the taxpayer's money and all these different cultures (language, religion, customs) as a threat to our British culture.

To emphasize the relevance of such issues for 'ordinary' people, the right-wing Press also assumes a clearly anti-intellectual stance, in which the scornful remarks about 'sociologists' nicely fit, and which at the same time conveys a philosophy of common sense. Topics, argumentation and the local meaning strategies studied in this chapter all focus on the persuasive communication of this ideology of common sense ("it is not fair"), reactions to the various 'threats' of immigration and the presence of ethnic minorities. It is not surprising therefore that when right-wing columnist Ms Lee-Potter summarizes such reactions of the readers, her column is headlined: "THANK GOD YOU HAVE WRITTEN WHAT WE THINK."

## Conclusion

Our analysis has gradually discovered further ideological coherence and foundation in the meanings and beliefs expressed by the conservative Press. At this local level of news reports and background stories we also find a host of indications of the interpretation basis of ethnic affairs. Along the familiar dimensions of in-group ('us') and out-group ('them') articulation, then, we find first that 'we', ordinary white British, are represented and defended as tolerant and peaceful, as people who love freedom of speech and enterprise, who love their country, respect authority (such as the police), and who are law-abiding and commonsensical. The opposite holds for 'them', including the immigrants (except, in some cases, the Asians), and especially the anti-racists and the loony left. They are portrayed as aggressive, tyrannical, and intolerant; they indoctrinate our youth, incite to race hatred and therefore are inverted racists (they hate the English); they are either criminal or condone and excuse crime, spend too much taxpayers' money, do not respect our values, and accuse us of prejudice and discrimination.

For the public at large especially, this negative portrayal of minorities, white anti-racists and the left, may be translated into a persuasive set of popular appeals based on an ideology of commonsense interpretations and evaluations of the ethnic situation. We have also seen that the interests that underlie this ideology can be explained in terms of a struggle for symbolic power, in which the Press competes with other groups (teachers, academics, writers, left-wing politicians, anti-racists) for control over the definition of the ethnic situation. However, this struggle at the same time appears to have important socio-economic implications, in which 'freedom of speech' is closely related to 'freedom of enterprise'. In the field of reporting about ethnic affairs, these two ideological goals not only define the dominant conservative ideology, but also the ideology of white group power in general.

# 8  Style and rhetoric

## THE RELEVANCE OF STYLE AND RHETORIC

After the analysis of several types of underlying structures in previous chapters, we finally turn to the so-called 'surface structures' or expression level of race reporting, that is, its style and rhetoric. Style has to do with the choice and variation of the words journalists use when writing about minorities, and with the sentence patterns that organize these words. Style is the trace in the text of the personal opinions of speakers as well as of the social context of language use. Rhetoric, as understood here, deals with special verbal ploys, such as alliterations and metaphors, that help catch the reader's attention, and which therefore are primarily used with a persuasive aim. An analysis of style tells us what the *appropriate* use of words is in order to express meaning in a specific situation or discourse genre. Rhetorical study tells us what the most *effective* way is when communicating our meanings and beliefs.

In reporting about ethnic affairs, style and rhetoric play an important function. We have repeatedly observed in the previous chapters that, even more so than for other subject matters, writing about race is riddled with opinions. Sometimes delicate topics and complex attitudes must be subtly and persuasively formulated in order both to inform and persuade the reading public. Similarly, the social context of race relations, including news reporting about it, involves writers and readers who belong to various social formations or institutions, and this membership of class, gender, and race shows not only in *what* journalists write about ethnic affairs, but also *how* they do that.

Little scholarly analysis is needed to establish that there are also significant style differences between conservative and liberal newspapers and especially between the 'quality' Press and the tabloids. In our analyses of headlines and local semantics, we already have seen that what for one paper is a "disturbance" may be a "murderous looting spree" for another, and also what meanings are attached to such words as "freedom" and "tolerance". This chapter focuses on such journalistic 'formulations' of ethnic events, and aims to make inferences from such stylistic and rhetoric devices about the meanings and opinions of journalists about these events.

## LEXICAL STYLE

Let us begin with the most obvious aspect of the study of 'formulation' in race reporting, the choice of words, that is, its lexical style. Above we defined the style of a text as those properties of its expression that may vary as a function of the personal and especially the social context (Scherer and Giles, 1979). This selection may vary with the text genre as well as with the opinions, the social situation, group membership, or culture of the writer. The use of "thug" rather than "demonstrator" signals different underlying opinions about the people referred to. That is, a journalist may choose between these two variants (and many others) to refer to the same person or group member, and this choice is controlled by socially shared opinions, attitudes, and ideologies (Chilton, 1988; Geis, 1987; Kress, 1985; Sandell, 1977).

Similarly, headlines may frequently use the short word "bid" where other discourse genres such as everyday conversations will rather use "attempt" or "try". This is a typical example of genre style. But even within the same newspaper, we may again find a variation between, for example, "PC", "policeman" (or "policewoman"), "bobby", "copper", or "cop", as is also the case in the many reports about the 'race riots' in Britain. These uses may differ according to the formality of the specific newspaper article, but may also signal different attitudes towards the police: "bobby" is obviously friendlier than "cop", which is again less negative than non-media words like "pig", which is only occasionally quoted as an expression of young people in conflict with the police.

The factor of social situation is closely tied to the role of text genre in the determination of lexical style. Mass media communication, despite its wide variation, is a specific type of social situation. It is public, more or less formal and monological, among other things, and this precludes the use of specific words and favours others (Lüger, 1983). Indeed, the wish of the *Sun* that Bernie Grant "may rot in hell" is remarkable in the sense that it borrows the 'colloquial' style from everyday informal conversation. Yet it crucially differs from such a conversation, or even from an informal letter or lecture, by the fact that the personal pronoun "I" is systematically absent from this editorial. If a personal pronoun is used at all, it will be "we". However, usually the writer will refer to the source of the message as the name of the newspaper, as is also suggested by the heading over the *Sun*'s editorials: THE SUN SAYS ...

Finally, the broader social context and culture may impinge on the choice of words. Newspapers in western Europe are mostly written by white men (and by a few, also white, women). These social factors determine their perspective and opinions on ethnic affairs, and will therefore also guide their choice of words.

Hence, most of the words used in the Press to describe social reality will thus signal the 'position' of the writer, that is, journalistic opinion, newspaper discourse genre, social or communicative situation, and group membership and culture. At the same time, within each of these contexts, such words may vary along several dimensions of informality, unfriendliness, solidarity, dominance, or power (Kramarae, Schulz, and O'Barr, 1984; van Dijk, 1989a). Thus, the choice of words will also reveal who is in control and what the relations are between writers and readers, or between writers and people they write about. Let us examine some of these style patterns in the Press reports about race relations in Britain.

### "Blacks", "West Indians", "Asians", or "English"?

A first important aspect of style concerns the identification of participants in ethnic events. We have seen that there are variations in the words used to refer to people of West Indian origin. Often, they are called "West Indians", sometimes "blacks" and occasionally "Afro-Caribbeans". The uses of these and related words have different implications and associations, also depending on the social position or beliefs of the user. Thus, "blacks" may be used generally for all people who have African ancestors, but its use may also specifically apply to West Indians, whether or not they are of West African, Asian and some of European background. For our analysis, however, it is even more relevant to note that "West Indians" is also used for those people who have British nationality and who were born in Britain. Such use, therefore, emphasizes the origin of ancestors or the membership of a specific community or ethnic group.

In many situations such references to ethnic group membership are irrelevant, and have been proscribed by the Code of Conduct of the National Union of Journalists, a prohibition which is however widely ignored. During the period of our analysis, there was a court case against *The Times*, which had used a reference to the ethnic background of a suspect. The case was won by *The Times* because the judge ruled that the issue was already widely known, and the suspect already often identified by his ethnic background. The judge also found that *The Times* did not use the reference to the ethnic background as an explanation for the crime committed. A similar case was won by the *Sun* who had identified somebody as 'Irish'. Whereas the liberal Press generally avoids making irreievant references to the ethnic background of crime suspects, the right-wing Press often identifies them as "black".

More generally, the irrelevant use of identifications of ethnic background in the right-wing Press is associated with negative opinions about the news actors. Interestingly, the reverse is also true. Black people, such as famous pop stars or sportsmen and women, may simply be called "British" (or "Dutch" in the Dutch Press), or not be identified by origin or nationality at all, when they have a non-controversial positive role. One reader of the *Telegraph* takes offence against this practice:

(Letter to the editor) Sir – Can you explain why black Englishmen and women who win Olympic medals or excel at games are described as 'English' while those who riot and throw petrol bombs are almost invariably 'West Indian'? (*Telegraph*, 13 September 1985)

It is not surprising that the editor of the Telegraph doesn't answer that question. Unless brought to court, newspapers (including liberal ones) never answer such questions, and never discuss in more general terms possible criticisms of their race reporting.

The use of "Asians" is even more general and confused than that of "West Indians". In the British Press, the term is mostly used as a catch-all phrase for all people who come from (or whose ancestors come from) the South Asian continent, even including people who immigrated from East Africa but whose ancestors are from South Asia. The term seldom includes East Asians, for instance, people from China, Japan, or Hongkong, nor people from South-East Asia, for example, from Vietnam or Thailand; in these cases the specific nationality is mostly used. Sometimes, "Asians" are specified as "Indians", "Pakistani", "Bangladeshis", or "Sri Lankans", especially in more personal, individualized reporting and interviewing. In reports about immigration, the overall term "new commonwealth citizens" may be used in this case.

In combination with, and to mark a distinction with "black", Asians are sometimes referred to as "brown" in the Press and by some news actors. On the other hand, the term "black" may also be used, in a more political sense, by those quoted news actors who use the term for any "non-white" (or non-European) person in Britain, that is, including all people of African, Asian (or Australian Aboriginal), Pacific, or Amerindian (or sometimes generally Latin American) origin.

For most of the Press, however, "black" means African (except the Arab countries of Northern Africa) or Afro-Caribbean. The uses of such terms in the Press, everyday conversation, and political rhetoric, are so varied, however, that a special study would be needed to track the precise associations and stylistic implications of these terms. Thus, whereas for black people and white anti-racists the term "black" may have neutral or positive implications, some of the right-wing Press and its readers may associate it with negative attitudes. That is, the implications of the use of the term are in that case closely tied to the attitudes about the people referred to.

In reporting about ethnic affairs, the white Press also needs a specific term to refer to its own in-group. When opposed to "black", the term "white" is of course common, but also "Britons" may be used, as if referring to a specific, white, European tribe. Confusion is rife here, because it usually does not refer to all people born in Great Britain, but to people of white British "stock", as right-wing writers sometimes say. Similarly, especially in reporting about the politics of immigration, we may find variations between "passport holders", which is mostly used to refer to non-white immigrants with a British passport, or British "nationals", which is often used to refer to white British people.

We see that writing about the "multi-ethnic" society also implies a complex panoply of terms, with many different associations depending on who exactly uses the term, in what situation, and about what topic. Note that these identifying descriptions of the 'other' also may be a form of problematization. Since 'white' is the norm, it is much less used than 'black', whereas identification of Europeans in terms of Anglo-Saxons or Caucasians is exceptional in the Press.

## Negativization

If variations in lexical style are a function of underlying opinions and attitudes, we may expect that there are many ways to express positive or negative feelings about news actors. Whereas the liberal Press usually avoids clearly negative terms in its reporting, the right-wing Press is much less reticent. In our discussion of the headlines, we already examined which terms are used to refer negatively to mostly black rioters. More generally, such uses are also found in the reports themselves, either to denote news actors or their properties or actions. Those youths participating in the urban disturbances, are routinely described with the words "thugs", "hooligans", "mobs", or related ones, and seldom with less negative terms such as "demonstrators". The most general term in this case is "rioter", often preceded by negative adjectives such as "crazed" or "raging", or in combination with negative nouns such as "bloodlust". A riot itself is invariably called an "orgy of destruction and looting", which emphasizes both the criminal and the irrational nature of the riots.

Whereas it is hardly surprising that negative terms are used to describe what is seen as criminal activity (looting, arson, murder), such terms are however also used for perfectly legitimate actions, such as demonstrating or protesting. For the right-wing Press, such terms are specifically reserved for the left and anti-racists, as we may predict from our semantic analyses of the last chapter. Thus, the conservative Press will often describe the demonstrators who protest against Honeyford as "noisy" (for example, *Times*, 17 September).

The description of leftists and anti-racists and their activities apparently stimulates the lexical inventiveness of the right-wing Press. Here is an abbreviated list of characteristic examples from July 1985–January 1986 (those in headlines are in capitals):

Snoopers (*Telegraph*, 1 August, editorial)
A noisy mob of activist demonstrators (*Telegraph*, 23 September)
These dismal fanatics, monstrous creatures (*Telegraph*, 26 September)
Unscrupulous or feather-brained observers (*Telegraph*, 30 September)
The British race relations pundits (*Telegraph*, 1 October)
Trotskyites, socialist extremists, Revolutionary Communists, Marxists and Black militants (*Telegraph*, 9 October)
Race conflict 'high priests' (*Telegraph*, 11 October)
Bone-brained Left-fascism (*Telegraph*, 30 November, editorial)
The multi-nonsense brigade (*Telegraph*, 11 January)
Mob of left-wing crazies (*Mail*, 24 September)
THE RENT-A-RIOT AGITATORS (*Mail*, 30 September)
What a goon (said about Bernie Grant) (*Mail*, 10 October, Frank Chapple)
He and his henchmen ... this obnoxious man, left-wing inquisitor (about Grant) (*Mail*, 18 October)
SNOOPERS, untiring busybodies (*Sun*, 2 August, editorial)
Blinkered tyrants (*Sun*, 6 September)
Left-wing crackpots (*Sun*, 7 September)
A pack trying to hound Ray Honeyford (*Sun*, 25 September)
Unleashing packs of Government snoopers (*Sun*, 16 October)
The hysterical 'anti-racist' brigade ... the Ayatollahs of Bradford, the Left-wing anti-racist mob (*Sun*, 23 October)

An analysis of these examples shows that the invectives tend to be chosen from very specific style registers, those of mental illness and irrationality, political and ideological intolerance and oppression, and finally that of threatening animals. We again witness the phenomenon of reversal, that is, the use of epithets that have been used against the tabloid Press itself.

## SYNTACTIC STYLE

After our analysis, in Chapter three, of some aspects of the syntactic structures of the headlines, and of the semantics of vagueness in the previous chapter, little need be said here about the ideological implications of sentence structure. As for syntactic complexity, measured, for instance, by the number of dependent clauses per sentence, it is not unexpected to find that the *Sun* has short, rather simple sentences, the *Mail* somewhat longer sentences, and the other newspapers the most complex ones, both in their editorials and in their news reports.

More interesting for our analysis is the syntactic realization of underlying meanings, such as the order and expression of participants in ethnic situations. We have witnessed before that negative acts of in-group members, such as the authorities or the police, may be reduced in effect by placing them later in the sentence or by keeping the agency implicit, for instance in passive sentences (Fowler *et al.*, 1979; Kress and Hodge, 1979; Sykes, 1985; van Dijk, 1988b, 1988c). Compare for instance the ways the Press tells the readers about the police shooting of an innocent black woman in Brixton (we include the Sunday papers because they had the first news of the event):

> The build-up to the riot in Brixton on Saturday evening began at about 2 pm in Normandy Road, where seven hours earlier a police officer shot Mrs Cherry Groce at her home. (*Guardian*, 30 September)

> Rioting mobs of youths set Brixton ablaze last night in an outburst of fury at the police for accidentally shooting a black woman. (*Sunday Times*, 29 September)

> On Saturday, police were petrol-bombed, shops looted and cars burned after the shooting of a West Indian woman. (*Times*, 30 September)

> YARD REGRET AFTER BLACK WOMAN IS SHOT IN RAID. A mob of about 300 youths, mainly black, went on the rampage in Brixton last night after Cherry Groce, a 38-year-old black woman, was shot and seriously wounded during a police raid on her home early yesterday. (*Sunday Telegraph*, 29 September)

> RIOT AFTER POLICE SHOOT MOTHER OF 6. (*Mail on Sunday*, 29 September)

> GRIM WAIT FACES THE SHOT MUM. Gun-raid victim Cherry Groce was told yesterday she faces a grim 72-hour wait before learning if she will ever walk again. (*Sun*, 30 September)

The use of passive sentences ("Mrs Groce was shot by police") or nominalizations ("the shooting of Mrs Groce") may be explained by several factors of news discourse structure. The main factor is previous knowledge: when the readers are supposed to already know what happened (for example, through television reporting, as is the case here), the shooting may be presupposed by a nomimal expression instead of a full sentence. Also, such an abbreviated proposition may be used when part of a larger sentence (as in "the shooting is being investigated by ...").

However, these examples also show that the Press uses several syntactic strategies in the accentuation of the negative role of black youths and the mitigation of the negative role of the police. Very few reports feature sentences such as "The police shot ..." as a main clause or headline. Rather, their role must be inferred by the reader from such expressions as "during a raid", or from an action in which "the police were involved". We have earlier seen that if the shooting cannot be denied it will be described as "accidental" or as a "tragic mistake". On the other hand, when the police have a positive role, as in the headline we have analysed before, "POLICE SAVE ASIANS", they are put in prominent first position (for earlier critical analyses of these syntactic strategies, see, for example, Fowler, Hodge, Kress, and Trew, 1979).

In the examples analysed above, as well as in other examples, we finally also found that events may be strategically played down by the syntactic structure of the sentence, for example, by referring to the event in a 'lower' (later, less prominent) embedded clause, or conversely by putting it in first position when the event needs extra prominence. The latter is typically the case in the Press for the contents of declarative sentences. Instead of saying, for instance, "The police claimed that black youths ...", we may frequently find "Black youths ... said the police"; in the latter case the main clause is put at the end, so that the contents of the allegation are put as if they were a fact, at the beginning of the sentence, especially when the actions of the black youths are negative.

# RHETORIC

Although the notion of 'rhetoric' may be interpreted in its classical way, that is, as the 'art of good speaking (or writing)', which would involve grammar, style, and many other aspects of discourse structure and language use, we here limit a rhetorical analysis to specific 'rhetorical' operations, such as the well-known figures of style (which in our analysis have little to do with 'style' as defined above) (for various contemporary approaches to rhetoric, see, for example, Corbett, 1971; Kahane, 1971).

Our analysis of the British Press shows that specific rhetorical features are especially frequent in the right-wing Press. The *Guardian* and *The Times* have an occasional metaphor and sometimes an alliteration in their headlines, but on the whole they avoid 'ornate' language use. The *Telegraph*, and especially the *Mail* and *Sun*, on the other hand, love it, and most of their headlines, lead sentences, and editorials offer rich grounds for rhetorical exploration.

It should be noted, however, that strictly speaking rhetoric is independent of meaning, and therefore only indirectly related to ideological readings. After all, ideological opponents may well make use of the same rhetorical strategies. Whether or not a proposition is expressed with an alliteration, or in the form of a syntactic parallelism, does not as such allow us to make inferences about the position or beliefs of the speaker. However, rhetorical 'figures' are non-obligatory additional structures in texts that may draw attention, and may therefore indirectly emphasize specific meanings. One result of this specific focus, for instance of a 'catchy' alliterative headline, is the heightened probability of recall by the readers, and therefore a more persistent influence of the news report, and its definition of the situation. Other rhetorical figures, for instance in editorials, may underscore the argumentation of the newspaper. Let us examine some examples, and see whether they may have specific functions in race reporting. It may be asked, for instance, whether rhetorical figures accompany specific content or opinions, or whether they tend to be associated with specific news actors.

## Repetition: alliteration, rhyme, parallelism

*Alliteration* is one of the most prominent figures in the popular Press. It typically occurs in headlines, lead sentences, editorials, and opinion articles, that is, in sentences that express evaluative meanings or opinions, and much less in the 'normal' reporting of events:

(Immigration) But far from acknowledging their colossal blunder, they *carry* on with the *cant and claptrap*, the illusion of race equality and the fiction that people are British if they choose to say so. (*Telegraph*, 19 October, column by Honor Tracy)

(Handsworth) FACE TO FACE WITH THE FEAR AND FURY OF LOZELLS ROAD. (*Mail*, 11 September)

(What are they teaching them?) If it isn't the three Rs, perhaps it is the three Ss instead: *sedition, subversion and sociological hogwash. (Mail*, 19 October)

(Tottenham) BOMBS, BULLETS, BLOOD IN BARRICADED BRITAIN. (*Mail*, 27 December)

The widow of Keith Blakelock, the *brave bobby butchered by black* rioters, said last night that she pitied the killers. (*Sun*, 8 October)

These examples show that alliterations are mainly used when describing alleged aggression or other negative acts of immigrants or minority groups or generally in situations of tension and conflict attributed to them, such as the riots. Their function in that case seems to be to emphasize the meaning or evaluation of the sentence or headline – which is indeed 'hammered home' by such alliterations: a "West Indian bomber" is less impressive than a "black bomber", "fear and fury" match better than 'fear and anger' and the pair "cant and claptrap" is even more negative than 'nonsense' alone. On the other hand, we have only an occasional positive use of an alliteration, such as a "brave bobby", which also serves to emphasize the evaluation. We have found only one example in which alliteration is used in a sentence where blacks are represented as victims (of unnamed actors!): BIAS "BARS BLACKS FROM JOBS" (*Mail*, 18 September). There is also occasional use of *rhyme*, for instance in the the *Mail* headline "RAY MUST STAY".

*Parallelism* is more frequent, and especially used in editorials and columns:

(Handsworth disturbances) It was, in essence, not a race riot ... It was not a 'spontaneous eruption' of human misery ... It was not 'caused' by unemployment, or poverty. (*Telegraph* 13 September, editorial)

(Honeyford) For speaking common sense he's been vilified; for being courageous he's been damned, for refusing to concede defeat his enemies can't forgive him. (*Mail*, 18 September, column by Lynda Lee-Potter)

(Tottenham) Now it is not merely sticks and stones and petrol bombs. Now it is shotguns and knives. Now it is not merely cuts and bruises. Now it is murder. (*Sun*, 8 October, editorial)

(Freedom of speech) We have tyranny in Britain. We have intimidation. We have a sinister attempt first to curb and then to destroy freedom of speech. We have racism too – and that is what is behind the plot. It is not white racism. It is black racism. (*Sun*, 24 October)

We see that parallelism especially serves argumentation, in all cases directed against young blacks and anti-racists. Sometimes the parallelism is accompanied by repeated negation ("it was not ... it was not ..."), or in a figure of contrast ("it was not ... it was ..."), sometimes even combined with other figures, such as alliteration ("vicious mob ... victims", "sticks and stones"). Special emphasis can be given to the parallelism by a climax, that is, when the subsequent propositions are placed higher on a scale of seriousness: from sticks and stones and petrol bombs to shotguns and knives, from cuts and bruises to murder. We see that parallelism and alliteration seem to have similar functions of emphasizing negative properties of opponents. Whereas alliteration however focuses on negative news actors and events, parallelism underscores argumentative steps made in evaluating such events.

## Hyperbole

Whereas the previous figures operate at the level of sound and sentence structure, most other figures are semantic and operate on meanings, as we already have seen in our local semantic analysis. Thus, meanings may be emphasized, for instance, by exaggeration or hyperbole, or de-emphasized, perhaps by understatement, litotes, or other forms of mitigation. It need hardly be repeated whose negative or positive actions will be emphasized or de-emphasized in this way. A few examples, selected from many others:

> (Honeyford) ... a *guerilla* campaign. (*Mail*, 16 September)

> (Broadwater Farm) Militant youths who masterminded the Tottenham riots planned the *mass murder of policemen in a blazing underground trap.* (*Mail*, 12 January)

> TORY'S MOB TERROR. A top Tory last night told of his terror when a mob of students spat and threw water at him. (*Sun*, November 9)

Such examples are hardly surprising in the tabloid Press and certainly not limited to race reporting. Dramatization, exaggeration, and hyperbole are the main rhetorical tricks of the popular Press to make the news more exciting. However, when race relations are involved, such exaggerations suddenly become highly selective: They are used especially to emphasize the aggression or other negative properties of black people. Thus, tackling another person becomes a "vicious attack" when a controversial black councillor like Bernie Grant does it, disturbances are not merely described as "riots" but even as "mob war" when young West Indians are involved, a policeman is not "stabbed", but "hacked down and mutilated in a fury of blood lust" – a description which is unthinkable when the police shoots a black woman. Being spat at, or being splashed with water, in a racist talk, is represented as terror. And so on.

Again, such rhetoric would be innocent or would just make juicy reading in the popular Press account of events, which is close to everyday exaggerations in conversation about mundane happenings. However, we have found that 'hyperbolism' it not a general rhetorical feature of the tabloids. Rather, it is selectively used to emphasize and dramatize the negative events and actions in which the left, blacks, and anti-racists are involved. Little psychology is needed to infer that particularly in the context of a racist society, such a dramatic emphasis on the real or alleged negative actions of minority groups "stirs up race hatred", rather than mitigates it. To get a more coherent impression of this form of hyperbolic rhetoric, consider the following example of what the *Sun* itself would probably call 'verbal terror', combining most of the stylistic and rhetorical structures analysed above:

> HATE OF A BLACK BOMBER. A black thug stalks a Birmingham street with hate in his eyes and a petrol bomb in his hand. The prowling maniac was one of the West Indian hoodlums who brought new race terror to the city's riot-torn Handsworth district yesterday. And as darkness fell over smoke-blackened ruins of a stunned community, fears of more mayhem loomed. Sullen gangs of coloured youths roamed the area watched warily by squads of weary police. (*Sun*, 11 September)

## Understatement

As soon as blacks or other minority are victims of white "terror", we seldom find such exaggerations. We have found that 'racism' as a word is taboo, and only used as a discrediting quote. Even discrimination may thus be mitigated to nearly innocent proportions of 'unfair' treatment or even 'bad luck', always without mentioning the white perpetrators of a crime, which is *never* called a crime in the Press:

> (CRE report on discrimination) HOME LOANS 'UNFAIR TO BLACKS' (*Telegraph*, 16 October)

> WHERE BLACKS LOSE OUT ON HOME LOANS (*Mail*, 16 October)

> 'BIAS' BARS BLACKS FROM JOBS (*Mail*, 18 September)

Analysis of the actions of the Tory administration, of the police or of other white authorities in power also show that while hyperboles are common in tabloid reporting, some form of whitewashing will also be subtly used to de-emphasize the responsibility of political in-group

members. In other words, we see again that although rh
themselves may be ideologically neutral, their use is hig
description of the ethnic situation: they emphasize th
'them', and play down 'our' 'mistakes'.

## Metaphor, comparison and metonymia

The final set of rhetorical devices amply used in evaluative writing in the
Press are metaphors and comparisons. Again, they are rare in standard
reporting, but often show up in editorials, columns, and background
features. We have already shown that traditional lexical metaphors are
used when describing the riots as a "war", and demonstrators as
"guerillas". That is, events and people are described by words that are
literally inappropriate in that situation, but which focus on a specific
dimension of these events, or people, such as their "warlike" nature.
Again, the riots especially inspire the more literary minded of the
journalists:

> (Handsworth) Malice and criminal inspiration stalked the streets of
> Handsworth that night ... In Handsworth itself there were innocent
> victims who perished in the flames of anarchy. (*Times*, 11 September)

> (Handsworth) Police chief tells of riot locusts in Handsworth (*Times*,
> 18 September)

> THE ENGLISH BECOME THE LOST TRIBE OF RACE RELATIONS.
> (*Telegraph*, 21 November)

> (Handsworth) FLAMES OF WRATH IN THE CITY OF FEAR (*Mail*, 11
> September)

> (Handsworth) SALVAGE THE TRUTH FROM THE FLAMES. On the
> high-stepping heels of carnival, came the killing ... After a long, wet
> summer, the sun at last shines warmly on smouldering rubble and
> recrimination, which mock both hope and good will. (*Mail*, 11
> September)

> (Immigration). All this is *weaponry for the class warriors*. (*Times*, 17
> October, Ronald Butt)

British race relations, for the tabloid Press, is defined as a "war of the
races", in which by the usual reversal we have earlier studied, the whites
are the victims ("the lost tribe of race relations"). When ethnic affairs are
marred by violent disturbances, we may expect all possible metaphors
that combine the domains of war, crime, catastrophe, and apocalypse.

...inspire expressions such as "the flames of anarchy" or, even ...inbeckian, the "flames of wrath" in Handsworth, variously called ...bleeding heart of England" or an "inner city jungle", apparently the ...osen location of black people. When speaking of rioters, police chief Dear prefers "locusts". Ronald Butt of *The Times* sticks to the war domain of metaphorization when calling the leftist enemy the "class warriors". The distribution of positive and negative metaphors dovetails with the allegiances of the right-wing Press. Where blacks are associated with war, crime, and anarchy, the police are said to "wear a badge of courage". We have earlier encountered comparisons between anti-racists and the Nazis, Goebbels, the ayatollahs or even "pocket Hitlers".

Metonymias are less frequent, but no less literary. Honeyford is thus "greeted by empty desks". However, sometimes they are less innocent, especially in newspaper shorthand. We have seen in the analysis of the headlines that short forms may often be used to describe a person or event, for example, Honeyford as the "race-row head". In this case this would be apt, because he actually caused the race-row. On other occasions however, such shorthands are confusing if not misleading. To call Mrs Jarrett the "riot woman" (*Mail*, 29 November) is no longer an innocent metonymia, but an association that ties an innocent victim to the riot as if she (and not the police) were the cause or the participant in the riot. The same is true for her son, called the "riot son" by the *Sun* (14 December). Conversely, the police victim of the same riot in Tottenham is never called the 'riot policeman'.

## CONCLUSIONS

The analysis of style and rhetoric, that is, of the formulation devices of news discourse, further supports the conclusions found in the previous chapters. What at first sight may be innocent variations of lexical selection or of rhetorical artistry, appears to be a subtle – and often not so subtle – way to vilify the enemies of the right-wing Press, and rhetorically to emphasize such evaluations. Whereas large parts of routine news reports may have a more neutral style, the crucial headlines and leads, which define and evaluate ethnic situations, will often be used by the right-wing Press to put a negative characterization of its participants firmly in place before the reader starts to interpret the rest of the report. Editorials, features and columns, in which opinions are expected, are even less reticent with lexical abuse, drawn especially from the areas of mental health, warfare, animal life, or political oppression. In that case, the enemies are either described as crazy, at best as irrational, and more often than not as top criminals: mass murderers, Nazis, ayatollahs, inquisitors, tyrants, and similar scum of the earth. There is little doubt about the position of the right-wing Press in this kind of reporting and editorializing.

Blacks, leftists, and anti-racists are not the only victims of these forms of white verbal aggression. The many millions of readers of the conservative Press also become involved when daily confronted with this rhetoric of race hate. In the next chapter we investigate how the reading public reacts to the more subtle kinds of reporting about race in the Netherlands. We may then also begin to answer the question whether it is the Press that instills or confirms latent prejudice and racism, or whether it simply reflects what most readers think anyway.

# 9 The reproduction of news about ethnic affairs

## THE PRESS AND ITS PUBLIC

The study of the role of the Press in the reproduction of racism cannot be limited to an analysis of the meanings and forms of its news reports about ethnic affairs. To understand this role, we need to know how news reports affect the readers. Therefore, this chapter briefly summarizes the results of a research project that examines one aspect of the notorious problem of media 'influence'. We carried out in-depth interviews with some 150 people in the Netherlands and asked them about a number of 'ethnic' issues they had learned about from their newspapers. Detailed discourse analysis of these interviews not only gives us some insight into the ethnic attitudes and ideologies of different kinds of readers, but also into the problem of how such social cognitions are shaped by the forms and contents of the Press stories about these issues.

### The problem of influence

The theoretical and empirical problems of such a study are immense. A year-long, multidisciplinary research project would be necessary to solve only a few of them. Research in mass communication and social psychology has for decades sought to uncover the complex mechanisms that underly the processes of media 'effects' (Klapper, 1960). This research tradition is known to have yielded confused if not contradictory results, ranging from early assessments about the vast influence of the mass media to more sceptical conclusions about the role of mass communication in the formation and change of social beliefs (McQuail, 1983; Robinson and Levy, 1986). This confusion soon led to new approaches to the problem. For instance, research on 'agenda-setting' proposed to investigate not so much how the media influence what people think, but rather what they think *about* (Iyengar and Kinder, 1987;

McCombs and Shaw, 1972; Rogers and Dearing, 1988).

Socio-political studies of media influence focused less on the study of specific, immediate changes of opinions on social issues, but emphasized the broader role of the media in the formation of ideological frameworks of interpretation (Cohen and Young, 1981; Collins *et al.*, 1986; Hall *et al.*, 1980). In the latter perspective of research, which also provides elements of the conceptual framework of our own research, the crucial question is not primarily how the media specifically influence *what* people think, or even what people think *about*, but it is which role the media play in determining *how* the public thinks about social and political reality, that is, what structural role the media have in the reproduction of culture and dominant ideologies. Whereas the media may have rather heterogeneous short-range effects on media users, this broader, structural influence on the formation of ideological frameworks of representation is probably fundamental.

## A new approach

Our own approach to the complex problem of media influence starts from our conclusion that most of the questions asked in the earlier directions of research may have been relevant, but that they were also often too simplistic, too general, and too vague. Indeed, even the most elementary notions of the process of media influence were ignored or dealt with only superficially. For instance, media influence implies an influence of various types of media discourse. However, apart from some attention paid to elementary structures of argumentation and rhetoric, none of the traditional approaches developed a systematic theory of the structures or strategies of such discourse. The influence of such discourse means the influence on the cognitions of media users. Despite earlier work on cognitions in cognitive and social psychology, however, we are only now beginning to understand some of the details of the processes involved in the understanding of text or talk and the transformation of knowledge and beliefs. And finally, the notion of media effects mostly focused on attitudes and ultimately on the actions of media users based on such attitudes. In traditional social psychology, there is a vast literature on attitudes and attitude change (for surveys, see, for example, Fishbein and Ajzen, 1975; Himmelfarb and Eagly, 1974; and, more recently, Eiser and van der Pligt, 1988). Yet, we still hardly know what such attitudes look like exactly, and by which cognitive processes, and in which social situations, these attitudes are formed and changed, or how precisely attitudes relate to action and interaction, for that matter (see also Zanna, Olson, and Herman, 1987). In other words, in order to answer the question of media influence, we first need to answer many other, more specific questions, and our answers need to be vastly more precise and detailed than those given in earlier work.

## Recent developments

Fortunately, recent developments in a number of disciplines allow us partly to answer some of these more specific questions. Thus, recent discourse analytical approaches have suggested how news texts may be analysed in a systematic and explicit way (van Dijk, 1988a, 1988b). The previous chapters have illustrated this approach in a more informal manner. That is, for our own research problem, we now know more or less what the properties are of news discourse about ethnic affairs: its main topics, its schematic organization, its local meanings, and its style and rhetoric.

Similarly, at various points in our analysis, we have already suggested that such a textual analysis is closely linked with a cognitive approach. After all, questions of meaning, interpretation, and understanding are not merely answered in semantics, but also have to do with people's minds, that is, involve the actual mental processing of texts by the readers. During the last fifteen years, these processes of understanding, memorizing, and using information from texts have been studied in detail (van Dijk and Kintsch, 1983), and the results of this work have recently also been applied in the study of the processing of news by media users (Graber, 1984; Gunter, 1987; Höijer and Findahl, 1984; van Dijk, 1988a).

## Social cognitions

The same cognitivistic framework has more recently had a decisive influence in social psychology (Fiske and Taylor, 1984; Wyer and Srull, 1984). This means that elusive notions such as 'attitudes', and the strategies of their actual use, can now be analysed in much more (though still far from adequate) ways, for instance in terms of what are called 'social cognitions' or 'social representations' (Farr and Moscovici, 1984). This means that we also finally have some idea about the important, but equally vague, notion of 'stereotype' or 'prejudice' (Hamilton, 1981; van Dijk, 1987a), or even about the broader (and even vaguer) notion of 'ethnic (or racial) ideology'. When we talk about the 'influence' of the Press on the readers, or more broadly, about the role of the Press in the reproduction of racism, we refer to this process: how media discourses contribute to the formation and change of the social representations of the readers about themselves as a group, about ethnic minorities, and about the relations between these groups. And this question needs to be answered before we can even begin to think of the next question, which partly lies outside the scope of discourse analysis proper: how do these social representations about ethnic groups monitor the actions of the media users, for instance in forms of everyday discrimination?

## From social representations to social talk

One dimension of this crucial, 'ultimate' question about the notion of influence, how do social representations influence action, does however fall within the scope of an interdisciplinary discourse analysis. That is, the 'actions' engaged in on the basis of social representations are very often also verbal actions, that is, forms of text and talk (van Dijk, 1990). Indeed, probably more often than interacting with ethnic minorities, most white people talk or write about them. We analysed thousands of such forms of discourse for the research reported in the previous chapters as well as in several earlier studies (see, for example, van Dijk, 1984, 1987a). This discourse may be analysed again in order to reconstruct, through a complex set of procedures, what white people actually think about ethnic minorities. Thus, one way of studying the complex process of media influence, is to ask people to talk informally about the ethnic issues they have read about in the paper and to analyse such interviews. This will yield suggestions about the detailed contents and structures of more general attitudes about minorities, as well as about some of the relations between these social representations and the social representations of journalists expressed and persuasively conveyed by news reports in the Press, as we have analysed them in the previous chapters.

## NOTIONS FROM A THEORETICAL FRAMEWORK

After this first, informal analysis of the problems of media influence and the reproduction of racism, a brief summary of our theoretical framework is in order before we summarize some results of the empirical study on readers' responses to Press reports about ethnic affairs.

A first assumption of this framework is that the formation or change of the ethnic beliefs of the readers as a function of news reports in the Press presupposes that the readers actually *understand* such news reports. That people first have to understand a text before being able to use its information seems obvious, but research shows that many people sometimes understand very little of news reports (Findahl and Höijer, 1984; Gunter, 1987). Hence, the process of influence must be based on that 'little' that readers *do* understand. Secondly, whatever people may understand of news reports, they can only use their relevant information later when they *remember* this information. Again, this may seem trivial, but research also shows that people remember very little of the news they see on television or read in the paper (Graber, 1984; Gunter, 1987; Robinson and Levy, 1986). Therefore, any influence of the Press must be based on the little people *do* memorize of what they read. Thirdly, most theories in cognitive and social psychology assume that understanding, remembering, and further uses made of textual information are neither passive, nor limited to the information people derive from discourse (van Dijk and Kintsch, 1983). Rather, they are engaged in the *active construction* of their 'own' interpretations of news reports, and they make massive use of many other sources of information during this process of understanding, notably of their already vast *knowledge* about the world. Finally, again not quite trivially, it must be realized that these active processes of understanding and memorization are embedded in a social, cultural, and political *context*. This means that we need to spell out in detail how the socio-cultural action of newspaper reading, media use, or the socio-political position of the readers affect these processes of understanding and belief formation. Unfortunately, we know very little about the detailed mechanisms of these socio-political constraints on news comprehension and recall.

These four assumptions, among many others, suggest why the relation between the news reports in the Press and the information people actually use in the formation and change of their ethnic beliefs is very indirect. They also explain why 'direct effects' of news reporting can seldom be observed and why experimental work on attitude and attitude change in the laboratory is so often inconclusive. The same is true for the role of the media in the formation and change of ethnic attitudes and ideologies. In other words, we must analyse in detail what processes are involved in understanding and memorization, and how knowledge and other social beliefs, as well as the communicative and socio-cultural context affect this process before they are themselves affected by it.

## Strategies

Let us introduce a few essential notions needed to talk somewhat more analytically about the processes involved. First, it must be stressed that all processes involved in the understanding and memorization of news (or other) discourse are *strategic* (van Dijk and Kintsch, 1983). This means that readers, unlike grammars or theories of discourse, do not try systematically or fully to analyse and understand a text, but only attend to those processes and information that may be used effectively to realize their goals. This means on the one hand that understanding may be partial and tentative, but on the other hand that it is very fast and usually adequate for most purposes. Thus, one of the strategies of news understanding may be to grasp only the overall meaning (topics, macrostructure) of the text, and readers may effectively realize that goal by only reading, or skimming the headlines and the lead. Note that many of these mental strategies are fully or semi-automated, and seldom 'conscious'. Another aspect of this strategic processing is that readers simultaneously obtain and combine information from different structural levels and sources at the same time, in a 'parallel' fashion. Thus, information about the lay-out, syntax, and semantics of the text may variously be attended to and combined with information from the context, or information derived from their knowledge about society. Hence, strategic processing is context dependent, goal oriented, flexible, multi-level, effective, and fast, but possibly incomplete.

It is in this strategic way that readers in principle go through a news discourse word by word, sentence by sentence, and gradually build a representation of the meaning of the text in memory. Especially when reading the newspaper, readers may also jump words, sentences, or whole fragments. Despite this occasionally fragmentary reading, high-level information in a text, such as its topics, tends to be memorized best, and research on news comprehension has repeatedly found the same effect. This means that even incomplete, partial understanding of a news report may well yield the crucial result that people understand the main topics of the news reports, even when they do not understand or ignore the details of a news report. We have also seen earlier that this process of interpretation makes use of vast amounts of knowledge, for example, of knowledge scripts, for instance about 'immigration' or 'riots'. Elements of these socially shared scripts may be used to understand and 'add' the missing information of news reports.

## Models

Finally, the goal of reading a news report is not just to understand it, that is, to build a meaning representation of it in memory, but to get to know and understand the events the news reports are about. We have earlier seen that this goal or function of newspaper reading means that readers must build *models* about such situations, that is, mental representations of the actors, actions, or events described by the text. Scripts and other types of general, social knowledge, are used to 'fill in' the relevant 'missing' parts of such models. Indeed, a news report only provides a very small fragment of the information the readers use to build a new model of a recent event. For instance, we saw earlier that each reader's model of the Handsworth 'riot' is built from fragments of news reports, combined with general knowledge about riots, the police, the inner cities, poverty, youth, and black people, and possibly with some knowledge about personal experiences in Birmingham and the disturbances in Handsworth.

Besides knowledge derived from the text, from scripts, or from their personal biography of experiences, people finally add evaluative propositions, that is opinions, to one or more elements of the model. Thus, when we read a news report in the Press, we form or activate opinions about events, about the news actors, and what they do. In the same way as knowledge about riots may be derived from the 'riot' script, readers use general opinions (perhaps those shared by their social group) about rioting or the police, organized in attitudes, to derive their current specific opinion about this particular riot.

## The expression of models

Crucial for the understanding of the results reported in the rest of this chapter is that whatever people say they remember about news in the Press is not so much directly derived from the mental representations of these news reports themselves (after some time these are no longer accessible), but on the models people have built during the reading process. With each news report on the same or a similar event or issue, people may update, recombine, or further generalize these models. As soon as they become general and abstract enough, and no longer characteristic for one specific context or reader, the models develop into more general types of knowledge, for example, scripts. Similarly, repeated specific opinions about particular events may be generalized to more complex social attitudes. In both cases, however, the processes of generalization and abstraction often involve discourse and communication. That is, people hear or read how other people understand and evaluate events and typically adapt their models to those of others, if only in order to be able to communicate, to interact successfully, or to feel a competent member of a group. Unfortunately, the same basic process takes place in the formation of ethnic prejudice (which does not mean that ethnic prejudices are cognitively 'necessary'!).

Thus, the interviews analysed in the remainder of this chapter are largely based on the models the readers have built while watching television, reading the paper, or talking with other people. Few of the interviewees have direct personal experiences with the ethnic events they learned about through public or personal communication. Hence, what they say is first of all an 'expression' or 'formulation' of their underlying 'media-mediated' models. For the reasons explained above, these models are personal (and therefore each interview is different), but these different models and interviews also share important social knowledge and beliefs with others. Indeed, they may share elements with the models as expressed by the journalists of the news reports in the Press. It is at this particular point that we examine the notion of 'influence' of news on the readers.

Note, however, that what people say in interviews not only derives from their models of news events, but also from the model they have about the present interview situation. That is, they have knowledge and opinions about themselves as speakers, about the interviewer, about the goal of the interview, and about the whole interaction. That is, what people tell us about ethnic affairs will be necessarily adapted to the constraints of the interview situation as it is represented in the model of the interviewee about that situation. Our earlier work on the expression of ethnic beliefs in everyday conversations has shown in detail that people often present themselves in a positive light (van Dijk, 1984; 1987a). This self-presentation strategy is essential when a socially 'delicate' issue such as minorities or race relations is brought up. Thus, most speakers will tend to show and stress, sometimes subtly, sometimes explicitly, that they 'are not racists'. Similarly, if they disagree with the interviewer, they will use persuasive strategies to convey their model of the situation. That is, they do not merely want to 'express' their model, but also to make their model (especially its opinions) credible and acceptable. In other words, the ways people express the models they have about ethnic events read about in the Press depend on the interview context, or rather on the model people have of that context, including the perceived beliefs of the interviewer.

## The Press and the formation and change of ethnic attitudes

There is a vast literature in social psychology on the formation and change of ethnic stereotypes and prejudices (see, for example, Allport, 1954; Bar-Tal, Graumann, Kruglanski, and Stroebe, 1989; Miller, 1982). Much of this work, however, is carried out within the broader framework of traditional attitude research, or within the perspective of inter-group theory (Tajfel, 1981). Only more recently, have more sophisticated theories of social cognition been brought to bear in the study of social representations about minority groups (Fiske and Taylor, 1984; Hamilton, 1981; van Dijk, 1987a). Research on the formation and change of ethnic cognitions due to discourse and communication is still in its infancy (see Chapter two). The same is true for the specific role of the mass media in this complex process, and this book and some of our earlier studies only provide a first step in acquiring this insight (see also Graber, 1984).

However, in their seminal study of racism and the mass media, Hartmann and Husband (1974) already pay extensive attention to the role of the media in the acquisition of beliefs about ethnic affairs in the UK. One of the results of their empirical survey is that although for specific topics, such as those of immigration or the extent of discrimination, white people largely draw upon the mass media for their knowledge, they also (they say) make extensive use of personal experiences, especially when they live in mixed neigbourhoods.

Although our own earlier research (van Dijk, 1987a) suggests that even such 'experiences' may be derived from conversations with family members, neighbours and friends, and although these conversations may in turn be partly based on media stories, the findings of Hartmann and Husband remind us of the complex nature of 'information sources' for social beliefs. That is, even when initially a large part of the information about new immigrants or minorities may be derived from the media, there will soon be a complex 'discourse environment' for the formation of ethnic opinions, featuring primarily a combination of media stories and everyday talk, but also textbooks, advertising, movies, literature, comics, etc. And although the 'cases' studied below are rare examples of fairly exclusive media influence, we need to bear in mind that news discourse is continuously mixed with other information sources about ethnic affairs.

## THE INTERVIEWS

Bearing in mind the theoretical background outlined above, and with the intention of investigating a few crucial aspects of the vast problem of the role of the Press in the reproduction of racism, we carried out some 150 interviews with white people in various neighbourhoods of Amsterdam, as well as in some other Dutch cities. Just like our earlier research on 'con- versations about minorities', these interviews, conducted in the spring of 1987, were highly informal, and as similar as possible to everyday conversations. Although the interviewers had a number of organizing questions about recent ethnic events reported in the Press, the people inter- viewed could talk freely about the various topics brought up. In order to avoid emphasis on the delicate ethnic issue, the interviews were presented as being about newspaper reading, not about ethnic affairs. After each interview, people were asked to provide some demographic data as well as information about their media use and contacts with minority groups.

The major topics chosen were about seven different issues and events.

One of these topics, the immigration of Tamils, was reported as far back as two years before, and others, such as the immigration of other refugee groups (notably Iranians) and the traffic in women, were more recent. Also, we selected four more specific events, namely the murder of a Turkish lawyer, a shooting during Kurdish new year festivities, an incident involving a fascist Turkish organization, and the transfer of a famous black soccer player, Ruud Gullit, to AC Milan. The choice of these topics was motivated by several considerations: the delay after reading about them, the number of news items about them, and the kind of negative or positive events and ethnic news actors involved.

The interviews were conducted by students who participated in a research seminar on the effects of ethnic affairs reporting in the Press. Most interviews were carried out in the homes of the interviewees. The interviews, which lasted on average about half an hour, were transcribed in detail, and these transcripts form the basis of the analysis. Since we were mainly interested, in this stage, in the 'contents' of the models of the readers, the interviews were first analysed in terms of their propositions, which then could be compared with the propositions of the news reports, as well as with the propositions of other interviews.

## THE READERS

Because of the method of contacting respondents (partly in the university), higher educated readers with better jobs are over-represented among the sample of people we interviewed. This also explains why there are more quality Press readers than popular newspaper readers among the interviewees. They spend 40 minutes on average each day reading their paper(s). Similarly, many readers also read weekly magazines and regularly watch current affairs programmes on television. At least half of the readers read more than one newspaper. The readers are moderately satisfied with their newspapers and usually agree with its editorial stance.

Most readers do not have close or daily contacts with minority groups, nor do they often speak about such groups or about ethnic affairs with their family members or colleagues. However, our data suggest that better educated readers have slightly more interest in ethnic issues than the other readers. The same is true for the factor of neighbourhood: people in mixed neighbourhoods tend to have more interests in ethnic affairs, independently of their level of education. There are virtually no age or gender effects: men and women, young and old people appear to have similar levels of interest or degrees of contact. However, since most ethnic contacts take place at work, and since about 25 per cent of the interviewees (especially among the younger ones and the women) are unemployed, these tended to have fewer contacts with minority groups.

For our research question it is interesting to note that choice of newspapers does seem to correlate somewhat with interest in ethnic affairs: readers of liberal *Volkskrant*, which publishes fairly frequent items about ethnic affairs, say they have more interest in minorities, speak about them more often, and use alternative information sources more often than readers of other newspapers. On the whole, however, we did not find dramatic differences between different social groups of readers as to their interest in, contact with, or communication about ethnic minorities, although higher education, leftist political orientation, reading a liberal paper, and living in a mixed neighbourhood do seem to have some influence on the interest and general involvement of the readers (see Fiske and Kinder, 1981).

## INFORMATION REPRODUCED

Although recall of specific information about news events is not directly related to the amount of influence that news reports have, we assume that information is more likely to influence opinions if it is available. That is, if people are able to reproduce specific information, especially after some time, it is more likely that such information has been, or could be, used to form evaluations about news events. Also, the ways the information is reproduced may give us important clues about the processes of belief formation.

One of the most interesting findings of the analysis of the amount of recall, measured by the number of propositions produced by the readers about the respective events, was that the Tamil case (see Chapter one for a summary of this event, and for analysis: van Dijk, 1988d), was recalled best, despite the fact that most news reports about it had appeared in the Press two years earlier. Of 148 readers, 128 still remembered the sudden arrival of Tamil refugees, as well as much of the details of the news stories about them (see Table 9.1). On average, the readers reproduced some 12 propositions about this event.

The obvious explanation for this remarkable score is that the Press had paid massive attention to this event. In particular, the conservative Press reproduced the panic displayed by the responsible authorities in The Hague. Many hundreds of news reports about the Tamils were published over a period of only a few months, and this barrage of reporting apparently had a lasting effect on the readers. Most of them know who the Tamils are, where they came from and why, and what happened to them in the Netherlands. Because the Dutch public did not know much

*Table 9.1* Amount of recall for seven 'ethnic events' in the Dutch Press, August 1985–January 1986

| Topics | Total no. of propositions | No. of diff. propositions | No. of unique propositions | No. of propositions occurring more than 5 times | Minimum no. of propositions | No. of readers | No. of propositions per reader |
|---|---|---|---|---|---|---|---|
| 1 Tamils | 1580 | 47 | 280 | 60 | 80 | 128 | 12.3 |
| 2 Refugees | 1352 | 478 | 314 | 46 | 54 | 135 | 10.0 |
| 3 Traffic of women | 450 | 160 | 115 | 12 | 49 | 108 | 4.2 |
| 4 Assault | 239 | 134 | 92 | 6 | 14 | 90 | 2.7 |
| 5 Soccer player | 298 | 100 | 74 | 9 | 48 | 114 | 2.6 |
| 6 Amicales | 281 | 125 | 89 | 9 | 23 | 74 | 3.8 |
| 7 Assassination | 165 | 92 | 69 | 4 | 12 | 58 | 2.8 |

about Tamils and the civil war in Sri Lanka before the arrival of the Tamils, most information about them must have come from the media, and especially from the Press. That is, we may speak of a rather clear effect of Press coverage in this case.

One of the prominent features of the information recalled was that, unlike for most news stories, many readers not only were able to reproduce the global outline (the main topics) of the Tamil story, but even could reproduce quite specific details, such as the precise route many Tamils followed to enter the Netherlands, how and where they were housed and under what conditions. This was information that was repeatedly emphasized in the Press. Note however that despite the large number of different propositions reproduced, many of these are unique for one reader. That is, besides a clear overlap in the recall of main topics of the stories, there is much personal variation in the recall of details: each reader has his or her own 'Tamil-model'.

Similar observations may be made for the closely related topic of refugee immigration in general. Again, most readers still know about this event, which had hit the headlines repeatedly during the previous two years. Scenes of Iranian refugees who had to stay for weeks in the arrival halls of Schiphol Airport, communicated through television news as well as photographs in the Press, were still fresh in the minds of many readers. In other words, issues such as refugees and immigration, if widely covered in the Press, appear to lead to well-established mental models of the readers.

As we can see in Table 9.1, this was much less the case for the other topics, although these were reported more recently. They were only occasionally, or even only once, reported, and many readers had either missed them, or simply could not remember them. Still, even these recent events were on average recalled by at least half of the readers. For these other issues, generally only the overall topics were still accessible. Details were often forgotten or confused with other stories.

When one considers the well-known fact that most information people read in the papers is soon forgotten, we may conclude that 'ethnic events' are rather prominently represented in memory. This is especially the case for 'structural' issues, because isolated events tend to be less accessible, even when reported recently. That is, repeated coverage in the Press effectively leads to specific knowledge formation. Most readers in the Netherlands now know about Tamils and other refugees, and much of their more specific recall may be prompted by this overall knowledge. In theoretical terms, we may say that repeated attention to an issue or an ethnic group allows readers continuously to update and 'rehearse' their models about them, and this will facilitate recall.

Also, in the case of the Tamils, there were events that stood out even more clearly, namely when some Tamils, frustrated by their treatment in the Netherlands, set fire to their temporary boarding houses. As expected, it is this negative event which is remembered most clearly. However, since some other, more recent ethnic events (the assassination and the shooting), were also negative and still much less well recalled, negative actions of minorities seem to be well recalled only when they can be fitted into a larger event framework, and when they are consistent with prejudiced attitudes, for instance, about the violence or ingratitude of non-white immigrants.

Interestingly, people not only recalled the events themselves but also the reporting about them. Some readers explicitly referred to the many negative stories in the Press about Tamils (see below). This amount of attention in the Press is not always related to prominence of recall, however. This may be concluded from the fact that although the conservative Press in particular emphasized the 'economic' (read: bogus) nature of Tamil immigration, this negative point was not very prominent among the readers, who focused more on the events than on the opinions conveyed by the Press.

If we consider differences in recall as a function of social reader characteristics, our data seem to suggest little variance (on average between 25 and 35 propositions for each reader). On the whole, and as may be expected, the better educated (who also have better jobs and live in wealthier neighbourhoods), who read more quality newspapers, and who claim to have more interest in ethnic affairs, also tend to recall more propositions on most topics. (This is with the exception of the sports item, broadly covered in the popular Press, which tended to be better recalled by men and by those, often of lower education, who were more interested in soccer.)

Some of these reader characteristics closely relate to the nature of their newspapers. Since the quality Press has more information about ethnic affairs, and the better educated mostly read the quality Press, both their education (and hence the degree of understanding of any news), as well as their newspapers may account for the higher number of propositions they recall about ethnic events. Thus, the proportion of propositions recalled by the readers of the popular Press (*Telegraaf*) is smaller than might be expected from their percentage of representation in the group of readers. The converse is true for the conservative quality newspaper *NRC-Handelsblad*, which at least initially also reported rather negatively about the refugees, but whose readers produce more propositions than average. Otherwise, there are few remarkable differences due to the respective newspapers read.

## OPINIONS

Most readers, in particular the better educated ones, still remember the top level information of most prominent ethnic events reported in the Press, especially when these events are covered extensively. Since most readers have few other sources of information about ethnic affairs, we must conclude that the media have an important role in conveying this kind of knowledge. This is the first important conclusion from our research. However, the question of media influence is mostly understood to apply more specifically to the formation or change of 'attitudes'. So, we should investigate more specifically what opinions the interviewees express about the events reported in the Press.

We here touch upon a more difficult question of this study. If no or few other information sources than the media (or the Press) are available about specific ethnic events, and if people know these events rather well, then it is permissible to conclude that most of their knowledge is due to the Press (or at least to conversations with others who are informed by the Press). However, this is not directly the case for opinions. True, before having read about them in the paper, most people not only did not know anything about Tamils, but most likely did not have an opinion about them either (although people sometimes do have opinions about ethnic groups they do not know anything about!). But once they have obtained some information about specific ethnic events, or about new immigrant groups, people may in principle accept or disregard the more neutral or negative bias associated with these stories in their newspapers.

Even more important, the opinion formation process may be partly independent of the specific bias thus conveyed. That is, right-wing readers of a right-wing newspaper have an ideological framework that facilitates the development of right-wing opinions whatever the opinion of their newspaper (the same could be said to be true for left-wing readers of left-wing papers). That is, they will tend to form biased models of situations reported in the Press if these situations can be interpreted in line with their dominant prejudiced attitudes. In actual practice, however, Press opinions and reader opinions will tend to be similar and reinforce each other, which is also obvious from the very choice of newspapers in the first place: we have seen that most readers say they support the editorial stance of the newspapers they read.

Thus, we assume that ideological frameworks, especially on issues such as ethnic affairs, that are not very prominent in the everyday lives of most white people, are not developed spontaneously, that is, without similar ideological frameworks expressed in the newspapers they read. That is, people do not 'neutrally' record the 'facts' and then autonomously build opinions about them, but are confronted with mediated media models of the situation that combine facts with interpretations and evaluations. If these opinions are coherent with existing attitudes and ideological frameworks, then they will tend to be accepted, and perhaps used to form attitudes that are in line with those expressed by the newspaper, whereupon they may operate autonomously in the interpretation and evaluation of new social events and groups.

Hence, theoretically speaking, there are several plausible arguments that predict that most readers adopt or accept the opinions on ethnic matters conveyed by the newspapers they read. However, since many other, media-independent factors are involved in opinion formation, there may be interesting exceptions and variations, perhaps due to personal experiences (Hartmann and Husband, 1974). Let us therefore examine in some more detail the opinions of the readers we interviewed about a number of ethnic issues and events.

One of the first observations of the opinion structures of the readers was that opinions tend to be formed and expressed especially for those topics people know most about. In our case, for instance, opinions were more extensive and pronounced about Tamils and refugees than about the other, more incidental events. Stories about incidents may have led to 'incidental' opinions during reading, but apparently these opinions are just as inaccessible as the knowledge about these events. Once an issue becomes important, it becomes associated with more complex, more deeply grounded, attitude structures and ideologies, which also allow more extensive, and more independent formulations of specific opinions.

## Attitude prototypes

The analysis of the hundreds of opinion propositions expressed about the Tamils and the refugees (to which we restrict ourselves here), yields an overall picture of three basic attitude 'prototypes', that is, attitudes that are overall against the immigration of more refugees, attitudes that are pro-immigration, and a mixed category of cautious, conditional acceptance of refugee immigration.

These prototypes are hardly specific for Tamils and refugees, and more generally reflect attitudes about minorities. Indeed, the contents are fairly similar to the ethnic opinions of Dutch people (and other white Europeans and North Americans) we have been able to infer from other fieldwork on ethnic attitudes (Van Dijk, 1987a). Hence, ethnic attitude structures are not arbitrary, but ideologically coherent.

The contra-refugee attitude prototype typically features the following propositions: refugees come to the Netherlands because they think it is a social paradise; they are economic and not real refugees; the Dutch authorities are too easy on immigration; too much is done for the refugees; we cannot afford more refugees; we have to pay for these refugees; and refugees are not grateful for what we do for them. Here is an example of the summarized opinions of two of the interviewees who share this attitude (we have added some demographic and media-use characteristics; the lower the figures for education and occupation, the lower the level of education or occupation, measured on a seven-point scale).

AK05 (man, 21, unemployed, education level: 3, paper: popular conservative)

If the Tamils set fire to their pensions, they should stay in their own country. Tamils are well housed and get enough pocket money. There are too many immigrants coming to this country, and further immigration should be stopped. Immigration policy is not strict enough. Refugees come here to find work in a rich country.

BI03 (man, 67, education level: 2, job level: 1, paper: popular-conservative)

If you say anything against them, they say you discriminate. If Tamils stay here, unemployment will rise. Refugees come here because this country is a social paradise. This country cannot even take care of its own people. Tamils come to this country and even set fire to their homes. Tamils are ungrateful. I would make a stricter selection of refugees. The government lets everybody in.

The pro-refugee prototypical attitude features the following opinion propositions: refugees come here because they are persecuted in their countries, or have other good reasons to come here; Dutch immigration policies are too strict, refugees are received stingily, and we should do more for them; it is understandable that the refugees protested violently against their treatment; many Dutch people are prejudiced against refugees and the media reported too negatively about them.

Note that this pro-refugee attitude has a partly paternalistic slant. Many people who favour the immigration of refugees pity the refugees, and do not always emphasize their rights. Here are the summarized opinions of an interviewee who shares this attitude:

HJ05 (Woman, 21, unemployed, education level: 4, paper: quality-leftist)

Tamils were pitiful. It is ridiculous to send Tamils back without legal appeal. The Netherlands is not as full as people say. I don't like the government making its policies stricter. I like all these different nationalities. We must solve the problem at the European level, but we cannot wait until such international decisions are made.

We see that the pro- and con-attitude structures are each others' mirror image. The opinions are not arbitrarily attached to many different events, actions, or situations, but seem to focus on the same aspects of the whole situation. Thus, the treatment of the refugees by the government may be approved of or not, and the same is true for the behaviour of the refugees themselves. In other words, we here seem to observe the kind of 'autonomous' attitude formation we mentioned above: given the 'facts', people may develop their opinion clusters in different directions, such that they form attitude schemata that are each others' complements. The attitude prototypes are seldom formulated precisely in the ways they are expressed in the papers. This is particularly clear, for instance, in the negative opinions about the media in the pro-refugees attitude, which was obviously not a major issue in the Press, not even in the liberal Press. However, what the papers *do* influence are the very propositions people take as a basis for opinion formation: the contents of the attitudes reflect the issues that were most extensively reported in the media.

The possible opinion *range* is also derived from the Press. That is, whether refugees are or are not called 'economic' refugees, is a binary opinion choice that derives from the Press (which in turn reproduced the terminology of the Ministry of Justice), simply because the very notion of 'economic refugees' had never come up in public discussion before. Specific opinion choices are completely ignored by the interviewees because they are never discussed in Press accounts of the events. Thus, people may be critical of specific Dutch immigration policies regarding Tamils and other refugees, but very few readers formulate the opinion that the general principles of Dutch immigration policy are racist. This is simply not part of the latitude of consensus opinions as discussed in the Press.

In sum, first analysis suggests that attitudes tend to polarize in coherent attitude clusters, that the basic opinion targets are suggested by the Press, but that the range of debatable opinions is also prestructured by the Press. That is, the Press not only influences what we think about, and not only what we form opinions about, but also among which opinions we must choose.

## Social factors

The attitude structures of the interviewees are clearly a function of various social characteristics. For a group of 60 interviewees for whom we had extensive opinion data, we thus established attitude profiles, which were assigned approximate scale values, ranging from 1 (anti-racist) to 7 (explicitly racist). As may be expected, the average prejudice level was about 3.6. We then examined whether rich or poor neighbourhood, age, gender, occupation, education, contacts with minority groups, newspapers, and amount of propositions recalled about the ethnic events were correlated with differences in positive or negative attitudes about Tamils and other refugees.

This analysis resulted in the familiar ideological differences between younger, politically more progressive and critical, better educated and better informed people, on the one hand, and those who lack these properties on the other hand. The first group displays more or less liberal views on immigration, whereas the latter group espouses a more negative, authoritarian view, mostly associated with resentment based on economic and cultural competition or threat.

However, that the relation between social position and social representations of immigration are more complex, may be gleaned from the finding that real social competition need not be at stake here. The unemployed, especially those with higher education, do not appear to have more negative opinions than the employed. Similarly, those in poor inner city neigbourhoods, the most likely place for many of the new immigrants to be housed (apart from small provincial villages), are not more prejudiced against refugees than those in wealthier areas. On the contrary, our data suggest that people in the latter areas may even harbour more negative feelings against immigrants.

## The role of the Press

There is a clear relation between attitudes and newspapers read: readers of leftist *Volkskrant* are less hostile (prejudice level 2.9) against refugees than the readers of popular conservative *Telegraaf* (prejudice level 4.3), which reported very negatively about the refugees. We have seen, before, however, that this relation is not necessarily direct: a conservative, anti-foreigner attitude is also a factor in the very choice of newspapers. On the other hand, there is also an independent newspaper effect. Tamils and refugees are new immigrant groups. Although attitudes about them may in part be developed as a function of more general ideologies about minorities and immigration, the newspaper provides the initial definition and evaluation of the new situation. There are cases, such as the Vietnamese 'boat people', and more recently the massive emigration of people from the German Democratic Republic, where refugees were defined as pitiful, and deserving of our help and sympathy, if only because they are fleeing from a communist regime. Through these dominant media definitions, especially in the right-wing Press, very different attitudes result. Whereas the Tamils are essentially defined as economic refugees, that is as 'scroungers', Vietnamese or white European refugees are primarily seen in a positive light. Hence, Eurocentrism or anti-communism, both of the Press and of its readers, may supersede otherwise negative attitudes about immigrants or refugees.

To examine the role of the Press in more detail, we not only correlated contents and level of the ethnic attitudes of the interviewees with the newspapers they read, but also analysed the 634 passages in which the interviewees commented upon the Press and other information sources. Although people do not always remember in detail whether their knowledge and opinions are based on the Press or on other information sources, such as television, weeklies, or everyday talk, there was a surprisingly detailed model of the communication context in the case of Tamil and refugee reporting. Thus, in 154 passages, more than half (78) of the readers referred to the Press accounts on these issues. Although some readers shared the opinion that coverage was superficial, most of the accounts concluded that there had been extensive information about Tamils and the refugees. Indeed, as we have found earlier, most readers found reporting about these issues satisfactory.

Interestingly, whatever newspaper they read, the readers also explicitly referred to the attitude range of the Press and other people.

When asked about their conversations about Tamils with other people, the interviewees first mention that since they mostly talk with people who have similar opinions to their own, their sources also often shared their opinions about these particular issues. On the other hand, in particular the readers who are pro-refugees, often mention that they spoke with people who are against refugees and that in fact 'public opinion' was against the Tamils. Thus, whether on the basis of conversations or through the media, most readers are aware of tendencies in public opinion. Also, they know the 'terms' of the debate (pro- or contra-refugees), and focus on the points of the debate as defined by the Press.

There was virtually no interviewee who had a completely different schema of interpretation of the events. In other words, as we suggested earlier, the diversity of the media does lead to a diversity of opinions, but these remain within the boundaries of a very clearly organized ideological framework. Alternative interpretation frameworks, in which refugee immigration and immigration policies are defined against the background of neo-colonialism, racism, the relations between the rich 'North' and the poor 'South', and the causes of the latter's poverty, are rare. Thus, the manufacture of consent, also through the Dutch Press, is such that the people have the illusion of freedom of opinion, but they do not realize how strongly ideological constraints set the latitude of attitude formation and the terms of public debate. Fundamental criticism of the dominant ideology, of government policies and newspaper contents, is exceptional, as elsewhere in western Europe and North America (Herman and Chomsky, 1988; Chomsky, 1989).

## CONCLUSIONS

The results of the research summarized in this chapter reflect the complexity of the notion of influence. We have emphasized that the traditional theory of media 'effects' needs to be replaced by a complex theoretical framework which takes into account the structures of media discourse, cognitive strategies of news text comprehension and memorization, and the structures and strategies of social representations of the readers. Within this framework, this chapter reported some results of a first study of what information readers reproduce from the Press about ethnic events. One major conclusion from the analysis of their recall protocols is that time delays are not always a main factor in such recalls. When an event, such as the arrival of Tamils and other refugees, is massively reported, the readers may effectively have integrated this story in their models and their more general knowledge and attitudes about a new group of immigrants. This is particularly the case if such a story has 'structural' implications, for instance for race relations in the country, and if the readers, through better education or closer personal contacts, have a more elaborate social representation of such socio-political events.

Hence, through extensive reporting, the media in general, and the Press in particular, are able to define a public debate and to communicate the essential contents of ethnic situation models that have a lasting effect on people's 'social knowledge'. Analysis of the opinions expressed in the interviews also showed, however, that the opinion structures adopted by the readers closely followed those made available by the Press. Thus, there are both positive and negative attitude prototypes about Tamils and other refugees, but the ways these are being argued for and persuasively formulated are very similar, with arguments and terms directly borrowed from the media, and not only based on extant anti-foreigner attitudes. Most people also know about these differences, whether those of the Press or those expressed in everyday conversations.

Whereas these findings are more or less in line with our expectations, the more important structural conclusion from our analysis is that, despite variations in attitude structures expressed and conveyed by the Press, there is a remarkable consensus about the main points and the margins of the debate and the organization of opinions underlying it. People may differ about specific points of policy, and have the illusion that there is a 'free debate' in the Press, as well as in everyday conversations. However, virtually no reader challenges the structural forces and the sustaining ideologies that condition the ethnic and immigration situation as it is defined by the authorities and the Press. That is, we find rather striking confirmation of the combined 'structural-ideological' approach to the study of the influence of the media. Specific newspapers do have specific effects on their readers, but because of other information sources (such as television and everyday conversations) and social characteristics this influence may be mitigated and diversified. However, the media as a whole define the internal structures, the points of relevance, and especially the ideological boundaries of social representations. They provide the ready-made models, that is, the facts and opinions, that people use partly in *what* to think, but more important which they also use in devising *how* to think about ethnic affairs.

# 10 General conclusions

## INTRODUCTION

After a brief summary of our major findings, this final chapter discusses some of the conclusions presented in this book, and interprets these conclusions in a broader theoretical framework. Our review of earlier studies showed that during the last decades the coverage of ethnic and racial affairs in the Press, on both sides of the Atlantic, has gradually become less blatantly racist, but that stereotypes and the definition of minorities as a 'problem' or even as a 'threat' is still prevalent, in particular in the popular newspapers, while minority journalists, especially in Europe, continue to be discriminated against in hiring, promotion and news story assignments.

This book has shown that for the coverage during the 1980s, the same conclusion may be drawn, and we have reason to assume that this is not only the case for the British and the Dutch Press coverage we analysed. Whereas earlier studies were limited to overall content analyses, our discourse analysis study also focused on the details of news reports about ethnic affairs, so that subtle aspects of organization, meaning, or style could also be taken into account.

Thus, the structure and style of headlines not only subjectively express what journalists or editors see as the major topics of news reports, but also tend to emphasize the negative role of ethnic minorities in such topics. Similarly, extensive analysis of the major subjects and topics showed that minorities continue to be associated with a restricted number of stereotypical topics, such as immigration problems, crime, violence (especially 'riots'), and ethnic relations (especially discrimination), whereas other topics, such as those in the realm of politics, social affairs, and culture are under-reported. Moreover, as is the case for education, if such topics become prominent at all, then again problems and conflicts get most attention. We have also seen that this negative description of ethnic affairs is not limited to news reports, but also characterizes background articles and editorials. Indeed, the editorials clearly show the dominant ideology at work in the media account of the ethnic situation. In the right wing Press, ethnic events are primarily evaluated as a conflict between 'us' and 'them', against the background of a conservative ideology that prominently features such concepts as order, authority, loyalty, patriotism, and 'freedom'. Besides ethnic minorities, anti-racists and the 'loony left' in particular are the target of such editorial attacks. It is not surprising, therefore, that ethnic minorities are consistently less quoted than majority group members and institutions, even on subjects, such as experiences of racial attacks or prejudice, on which minorities are the experts.

Similarly, our analysis of local meanings (implications, pre-suppositions, disclaimers such as denials of racism, etc.) of news reports showed that minorities and anti-racists are systematically associated with conflict, crime, intolerance, unreliability or even reverse 'racism', whereas the negative actions of white authorities and organizations tend to be ignored or minimized. The expression of these underlying meanings in the various structures and figures of style and rhetoric emphasizes such an ideological position, especially in the tabloids, typically so with terms such as "mob", "fanatics", or "snoopers", or by the use of rhetorical devices such as alliteration, parallelism, and metaphor.

Finally, an empirical study among readers suggested that the reproduction of racism by the Press is largely effective, not so much because all readers always adopt the opinions of the Press, which they often do and sometimes do not, but rather because the Press manages to manufacture an ethnic consensus in which the very latitude of opinions and attitudes is quite strictly constrained. They not only set the agenda for public discussion (what people should think *about*) but, more important, they strongly suggest *how* the readers should think and talk about ethnic affairs.

## QUALIFICATIONS

### Differences between newspapers

Whereas these overall conclusions from our findings have strong empirical support, they need qualification and further interpretation and explanation. A first major qualification pertains to the generalization of these findings. Many of the examples and observations in this book examine the right-wing British Press, and especially the tabloids. But as we know, the right-wing British tabloids do not represent the whole

British Press, nor are they typical of the Press in general. Indeed, we have repeatedly emphasized that the quality Press, and especially the more liberal quality Press, represented by such newspapers as the *Guardian* in the UK, the *New York Times* in the USA, *Le Monde* in France, *La Repubblica* in Italy, *El País* in Spain, the *Frankfurter Rundschau* in West Germany, and *De Volkskrant* in the Netherlands, among others, have a much more subtle way of writing about ethnic affairs. At present, offensively prejudiced topicalization and style are exceptional in such newspapers. Similarly, they also tend to print more background information about ethnic relations, report more often about topics that are relevant for minorities, quote minority spokespersons more often, and even occasionally publish non-establishment, anti-racist views.

There are even considerable differences within newspapers. Thus, it is not uncommon for conservative quality newspapers, such as *The Times* in the UK, or *NRC-Handelsblad* in the Netherlands, occasionally to publish a discussion of ethnic events that may be exceptional even in a more leftist-liberal newspaper. However, these are usually exceptions to the overall ideology of these newspapers, due to the presence of a good journalist who has special interest and competence in ethnic affairs coverage. (See also the NUJ guidelines on pp. 255–7.)

However, these qualifications are necessarily followed (as in the disclaimers we studied), by a restrictive *but*, that is, by a second order qualification. Firstly, in most of the countries just mentioned, such newspapers may be influential for the liberal elites, but they are read by a relatively small minority of the population, say by about at most 20 per cent of the national readership, and often by less than 5 per cent of the readers. Indeed, as is the case for the *Guardian*, such papers may be dwarfed by the mass circulation tabloids, whereas they generally have fewer readers than the conservative quality Press. In other words, if judged by the number of readers, the conservative or right-wing perspective on ethnic relations is usually prominent in western countries.

Secondly, prestigious liberal newspapers are not exactly mouthpieces of an explicitly anti-racist perspective. Rather, they represent the more 'tolerant' wing of the ethnic consensus. Thus, as to hiring and promotion policies, we have already seen that, especially in Europe, they seldom employ minority journalists, let alone leading minority editors, and few if any of them have affirmative action policies. As to their coverage, we find that although they exhibit a more varied set of topics, and a more regular expression of the views and interests of minority groups and especially of 'sympathetic' white organizations, their major topics do not fundamentally differ from those in the rest of the Press. That is, in the quality Press too, stereotypical topics dominate, such as crime (drugs) and violence, cultural differences, and especially the many real or imaginary problems associated with a multi-ethnic society. Again in the liberal Press, the views of white authorities and institutions dominate the news about ethnic affairs. The everyday lives of minority groups, and their experiences in a white-dominated society are seldom a prominent topic, although times of crises (for instance, after serious 'riots') may occasion brief discussion of the 'background' of current events.

Discrimination is a frequent topic in the liberal Press, but we have also seen that it is usually covered in terms of 'deplorable' events, especially in business, and seldom from the point of view of the daily experiences of blacks. It is seldom discussed as an inherent structural property of a racist society. On the contrary, much of the liberal Press and its commentators tend to deny the prevalence of racism, and are inclined to associate racism with the extreme right. Since the liberal quality Press is also an elite Press, forms of elite discrimination and racism, as in politics, education, scholarly research, the state bureaucracy, social affairs, and especially in the media itself, are ignored, minimized, or even emphatically denied, even when journalists are confronted with incontrovertible research evidence to the contrary.

In other words, the social and ethnic ideologies and practices of the liberal Press are firmly within the dominant ethnic consensus. Its liberal position is expressed most clearly in critical reports or editorials about crude right-wing views on immigration and ethnic affairs, such as those of the KKK and similar groups in the USA, of Enoch Powell or the National Front in the UK, of Le Pen and the *Front National* in France, or of the *Republikaner* in West Germany. Both in the USA and Europe, the prevailing influence of 'no-nonsense' social politics of dominant market liberalism also brought a powerful backlash in ethnic affairs, which has regularly been expressed in the liberal Press. Civil rights, the struggle against racism, and especially the socio-economic position of minorities are hardly prominent concerns for such an ideology, as we see in the diminishing attention for such topics in the Press (unless they lead to overt crisis or spectacular events). Thus, in the USA, the Civil Rights Movement is seen as no longer relevant since large numbers of blacks and other minorities have been able to reach middle-class status. In this perspective, racism is seen as a thing of the past, and only occasionally relevant when emerging in tragic, but isolated incidents.

In this perspective, the more subtle, everyday forms of prejudice, discrimination, and racism are played down as occasional expressions of personal intolerance, as 'natural' ethnic competition, or attributed to the alleged over-sensitivity of minorities. Indeed, in other situations, for instance in educational 'under-achievement', these minorities are often themselves blamed for such forms of inequality. It is not surprising that, especially in Europe, most of the liberal Press is not exactly in favour of serious affirmative action policies (least of all in the news room) or of stringent anti-racist legislation. Like most other white liberals, and academics, journalists of these newspapers will reject blatant discrimination and racism (so they will condemn official racism and apartheid, especially when far away, in South Africa), but the lives and experiences of blacks and other minorities hardly ever touch them personally, and their concern is therefore mostly incidental or occasional. It is this form of no-nonsense liberalism that also characterizes many journalists and news reports of the liberal Press, and which effectively neutralizes and marginalizes the struggle against ethnic dominance by the white group. Indeed, this apparent 'tolerance' may even take the form of a much more insidious 'modern racism', simply because 'good intentions' or subtle practices of stereotyping or discrimination (for instance, in textbooks, the media, everyday talk, hiring) are much more difficult to combat.

## Differences between countries

What holds for different newspapers is also true for different countries. Our comparisons between the British and the Dutch Press have already shown that the right-wing popular Press in the UK does not have a direct counterpart in the Netherlands, where race relations, as well as its coverage in the Press, tends to be less dramatic and extreme. On the other hand, as is the case with the liberal view of race relations discussed above, this may mean that in the Netherlands civil rights gains are at the same time slower precisely because the Dutch elites largely cherish the myth of themselves as tolerant. Forms of affirmative action, whether in favour of women or of minorities, are much more difficult to realize than, for example, in the USA. Positions of the liberal Press vary accordingly. Similar remarks hold for the Press in other European countries. It may generally be observed that the larger the adherence to extremist right-wing or racist parties and positions among the population at large, as well as among the elites, the more likely it is that there are newspapers that support this ideology. What can be read daily about minority groups in right-wing newspapers in the UK, Germany, and France, would be exceptional in the Netherlands, Scandinavia or the USA, but it should be emphasized that such differences are not fundamental, but rather of degree, that is, usually stylistic and rhetorical. We need however more research to make such comparisons more detailed.

## INTERPRETATION

The research of this and earlier studies about the role of the Press in ethnic affairs has been placed in a broader theoretical framework that focuses on the reproduction of racism in white, western society. Thus, it was assumed that processes of reproduction, both at the micro- and at the macro-levels of social organization, not only have a 'material' dimension of overall structures (or processes) and local practices, but also a fundamental cognitive–ideological dimension. This ideological dimension and its reproduction are closely related to forms of discourse and communication. Indeed, both at the ideological macro-level of general group attitudes and consensus, as well as at the ideological micro-level of individual ethnic prejudices, text and talk play a crucial role in the acquisition, uses, confirmation, legitimation, and change of the ideological system that supports the ethnic dominance of the white group. It was further assumed that at present the media, including the Press, play a crucial role in this process of discursive reproduction. How should our empirical findings be interpreted relative to the central thesis of this book?

In the various chapters of this study we have found evidence for the close relationship between the Press and other major institutions and elite groups in society. This is also true for the mutual influence of these institutions in the realm of ethnic affairs. Thus, in the UK, the conservative Press consistently reported favourably the ethnic policies of the Thatcher government, for instance on the severe restriction of immigration, the rejection of affirmative action, and the reactions to the 'riots'. The combined selection, frequency or ignoring of topics, as well as quotation patterns, local meaning, and rhetoric manifested an ideology that is broadly shared, with some minor variations, among the leading elites in politics and business. This was particularly clear in the virulent attacks made by the right-wing Press on any form of state-enforced affirmative action policy, especially in employment and business, as may be expected in a non-interventionist liberal-market ideology.

Although such ideologies may be generally shared among the conservative elites, and although therefore conservative politics and the conservative Press mutually influence and reinforce each other, the conservative Press also has its proper role in this reproduction process. It does not simply passively and favourably report the actions and opinions of conservative politicians or corporate business. On the contrary, it actively contributes to the construction of dominant ideologies and a broader consensus about them. The sources of this power of the Press within the dominant power framework are manifold.

Thus, firstly and not quite trivially, the Press, and especially the quality Press, is the dominant communication medium for the elites themselves. That is, the many power centres of the polity or economy need to know the policies and especially the possibly changing ideological positions of the others, and the Press provides this knowledge. However, even this role as the major communication medium among the elites is not merely a passive, mediating role, but is engaged in actively. That is, we have found that not all leading elites have equal access to the newspaper, and that the Press manipulates the exchange of elite views by favouring stories, topics, quotations, or styles of those politicians or other elites who are confirming its own ideologies. Thus, in the right-wing Press the interests and concerns of right-wing politicians or corporate leaders are systematically covered more sympathetically than those of the 'softer', more liberally or socially inspired conservative elites. "Lenient" judges, "snooping" state agencies such as the CRE, and other establishment institutions that are seen as 'favouring' minorities, may thus find themselves criticized, marginalized, or simply ignored. The same is true, but more forcefully so, for Labour and union policies.

Secondly, this autonomous role of both the quality and the popular Press is especially powerful in the persuasive role it has in the formation of public opinion. Stories, topics, style, and rhetoric are all geared towards a definition of the ethnic situation that tends to confirm prevalent stereotypes and attitudes among large segments of the readers of the conservative Press. In this perspective, the many crime and violence stories, and especially the dramatic 'riot' coverage, appeal to and confirm feelings of insecurity among many readers. Similarly, the stories on the problems of immigration, alleged 'positive discrimination' in housing and employment, or the anti-racist policies of left-wing councils, are primarily defined as a threat to the interests of 'ordinary' British taxpayers.

These stories are able to form or reinforce a public opinion about immigration and ethnic affairs that the politicians need to take into account in order to be re-elected. In other words, the Press not only is powerful in its manipulation of inter-elite communication, but also and especially in the crucial role it has in the persuasive definition of the ethnic situation for the public at large. Whereas the elites at least have access to other sources of information and communication, this is only occasionally the case, at least for an issue such as ethnic affairs, for the white public at large (even for those in 'mixed' neighbourhoods). It may be expected, therefore, that there is a close resemblance between the ethnic opinions of the popular Press and those of most of the readers. Since most white readers obtain their information about minorities largely from the media, the alternative hypothesis, that the Press writes 'what the people think' may safely be rejected. Not only our discourse analyses, but also our fieldwork has shown that media users form sometimes detailed knowledge about ethnic events, and that despite obvious variations in their ethnic opinions and attitudes, this variation is quite closely constrained by the latitude of opinions that have access to the media. Further comparison between the coverage of different immigration cases in the Press, for example, of Vietnamese boat refugees and Tamils, also supports the assumption that once defined as positive or negative by the Press (and dominant politicians), such groups generally are confronted with similar attitudes from the population at large.

Note that in order to manipulate public opinion, the Press also tends to select those letters and 'spontaneous' opinions of 'ordinary people' that are consistent with its own ethnic ideology. In other words, the Press has a number of institutional and symbolic resources that allow it to play a powerful role in the formation of a widely shared ethnic consensus. Since racism first of all has an ideological nature (presupposed by racist practices), it is precisely this ideological and discursive power of the Press that is essential in the formation and legitimation of such a consensus.

Thirdly, this particular ideological role, especially of the right-wing Press, becomes particularly clear in its vicious attacks against its most influential ideological competitors in the definition of the situation, educators and researchers and, to a lesser extent, liberal writers or other opinion leaders, including left-wing politicians. The unconditional support of Honeyford in the UK, and the consistent attacks against anti-racist teaching or even against multi-cultural curricula, show that education is seen as a dangerous medium of indoctrination, especially of those the newspapers can't reach – children – or of those whose political orientations are often more to the left, the students. Such attacks may not always have immediate effects (as the Honeyford affair also showed), but they will undoubtedly influence both the parents of these children, as well as the politicians who are responsible for education policies. Thus, it is unlikely that without the massive Press campaign, Honeyford would ever have been able to cross, as he did, the threshold of 10 Downing Street. More seriously, social science research programmes, anti-racist projects, or more generally a policy of multi-cultural education, appear to be negatively affected by constant Press accusations of 'anti-English' indoctrination. In sum, even if there are some domains where the Press has less symbolic power, it will go a long way to limit the power or the influence of its competitors.

These conclusions and interpretations regarding the role of the Press are particularly relevant for the blatantly negative coverage of ethnic affairs in the right-wing tabloid Press, but many examples have shown that in a more subtle way the same is true for the conservative quality Press. We have suggested that even the liberal Press does not exactly favour the interpretations of the ethnic situation by its own competitors, such as anti-racist scholars. There is evidence that anti-racist research (especially about the Press itself) is often ignored or ridiculed by the liberal newspapers too, whereas research findings that can be seen as confirming prevalent stereotypes tend to be given more attention, as is the case for research about problematic cultural differences or deviant behaviour of some segments of minority groups.

Finally, this study about the Press, as well as our earlier work on the reproduction of racism in textbooks and conversation, support the claim of much other recent work on racism, that is that the reproduction processes involved are essentially controlled by the elites. This does not imply that there is no racism among 'ordinary' people, nor that feelings of resentment against other racial or ethnic groups may not arise at grassroots level, especially in situations of real or apparent group competition and conflict arising in direct inter-ethnic contacts. However, we have repeatedly found that the main direction of influence is top down. Racist ideologies are not innate, but learned. A large part of this social learning process operates through formal education and the mass media. Biased stories in the tabloids are not the responsibility of reporters alone, but assigned and accepted by chief editors. Racist parties and their ideologies are usually inspired by intellectuals or leading politicians, as was typically the case for Enoch Powell in the UK. That such parties are seldom prohibited is due to the often opportunistic policies of the political elites, not only of the right. Although at present such extremist views do not represent the consensus among the elites, they seldom are of popular origin. The same is true for the more subtle, consensus views on ethnic affairs. The analysis, given above, of the socio-political position of the Press, and of the direction of its persuasive influence on the readers, thus warrants the conclusion that the Press plays a central role in the initial reproduction of racism by the elites.

## FINAL REMARKS

From these conclusions and interpretations it has become clear firstly that the theoretical framework in which our results are to be interpreted is vastly complex. The role of the Press in the reproduction of racism in society can no longer simply be assessed by listing its stereotypical topics or by giving examples of obvious bias against minorities or anti-racists. Since its role is largely symbolic and ideological, and hence based on discursive practices, we first of all need a thorough discourse analytical approach that is able systematically to describe and explain the subtleties of ethnic reporting.

Secondly, we have found that this reproductive and symbolic role of the Press is not isolated, but linked in many ways to political, economic, or other power institutions or the elites in general. The implications for the process of reproduction of this structural and ideological position of the Press relative to other institutions need to be further examined in a theoretical framework of which this book has only presented some brief elements, for instance in terms of the political economy and sociology of the media.

Finally, we need much more insight into the most complex question of the problem of reproduction, that is, the role of the Press, and in particular of the detailed structures and meanings of its reporting, in the process of opinion and attitude formation among the public at large. Such an account needs a complex interdisciplinary framework of theories about the acquisition, structures, uses, and changes of social cognitions of media users, and their social, political and cultural contexts.

In sum, although this book has tried to give some answers about one core question – about the discursive nature of the reproduction of racism by the Press – most of the other fundamental questions of this problem are still on the agenda.

# Appendix

## GUIDELINES ON RACE REPORTING

The National Union of Journalists has ratified guidelines for all its members to follow when dealing with race relations subjects. If you are a member these are your guidelines.

### Race reporting

1 Only mention someone's race if it is strictly relevant. Check to make sure you have it right. Would you mention race if the person was white?

2 Do not sensationalize race relations issues, it harms black people and it could harm you.

3 Think carefully about the words you use. Words which were once in common usage are now considered offensive, e.g. half-caste and coloured. Use mixed-race and black instead. Black can cover people of Arab, Asian, Chinese and African origin. Ask people how they define themselves.

4 Immigrant is often used as a term of abuse. Do not use it unless the person really is an immigrant. Most black people in Britain were born here and most immigrants are white.

5 Do not make assumptions about a person's cultural background – whether it is their name or religious detail. Ask them or where this is not possible check with the local community relations council.

6 Investigate the treatment of black people in education, health, employment, and housing. Do not forget travellers and gypsies. Cover their lives and concerns. Seek the views of their representatives.

7 Remember that black communities are culturally diverse. Get a full and correct view from representative organisations.

8 Press for equal opportunities for employment of black staff.

9 Be wary of disinformation. Just because a source is traditional does not mean it is accurate.

## Reporting racist organisations

1 When interviewing representatives of racist organisations or reporting meetings or statements or claims, journalists should carefully check all reports for accuracy and seek rebutting or opposing comments. The anti-social nature of such views should be exposed.

2 Do not sensationalize by reports, photographs, film, or presentation the activities of racist organisations.

3 Seek to publish or broadcast material exposing the myths and lies of racist organisations and their anti-social behaviour.

4 Do not allow the letters column or 'phone-in' programmes to be used to spread racial hatred in whatever guise.

## NUJ/NGA agreement on race reporting

1 The NGA and the NUJ believe that the development of racist attitudes and the growth of the fascist parties pose a threat to democracy, the right of trade union organizations, a free press, and the development of social harmony and well-being.

2 The NGA and the NUJ believe that members of their unions cannot avoid a measure of responsibility in fighting the evil of racism as expressed through the mass media.

3 The NGA and the NUJ reaffirm their total opposition to censorship but equally reaffirm their belief that press freedom must be conditioned by responsibility and an acknowledgement by all media workers of the need not to allow press freedom to be abused to slander a section of the community or to promote the evil of racism.

4 The NGA and the NUJ believe that the methods and the lies of the racists should be publicly and vigorously exposed.

5 The NGA and the NUJ believe that newspapers and magazines should not originate material which encourages discrimination on grounds of

race or colour as expressed in the NUJ's Rule Book and Code of Conduct.

6 The NGA and the NUJ recognise the right of members to withhold their labour on grounds of conscience because employers are providing a platform for racist propaganda.

7 The NGA and the NUJ believe that the editors should ensure that coverage of race stories should be placed in a balanced context.

8 The NGA and the NUJ will continue to monitor the development of media coverage in this area and give mutual support to members of each union seeking to enforce the aims outlined in this joint statement.

## Guidelines on travellers

1 Only mention the word gypsy or traveller if strictly relevant and accurate;

2 Give balanced reports seeking travellers' views as well as those of others, consulting the local travellers where possible;

3 Resist the temptation to sensationalize issues involving travellers, especially in their relations with settled communities over issues such as housing and settlement programmes and schooling;

4 Try to give wider coverage to travellers' lives and the problems they face;

5 Strive to promote the realization that the travellers' community is comprised of full citizens of Great Britain and Ireland whose civil rights are seldom adequately vindicated, who often suffer much hurt and damage through misuse of media and who have a right to have their special contributions to Irish and British life, especially in music and craft work and other cultural activities properly acknowledged and reported.

# References

Abercrombie, N., Hill, S. and Turner, B.S. (1980) *The Dominant Ideology Thesis*, London: Allen & Unwin.

Alexander, J.C., Giesen, B., Münch, R. and Smelser, N.J. (eds) (1987) *The Micro-macro Link*, Berkeley, CA: University of California Press.

Allport, G.W. (1954) *The Nature of Prejudice*, New York: Doubleday, Anchor Books.

Althusser, L. (1971) 'Ideology and ideological state apparatuses', in *Lenin and philosophy and other essays*, London: New Left Books.

Bagdikian, B.H. (1983) *The Media Monopoly*, Boston, MA: Beacon Press.

Bagley, C. (1973) *The Dutch Plural Society*, Oxford: Oxford University Press.

Balbi, R. (1988) *All'erta siam razzisti*, Milan: Mondadori.

Banton, M. (1977) *The Idea of Race*, London: Tavistock.

Barker, M. (1981) *The New Racism*, London: Junction Books.

Barrett, M., Corrigan, P., Kuhn, A. and Wolff, J. (eds) (1979) *Ideology and Cultural Production*, London: Croom Helm.

Bar-Tal, D., Graumann, C.F., Kruglanski, A.W. and Stroebe, W. (eds) (1989) *Stereotyping and Prejudice. Changing Conceptions*, New York: Springer.

Ben-Tovim, G., Gabriel, J., Law, I. and Stredder, K. (1986) *The Local Politics of Race*, London: Macmillan.

Benyon, J. (1987) 'Interpretations of civil disorder', in J. Benyon and J. Solomos (eds) *The Roots of Urban Unrest*, Oxford: Pergamon Press.

Benyon, J. and Solomos, J. (eds) (1987) *The Roots of Urban Unrest*, Oxford: Pergamon Press.

Bhat, A., Carr-Hill, R. and Ohri, S. (eds) (1988) *Britain's Black Population: A new Perspective*, 2nd edn, Aldershot: Gower.

Blauner, B. (1989) *Black Lives, White Lives: Three Decades of Race Relations in America*, Berkeley, LA: University of California Press.

Bonnafous, S. and Fiala, P. (1984) 'L'argumentation dans les éditoriaux de droite et d'extrême droite (1973–1982)', Papers of the Third International Colloquium of Political Lexicology, Paris: Institut de langue française (CNRS) and École Normale Supérieure.

Bourdieu, P. (1977) *Outline of a Theory of Practice*, Cambridge: Cambridge University Press.

Bourdieu, P. (1984) *Homo Academicus*, Paris: Minuit.

Bourdieu, P. and Passeron, J. -C. (1977) *Reproduction in Education, Society and Culture*, Beverly Hills, CA: Sage Publications.

Braham, P., Rhodes, E. and Pearn, M. (eds) (1981) *Discrimination and Disadvantage in Employment: The Experience of Black Workers*, London: Harper & Row (in association with the Open University Press).

Brandt, G.L. (1986) *The Realization of Anti-racist Teaching*, London: Falmer Press.

Breed, W. (1955) 'Social control in the newsroom', *Social Forces* 33, 326–335.

CCCS (Centre for Contemporary Cultural Studies) (1978) *On Ideology*, London: Hutchinson.

CCCS (Centre for Contemporary Cultural Studies, Birmingham) (1982) *The Empire Strikes Back. Race and Racism in 70s Britain*, London: Hutchinson.

Castles, S. (1984) *Here for Good. Western Europe's New Ethnic Minorities*, London: Pluto Press.

Chibnall, S. (1977) *Law-and-Order News*, London: Tavistock.

Chilton, P. (1988) *Orwellian Language and the Media*, London: Pluto Press.

Chomsky, N. (1989) *Necessary Illusions: Thought Control in Democratic Societies*, Montreal: CBC Enterprises.

Cicourel, A.V. (1973) *Cognitive Sociology*, Harmondsworth: Penguin Books.

Cohen, S. (1980) *Folk Devils and Moral Panics*, 2nd, revised edn, Oxford: Robertson.

Cohen, S. and Young, J. (eds) (1981) *The Manufacture of News: Deviance, Social Problems and the Mass Media*, 2nd edn, London: Constable; Beverly Hills, CA: Sage.

Collins, R., Curran, J., Garnham, N., Scannell, P., Schlesinger, P. and Sparks, C. (eds) (1986) *Media, Culture and Society*, London: Sage.

Corbett, E.P.J. (1971) *Classical Rhetoric for the Modern Student*, New York: Oxford University Press.

Coulmas, F. (ed.) (1986) *Direct and Indirect Speech*, Berlin: Mouton De Gruyter.

Cox, J. R. and Willard, C.A. (eds) (1982) *Advances in Argumentation Theory and Research*, Carbondale, IL: Southern Illinois University Press.

Critcher, C., Parker, M. and Sondhi, R. (1977) 'Race in the provincial Press: A case study of five West Midlands papers', in UNESCO, *Ethnicity in the Media*, Paris: Unesco. 25–192.

Daniel, J. and Allen, A. (1988) 'Newsmagazines, public policy, and the Black agenda', in G. Smitherman-Donaldson and T.A. van Dijk (eds) *Discourse and Discrimination*, Detroit, MI: Wayne State University Press, 23–45.

Davis, H. and Walton, P. (eds) (1983) *Language, Image, Media*, Oxford: Blackwell.

Delgado, M. (1972) *Gastarbeiter in der Presse [Guestworkers in the Press]*, Opladen: Westdeutscher Verlag.

Dovidio, J. F. and Gaertner, S.L. (eds) (1986) *Prejudice, Discrimination and Racism*, New York: Academic Press.

Downing, J. (1984) *Radical Media*, Boston, MA: Southend Press.

Dubbleman, J.E. (1987) 'Tamils in Luilekkerland?' MA Thesis, Free University of Amsterdam.

Ebel, M. and Fiala, P. (1983) *Sous le consensus, la xénophobie [Under the consensus, the xenophobia]*, Mémoires et documents 16, Lausanne: Institut de sciences politiques.

Eiser, J. R. and van der Pligt, J. (1988) *Attitudes and Decisions*, London: Routledge.

Essed, P.J.M. (1984) *Alledaags racisme [Everyday racism]*, Amsterdam: Sara (American edition: *Everyday Racism*, Claremont, CA: Hunter House, 1990).

Essed, P.J.M. (1987) *Academic racism: Common sense in the social sciences*, Universiteit van Amsterdam: Centrum voor Etnische Studies. CRES Publications, No. 5.

Essed, P.J.M. (1991) *Understanding Everyday Racism*, Newbury Park, CA: Sage.

European Parliament (1986) *Report of the research committee for the rise of fascism and racism in Europe*, reported by D. Evrigenis, Brussels: European Parliament.

Farr, R.M. and Moscovici, S. (eds) (1984) *Social Representations*, Cambridge: Cambridge University Press.

Findahl, O. and Höijer, B. (1984) *Begriplighetsanalys (The analysis of comprehensibility)*, Stockholm: Studentlitteratur.

Fishbein, M. and Ajzen, I. (1975) *Belief, attitude, intention and behaviour*, Reading, MA: Addison-Wesley.

Fisher, P.L. and Lowenstein, R.L. (eds) (1967) *Race and the News Media*, New York: Praeger.

Fiske, S.T. and Kinder, D.R. (1981) 'Involvement, expertise and schema use: Evidence from political cognition', in N. Cantor and J.F. Kihlstrom (eds) *Personality, Cognition, and Social Interaction*, Hilldale, NJ: Erlbaum, 171–90.

Fiske, S.T. and Taylor, S.E. (1984) *Social cognition*, Reading, MA: Addison-Wesley.

Fowler, R., Hodge, B., Kress, G. and Trew, T. (1979) *Language and Control*, London: Routledge & Kegan Paul.

Galtung, J. and Ruge, M.H. (1965) 'The structure of foreign news', *Journal of Peace Research* 2, 64–91.

Gans, H. (1979) *Deciding What's News*, New York: Pantheon Books.

Garst, R.E. and Bernstein, T.M. (1982) *Headlines and Deadlines*, 4th edn, New York: Columbia University Press.

Geis, Michael L. (1987) *The Language of Politics*, New York: Springer.

Giddens, A. (1979) *Central Problems in Social Theory*, London: Macmillan.

Gifford, Lord, QC (1986) *The Broadwater Farm Inquiry*: Report of the independent enquiry into disturbances of October 1985 at the Broadwater Farm Estate, Tottenham, chaired by Lord Gifford, QC., London: Karia Press.

Gilroy, P. (1987) *There Ain't No Black in the Union Jack*, London: Hutchinson.

Glasgow University Media Group (1976) *Bad News*, London: Routledge & Kegan Paul.

Glasgow University Media Group (1980) *More Bad News*, London: Routledge & Kegan Paul.

Golding, P. and Elliott, P. (1979) *Making the News*, London: Longman.

Golding, P., Murdock, G. and Schlesinger, P. (1986) *Communicating Politics*, Leicester: Leicester University Press.

Gordon, P. (1983) *White Law: Racism in the Police, Courts and Prisons*, London: Pluto Press.

Gordon, P. (1985) *Policing Immigration: Britain's Internal Controls*, London: Pluto Press.

Gordon, P. and Klug, F. (1986) *New Right, New Racism*, London: Searchlight Publications.

Gossett, T.F. (1963) *Race: The History of an Idea in America*, New York: Schocken Books.

Graber, Doris A. (1980) *Crime News and the Public*, New York: Praeger.

Graber, Doris A. (1984) *Processing the News*, 2nd edn (1988), New York: Longman.

Greenberg, B.S. and Mazingo, S.L. (1976) 'Racial issues in mass media institutions', in P.A. Katz (ed.), *Towards the Elimination of Racism*, New York: Pergamon Press, 309–340.

Gunter, B. (1987) *Poor Reception: Misunderstanding and Forgetting Broadcast News*, Newbury Park, CA: Sage.

Hall, S. (1987) 'Urban unrest in Britain', in J. Benyon and J. Solomos (eds), *The Roots of Urban Unrest*, Oxford: Pergamon Press, 45–50.

Hall, S. (1988) *The Hard Road to Renewal: Thatcherism and the Crisis of the Left*, London: Verso.

Hall, S., Critcher, C., Jefferson, T., Clarke, J. and Roberts, B. (1978) *Policing the Crisis: Mugging, the State and Law and Order*, London: Methuen.

Hall, S., Hobson, D., Lowe, A. and Willis, P. (eds) (1980) *Culture, Media, Language*, London: Hutchinson.

Halloran, J.D., Elliott, P. and Murdock, G. (1970) *Demonstrations and Communication: A Case Study*, Harmondsworth: Penguin Books.

Hamilton, D.L. (ed.) (1981) *Cognitive Processes in Stereotyping and Intergroup Behaviour*, Hillsdale, MA: Erlbaum.

Hansen, A. (1982) 'Press coverage of the summer (1981) riots', Unpublished MA dissertation, University of Leicester: Centre for Mass Communication Research.

Hartmann, P. and Husband, C. (1974) *Racism and the Mass Media*, London: Davis-Poynter.

Hartmann, P., Husband, C. and Clark, J. (1974) 'Race as news: a study in the handling of race in the British national Press from 1963–1970', in Unesco, *Race as News*, Paris: Unesco, 91–174.

Hedman, L. (1985) 'Invandrare i tystnadspiralen' ['Immigrants in the spiral of silence'], in *Journalisten som verklighetens dramaturg [The Journalist as reality's playwright]*, En rapport från Diskrimineringsutredningen [A report from the Discrimination Commission]. Stockholm: Regeringskansliet Offsetcentral.

Herman, E.S. and Chomsky, N. (1988) *Manufacturing consent: The Political Economy of the Mass Media*, New York: Pantheon Books.

Himmelfarb, S. and Eagly, A.H. (eds) (1974) *Readings in Attitude Change*, New York: Wiley.

Hoffmann, L. and Even, H. (1984) *Soziologie der Ausländerfeindlichkeit*, Weinheim and Basle: Beltz.

Höijer, B. and Findahl, O. (1984) *Nyheter, förståelse, och minne (News, understanding and memory)*, Stockholm: Studentlitteratur.

Hollingsworth, M. (1986) *The Press and Political Dissent*, London: Pluto Press.

Husband, C. (ed.) (1982) 'Race' in Britain, London: Hutchinson.

Huth, L. (1978) 'Zur Rolle der Argumentation im Texttyp Korrespond-entenbericht', in M. Schecher (ed.) *Theorie der Argumentation*, Tübingen: Niemeyer, 357–88.

Indra, D.M. (1979) 'Ethnicity, social stratification and opinion formation: An analysis of ethnic portrayal in the Vancouver Press', 1905–1976, Ph.D. dissertation, Simon Fraser University, Burnaby, British Columbia.

Institute of Race Relations (1985) *Policing against Black People*, London: Institute of Race Relations.

Iyengar, S. and Kinder, D.R. (1987) *News that Matters: Television and American Opinion*, Chicago: University of Chicago Press.

Jaynes, G.D. and Williams, Jr., R.M. (eds) (1989) *A Common Destiny: Blacks and American Society*, Washington DC : National Academy Press.

Jenkins, R. and Solomos, J. (eds) (1987) *Racism and Equal Opportunity Policies in the 1980s*, Cambridge: Cambridge University Press.

Johnson, K.A. (1987) 'Media images of Boston's Black Community', Research report, Boston, MA, University of Massachusetts: William Monroe Trotter Institute.

Johnson, P.B., Sears, D.O. and McConahay, J.B. (1971) '"Black invisibility", the Press and the Los Angeles riot', *American Journal of Sociology* 76, 698–721.

Johnson-Laird, P.N. (1983) *Mental Models*, Cambridge: Cambridge University Press.

Jordan, W.D. (1968) *White over Black*, New York: Norton.

Kahane, H. (1971) *Logic and Contemporary Rhetoric*, Belmont, CA: Wadsworth.

Katz, P.A. and Taylor, D.A. (eds) (1988) *Eliminating Racism: Profiles in Controversy*, New York: Plenum Press.

Kettle, M. and Hodges, L. (1982) *Uprising! The Police, the People and the Riots in Britain's Cities*, London: Pan Books.

Klapper, J.T. (1960) *The Effects of Mass Communication*, New York: Free Press.

Knopf, T.A. (1975) *Rumors, Race and Riots*, New Brunswick, NJ: Transaction Books.

Knorr-Cetina, K. and Cicourel, A.V. (eds) (1981) *Advances in Social Theory and Methodology, Towards an Integration of Micro- and Macrosociologies*, London: Routledge & Kegan Paul.

Kochman, T. (1981) *Black and White Styles in Conflict*, Chicago: University of Chicago Press.

Kramarae, C., Schulz, M. and O'Barr, W.M. (eds) (1984) *Language and Power*, Beverly Hills, CA: Sage.

Kress, G. (1985) 'Ideological structures in discourse', in T.A. van Dijk (ed.), *Handbook of Discourse Analysis*, vol. 4, *Discourse analysis in society*, London: Academic Press, 27–42.

Kress, G. and Hodge, B. (1979) *Language and Ideology*, London: Routledge & Kegan Paul.

Krippendorf, K. (1980) *Content Analysis*, Beverly Hills, CA: Sage.

Kuper, L. (ed.) (1975) *Race, Science and Society*, Paris: Unesco Press; and London: Allen & Unwin.

Larrain, J. (1979) *The Concept of Ideology*, London: Hutchinson.

Levitas, R. (ed.) (1986) *The Ideology of the New Right*, Cambridge: Polity Press.

Lüger, H.-H. (1983) *Pressesprache*, Tübingen: Niemeyer.

Lukes, S. (ed.) (1986) *Power*, Oxford: Blackwell.

Lyle, J. (ed.) (1968) *The Black American and the Press*, Los Angeles: Ward Ritchie.

Lyons, J. (1977) *Semantics*, 2 vols, Cambridge: Cambridge University Press.

Martindale, C. (1986) *The White Press and Black America*, New York: Greenwood Press.

Mazingo, S. (1988) 'Minorities and social control in the newsroom: thirty years after Breed', in T.A. van Dijk and G. Smitherman-Donaldson (eds), *Discourse and Discrimination*, Detroit, MI: Wayne State University Press, 93–130.

McCombs, M.E. and Shaw, D.L. (1972) 'The agenda-setting function of the Press', *Public Opinion Quarterly* 36, 176–87.

McQuail, D. (1983) *Mass communication theory: An introduction*, Beverly Hills, CA: Sage.

Merten, K. *et al.* (1986) *Das Bild der Ausländer in der deutschen Presse [The image of foreigners in the German Press]*, Frankfurt: Gagyeli Verlag.

Miles, R. (1982) *Racism and Migrant Labour*, London: Routledge & Kegan Paul.

Miles, R. (1989) *Racism*, London: Routledge.

Miller, A.G. (ed.) (1982) *'In the Eye of the Beholder': Contemporary Issues in Stereotyping*, New York: Praeger.

Minnema, F. (1989) 'Wie graag in ons vrije land is komen wonen ..., Moslims, media en de Rushdie-affaire' ['Who liked to come and live in our free country ... Muslims, media and the Rushdie affair']. MA thesis, University of Amsterdam, Dept. of Communication.

Minority Participation in the Media, (1984). Hearings before the subcommittee on telecommunications, consumer protection and finance, of the Committeee on energy and commerce, House of Representatives, 98th Congress, 19 and 23 September (1983).

Morley, D. (1983) 'Cultural transformations: the politics of resistance', in H. Davis and P. Walton (eds), *Language, Image, Media*, Oxford: Blackwell, 104–17.

Morrison, L. (1975) 'A black journalist's experience of British journalism', in C. Husband (ed.), *White Media and Black Britain*, London: Arrow Books.

Mullard, C. (1985a) *Race, Class and Ideology*, London: Routledge & Kegal Paul.

Mullard, C. (1985b) *Race, Power and Resistance*, London: Routledge & Kegal Paul.

Mullard, C. (1986) *Pluralism, ethnicism and ideology: Implications for a tranformative pedagogy*, University of Amsterdam, Centre for Race and Ethnic Studies, CRES Publication Series, Working Paper No. 2.

Murdock, G. (1984) 'Reporting the riots', in J. Benyon (ed.), *Scarman and After*, London: Pergamon Press, 73–95.

Murray, N. (1986) 'Anti-racists and other demons: the Press and ideology in Thatcher's Britain', *Race and Class* XXVII, 3, 1–20.

Omi, M. and Winant, H. (1986) *Racial Formation in the United States: From the 1960s to the 1980s*, New York and London: Routledge.

Paletz, David L. and Entman, Robert M. (1981) *Media, Power, Politics*, New York: Free Press.

Prince, G. (1982) *Narratology, The Form and Function of Narrative*, Berlin: Mouton.

Reeves, F. (1983) *British Racial Discourse*, Cambridge: Cambridge University Press.

Report of the National Advisory Commission on Civil Disorders (1988) 'The Kerner Report', New York: Bantam Books (first published 1968).

Rich, P.B. (1986) 'Conservative ideology and race in modern British politics', in Z. Layton-Henry and P.B. Rich (eds), *Race, Government and Politics in Britain*, London: Macmillan, 45–72.

Robinson, J.P. and Levy, M.R. (1986) *The Main Source: Learning from Television News*, Beverly Hills, CA: Sage.

Rogers, E.M. and Dearing, J.W. (1988) 'Agenda-setting research: Where has it been, Where is it going?', in J. Anderson (ed.), *Communication Yearbook 11*, Newbury Park: Sage, 555–94.

Rosenberg, S.W. (1988) *Reason, Ideology and Politics*, London: Polity Press.

Ruhrmann, G. and Kollmer, J. (1987) *Ausländerberichterstattung in der Kommune [Reporting foreigners in the community]*, Opladen: Westdeutscher Verlag.

Said, E.W. (1981) *Covering Islam*, Henley, Oxfordshire: Routledge & Kegan Paul.

Sandell, R. (1977) *Linguistic Style and Persuasion*, London: Academic Press.

Scarman, Lord (1981) *The Brixton disorders, 10–12 April (1981)*, London: HMSO.

Schank, R.C. and Abelson, R.P. (1977) *Scripts, Plans, Goals and Understanding*, Hillsdale, NJ: Erlbaum.

Scherer, K.R. and Giles, H. (eds) (1979) *Social Markers in Speech*, Cambridge: Cambridge University Press.

Schumacher, P. (1987) *De minderheden, 700,000 minder gelijk [Ethnic minorities, 700,000 migrants less equal]*, Amsterdam: Van Gennep.

Schuman, H., Steeh, C. and Bobo, L. (1985) *Racial Attitudes in America*, Cambridge, MA: Harvard University Press.

Schwarz, M.N.K. and Flammer, A. (1981) 'Text structure and title-effects on comprehension and recall', *Journal of Verbal Learning and Verbal Behaviour*, 20, 61–6.

Seidel, G. (1987) 'The white discursive order: the British New Right's discourse on cultural racism, with particular reference to the *Salisbury Review*', in I. Zavala, T.A. van Dijk and M. Diaz-Diocaretz (eds) *Approaches to Discourse, Poetics and Psychiatry*, Amsterdam: Benjamins.

Seidel, G. (1988a) 'The British New Right's "enemy within": the anti-racists', in G. Smitherman-Donaldson and T.A. van Dijk (eds) *Discourse and Discrimination*, Detroit, MI: Wayne State University Press.

Seidel, G. (ed.) (1988b) *The Nature of the Right. A Feminist Analysis of Order Patterns*, Amsterdam: Benjamins.

Seuren, P.A.M. (1985) *Discourse Semantics*, Oxford: Blackwell.

Smith, S.J. (1989) *The Politics of 'Race' and Residence*, Cambridge: Polity Press.

Snorgrass, J. W. and Woody, G.T. (1985) *Blacks and Media: A Selected, Annotated Bibliography, (1962–1982)*, Tallahassee: Florida A&M University Press.

Solomos, J. (1989) *Race and Racism in Contemporary Britain*, London: Macmillan.

Sumner, C. (1982) '"Political hooliganism"; and "rampaging mobs": The national press coverage of the Toxteth "riots"', in C. Sumner (ed.), *Crime, Justice and the Mass Media*, University of Cambridge: Institute of Criminology.

Sykes, M. (1985) 'Discrimination in discourse', in T.A. van Dijk (ed.), *Handbook of Discourse Analysis*, vol. 4, *Discourse Analysis in Society*, London: Academic Press, 83–101.

Taguieff, P.-A. (1988) *La force du préjugé. Essai sur le racisme et ses doubles*, Paris: Editions de la Découverte.

Tajfel, H. (1981) *Human Groups and Social Categories*, Cambridge: Cambridge University Press.

Todorov, T. (1989) *Nous et les autres. La réflexion française sur la diversité humaine*, Paris: Seuil.

Troyna, B. (1981) *Public Awareness and the Media: A Study of Reporting on Race*, London: Commission for Racial Equality.

Troyna, B. and Williams, J. (1986) *Racism, Education and the State*, London: Croom Helm.

Tuchman, G. (1978) *Making News*, New York: Free Press.

Tuchman, G., Kaplan Daniels, A. and Benét, J. (eds) (1978) *Hearth and Home: Images of Women in the Mass Media*, New York: Oxford University Press.

Tumber, H. (1982) *Television and the Riots*, London: British Film Institute.

UNESCO, (1983) *Racism, Science and Pseudo-science*, Paris: Unesco.

van Dijk, T.A. (1972) *Some Aspects of Text Grammars: A Study in Theoretical Poetics and Linguistics*, The Hague: Mouton.

van Dijk, T.A. (1977) *Text and Context: Explorations in the Semantics and Pragmatics of Discourse*, London: Longman.

van Dijk, T.A. (1980) *Macrostructures: An interdisciplinary study of global structures in discourse, interaction, and cognition*, Hillsdale, NJ: Erlbaum.

van Dijk, T.A. (1983) *Minderheden in de media [Minorities in the media]*, Amsterdam: Socialistische Uitgeverij Amsterdam.

van Dijk, T.A. (1984) *Prejudice in Discourse*, Amsterdam: Benjamins.

van Dijk, T.A. (ed.) (1985a) *Handbook of Discourse Analysis*, 4 vols, London: Academic Press.

van Dijk, T.A. (ed.) (1985b) *Discourse and Communication*, Berlin and New York: de Gruyter.

van Dijk, T.A. (1985c) 'Cognitive situation models in discourse processing: The expression of ethnic situation models in prejudiced stories', in J.P. Forgas (ed.), *Language and Social Situations*, New York: Springer, 61–79.

van Dijk, T.A. (1985d) 'Semantic discourse analysis', in van Dijk (ed.) *Handbook of Discourse Analysis*, vol. 2, London: Academic Press, 103–36.

van Dijk, T.A. (1987a) *Communicating Racism, Ethnic Prejudice in Thought and Talk*, Newbury Park, CA: Sage.

van Dijk, T.A. (1987b) *Schoolvoorbeelden van racisme. De reproduktie van racisme in maatschappijleerboeken [Textbook examples of racism. The reproduction of racism in social science textbooks]*, Amsterdam: Socialistische Uitgeverij Amsterdam.

van Dijk, T.A. (1987c) 'Episodic models in discourse processing', in R. Horowitz and S.J. Samuels (eds), *Comprehending Oral and Written Language*, New York: Academic Press, 161–96.

van Dijk, T.A. (1987d) 'Elite discourse and racism', in I. Zavala, T.A. van Dijk and M. Diaz-Diocaretz (eds), *Approaches to Discourse, Poetics and Psychiatry*, Amsterdam: Benjamins, 81–122.

van Dijk, T.A. (1988a) *News as Discourse*, Hillsdale, NJ: Erlbaum.

van Dijk, T.A. (1988b) *News Analysis: Case studies of international and national news in the press*, Hillsdale, NJ: Erlbaum.

van Dijk, T.A. (1988c) 'How "They" hit the headlines: ethnic minorities in the Press', in G. Smitherman-Donaldson and T.A. van Dijk (eds), *Discourse and discrimination*, Detroit, IL: Wayne State University Press, 221–62.

van Dijk, T.A. (1988d) 'The Tamil panic in the press', in T.A. van Dijk, *News Analysis: Case studies of international and national news in the press*, Hillsdale, NJ: Erlbaum, 215–54.

van Dijk, T.A. (1989a) 'Structures of discourse and structures of power', in J.A. Anderson (ed.), *Communication Yearbook* 12, Newbury Park, CA: Sage, 18–59.

van Dijk, T.A. (1989b) 'Critical news analysis', *Critical Studies* 1, 103–26.

van Dijk, T.A. (1989c) *Select Bibliography on Racism in the Press*, University of Amsterdam, Section on Discourse Studies: unpublished MS.

van Dijk, T.A. (1990) 'Social cognition and discourse', in H. Giles and P. Robinson (eds), *Handbook of Social Psychology and Language*, pp. 163–83, Chichester: Wiley.

van Dijk, T. A. and Kintsch, W. (1983) *Strategies of Discourse Comprehension*, New York: Academic Press.

van Dijk, T.A. and Smitherman-Donaldson, G. (1988) 'Introduction: Words that hurt', in G. Smitherman-Donaldson and T.A. van Dijk (eds), *Discourse and Discrimination*, Detroit, IL: Wayne State University Press, 11–22.

van Eemeren, F.H., Grootendorst, R. and Kruiger, T. (1984) *The Study of Argumentation*, New York: Irvington.

Wilson, C.C. and Gutiérrez, F., (1985) *Minorities and the Media*, Beverly Hills, CA and London: Sage Publications.

Windisch, U. (1978) *Xénophobie? Logique de la pensée populaire [Xenophobia? Logic of Popular Thought]*, Lausanne: L'Age d'Homme.

Windisch, U. (1982) *Pensée sociale, langage en usage et logiques autres [Social thought, language and other logics]*, Lausanne: L'Age d'Homme.

Windisch, U. (1985) *Le raisonnement et le parler quotidiens [Reasoning and everyday talk]*. Lausanne: L'Age d'Homme.

Windisch, U. (1987) *Le K.O. verbal, la communication conflictuelle [Verbal Knock Out: Conflictual Communication]*, Lausanne: L'Age d'Homme.

Wren-Lewis, J. (1981–2) 'The story of a riot: the television coverage of civil unrest in 1981', *Screen Education* 40, 26.

Wyer, Jr., R. S. and Srull, Thomas K. (eds) (1984) *Handbook of Social Cognition*, 3 vols, Hillsdale, NJ: Erlbaum.

Zanna, M.P., Olson, J.M. and Herman, C.P. (eds) (1987) *Social influence. The Ontario Symposium*, vol. 5, Hillsdale, NJ: Erlbaum.

# Author index

# Subject index